HEINRICH HEINE

GARLAND REFERENCE LIBRARY
OF THE HUMANITIES
(VOL. 302)

HEINRICH HEINE
A Selected Critical Bibliography
of Secondary Literature, 1956–1980

Jeffrey L. Sammons

GARLAND PUBLISHING, INC. • NEW YORK & LONDON
1982

Library of Congress Cataloging in Publication Data

Sammons, Jeffrey L.
  Heinrich Heine : a selected critical bibliography
of secondary literature, 1956–1980.

  (Garland reference library of the humanities ;
v. 302)
  Includes indexes.
  1. Heine, Heinrich, 1797–1856—Bibliography.
I. Title. II. Series.
Z8395.S24 [PT2328]   016.831′7   81-43346
ISBN 0-8240-9286-4   AACR2

Printed on acid-free, 250-year-life paper
Manufactured in the United States of America

CONTENTS

Introduction   vii

List of Abbreviations and Short Titles   xvii

  I. Editions
    1. Complete   3
    2. Selected   7

 II. Bibliography and Research Reports   11

III. Biographical Studies   19

 IV. Philological Studies   37

  V. Letters   45

 VI. General Expositions and Commentary   49

VII. Criticism
    1. General   55
    2. Lyric Poetry   73
      Musical Settings   90
    3. Epic and Political Poetry   92
    4. Fiction   101
    5. Dramas and Ballets   110
    6. Literature, Art, Music, Religion, Philosophy,
      Politics, Journalism   111

VIII. Reception, Reputation, Influence, and
    Comparative Studies   143

Index of Authors and Editors   173

Index of Works and Subjects   181

INTRODUCTION

Heinrich Heine is an unusual case in the history of world literature. While much worthwhile literature of the past seems to owe
its enduring life mainly to academic study, educational canons,
and the continuous attention of connoisseurs, Heine has been a
living presence in the cultural life of the world for a century and
a half. In this he resembles, in smaller compass, though with
greater virulence, Shakespeare and Goethe, but hardly any
others. Of all German poets he is undoubtedly the most widely
read in the world at large. He has been translated into every
language of the civilized world, and new translations, along with
studies of his influence in a wide variety of national cultures,
appear regularly. It is said that no other poet excepting the
Biblical Psalmist has been set to music as often as Heine. His
satirical verse and his pungently activist prose have reemerged
constantly as an inspiration in struggles against oppression and
for revolution. At the same time he is an object of inexhaustible
contentiousness, and the passion of debate concerning him is in
no way diminished in modern times from the uproar and conflict he generated in his own lifetime.

Much of this wide international involvement is gratifying,
not only for admirers of Heine, but for anyone who hopes that
the creations of the imagination and the intellect might per-
meate the larger fabric of civilization. But for the bibliographer
of Heine the situation has a nightmarish aspect, and for the
critical bibliographer it throws up challenges that are not easily
met. No one, I should imagine, could read everything written
about Heine in any one year in the course of that year, not only
because of its sheer bulk, but also because of its international
range and the likelihood that it will emerge in any format and
any medium. Studies of and commentary on Heine may be written in Hungarian, or Japanese, or Hebrew. They may appear in
newspapers or novels, in highly specialized scholarly works or in

television programs, in refined critical discourse or crude political agitation. Heine is one of the best served writers in literature in point of bibliography, yet the most professional bibliographer (which I am not) is always behind, always supplementing missed items from previous years and decades, always subject to correction. The East German bibliographer Siegfried Seifert, after having compiled a 343-page list for a period of eleven years, expressed a doubt in the preface whether comprehensive bibliographies of Heine would be feasible any more.

For the critical bibliographer this great mass of material obviously presents a problem of just selection. But for additional reasons a just selection is more difficult with Heine than with any other writer known to history. His reputation is the most embattled, the most highly charged of any major writer. He has sometimes been compared to Byron in this regard, and there are certain similarities in the history of their reputations in the nineteenth century, but Heine has long since outdistanced Byron in contentiousness. No one marches in the streets in Byron's behalf; no one challenges public institutions in Byron's name; no one engages Byron in the conflicts among modern nations. These things occur with Heine all the time.

This has been true virtually since the beginning, though the issues have shifted from past to present. In the nineteenth century Heine challenged the pieties and conventions of society, and, though this is not always admitted today, he challenged those of all social classes. Most fundamentally, he was at one with the restless and frustrated German middle class in his fierce hatred of the aristocracy that had clamped a reactionary, repressive rule on Central Europe in the post-Napoleonic era. He surpassed everyone in the fierceness of his denunciation and his contempt for kings, nobles, and governments. Since this dominant reactionary force was in explicit alliance with established religion, he mounted a life-long attack on what he conceived to be the repressive foundations of Christianity and especially Roman Catholicism. Unremittingly he called up before the rulers the spectre of the French Revolution, the Terror, and the conqueror Napoleon, the heroic model of much of his life. At the same time he would not ally himself with the German middle class, which he found philistine and dim. He cried anathema on the early phases of capitalism and, more ominously, he scourged every manifestation of nationalistic feeling, thus setting his teeth against the profoundest aspirations of the German middle class. What were for it categories of virtue were for Heine categories of repression. He seemed utterly without piety: he was rude about religion; he denounced Romanticism and was impudent toward Goethe; he confronted middle-class sexual sensitivities with an elaborately argued doctrine of sensualism, occasionally accompanied by studied salaciousness; he attacked individuals publicly in the fiercest manner, so that his life was a chain of scandals, punctuated by not a few duels. But no more was he an ally of the emerging proletariat, as he is often presented today. He wished to be understood as a spokesman for the "people," for he sensed in the people and their traditions a liberating sensual force distorted by centuries of religious and political oppression. But in the concrete case he wanted nothing to do with the working class or its radical spokesmen, whom he suspected of a barbaric puritanism inimical to poesy, to gratification and plentitude. In one phase he made common cause with some of the radicals of his time—especially with Karl Marx—to give his own struggles some resonance, but he did so within an often reiterated bad conscience.

Thus it is not surprising that he had few friends, and it must be admitted that his egocentric lack of self-control and his sometimes spectacular absence of ethical sensitivity contributed to the difficulties in his life and subsequent reputation. Nevertheless, he came to be the major German writer of his time, as he himself frankly stated and many others acknowledged, one way or another, often grudgingly. Matthew Arnold said that he was the most important European writer in the quarter century following upon the death of Goethe; while that may be an exaggeration, his eminence could not be denied and in fact it was just this eminence that complicated his reception by an often hostile public. Parts of that public came in time to deal with the difficulty by separating out from the rest of his life and work the poetry, especially that of *Buch der Lieder*, as though it had been written by a disembodied spirit of German poesy. His relationship to his posterity came to be an exact analogue to the satirical lines he wrote on the liberal poet Georg Herwegh's contretemps with the

King of Prussia: "In verses I charmed him / But he didn't like my prose." In time this preference for the poetry, often re-Romanticized and sentimentalized, turned out to be a delayed disaster for Heine's reputation, for over the generations people grew tired of it, and the rise of a more subtle, modernist poetry in Germany after the turn of the century brought about a precipitate drop in Heine's reputation around the time of World War I. In addition, the often moralistic resistance to Heine's fierce opposition to dominant German values and institutions began increasingly to acquire an anti-Semitic cast. Heine had always had to contend with a certain amount of anti-Semitism. In his lifetime it was irritating if not crippling, but in the latter part of the nineteenth century anti-Semitism became much shriller; it fell with special force upon Heine's reputation because of his allegedly un-German, pro-French posture. The waves of this development are much too complicated to describe briefly, and in fact the anti-Semitic and anti-democratic opposition to Heine was not as universal as is sometimes believed today, but it was real, symbolized in the famous long farce surrounding efforts to erect monuments to him in Germany, which led to riots and government crises. The Nazis, of course, attempted to consign him to oblivion as far as their arm could reach.

The post–World War II situation has sometimes been perceived as a modern continuation of this history; but this is a misapprehension that has caused confusion in the public discussion. It is true that Heine's visibility in Germany was seriously diminished by two only tangentially connected features of this history: the anti-Semitic, nationalist, and fascist repression on the one hand, and the failure of his poetry to stand up to modernist critical standards on the other. While there was a brief flurry of Heine publications and editions immediately after the war, for some time it appeared that his reputation was more secure outside of Germany, especially, though not exclusively, in English-speaking countries. Within about a decade, however, it became increasingly apparent that a rehabilitation of Heine was a matter of high priority in the Germans' effort to come to terms with the horrors of the recent past and to rejoin the community of civilized nations. But this laudable purpose immediately became a battlefield of the Cold War. The test came in 1956, the

centenary of Heine's death. In West Germany there were cere-
monies, memorial articles, and the like, but little more than
would be usual for any anniversary of any writer; it was clear
that Heine was largely absent from school and university cur-
ricula and from the consciousness of the wider public. But in
East Germany there was an enormous initiative, which had been
gathering momentum since shortly after the end of the war and
reached a peak of intensity in the centenary year. There can be
no doubt that there was an element of sincerity in the East
German propagation of Heine, where publications and cere-
monies proliferated and texts were published in millions of
copies. Heine was an icon of the anti-fascist steadfastness urgent
to many East German intellectuals and writers. But he rapidly
became a tool of official East German cultural politics. With a few
important exceptions, there was relatively little analytic or
critical discussion; most East German writing on Heine is rhetorical, assertive, and affirmative, making him a key figure in East
Germany's claim to be the true inheritor of the democratic and
revolutionary tradition in German literature and thought. Increasingly he was molded into a proto-Marxist posture and by
selective quotation and interpretation his complex views were
accommodated to orthodox Communist historiography. He was
especially useful as a stick with which to beat West Germany as
the successor to the fascist-capitalist *Reich,* for the lively East
German activity was regularly played off against the relative
quiescence in West Germany, and this contrast continued to be
asserted long after it had ceased to be true. That the official
propagation of Heine in East Germany was largely political and
opportunist has become clearer today, for, with the shift of the
center of gravity of Heine studies to the West, Heine has become
much less interesting in the East and the campaign has died
down; a major monograph on Heine has not appeared in East
Germany since 1967. As a policy, however, the campaign was
eminently successful, for there are still people all over the world,
even in the West German media, who believe that the Heine
tradition is nurtured in the East and neglected in the West.

It is likely that the pressure from East Germany helped to
accelerate the revival of serious Heine studies in the West. The
development may be dated from 1962, the year of the first an-

nual *Heine-Jahrbuch*, which, along with other studies and materials, has made the Heinrich Heine–Institut in Düsseldorf the major center of Heine studies in the West; to be sure, the Düsseldorf scholars cooperate with those in the East as well as with the team working on the third major center of Heine materials in the Bibliothèque Nationale in Paris. The flow of West German studies and editions has rapidly risen to a flood. This development became a prominent part of the aggressive revival of Marxism in West German literary studies in the late 1960s. Marxist perspectives have much to contribute to the study of Heine as of all literature. But certain rigidities of the Marxist position have led to a new conventionality in the outlook on Heine and sometimes to the transmission of clichés from one study to the next. The spirit of inquiry grows feeble when the answers to the questions put are known in advance and scholarship is employed to secure them illustratively. In many cases, in the West and in the East, there is a lack of analytic and critical judgment in favor of enrolling Heine as an ally for contemporary activist purposes. In my opinion there has been much serious and elaborate distortion as a consequence, although there are signs that West German Heine scholarship is slowly becoming more attentive to historical, biographical, and textual realities. On the other hand, there has from time to time been resistance, in and out of Germany, to the Marxist positions, sometimes judicious, sometimes intemperate.

It is easy to see that the critical bibliographer of Heine is in a quite different position from that of the observer of most other literary phenomena. There is no conscientious escape from the contentiousness. The bulk of modern Heine discussion is polemical in mode and ulterior in motive, demanding an ideological assent that must be either granted or withheld. My own criticisms proceed quite obviously from a liberal democratic ground and from a resistance to the practice of reshaping the meaning of past texts for present purposes. There is admittedly something unsatisfactory about criticisms and characterizations of often quite complex and carefully wrought studies phrased in a few sentences. I believe my opinions have a right to be taken as serious and thoughtful, based upon more than twenty years of experience with Heine and Heine scholarship. But they are not the only possible opinions, and the thorough student of Heine should not be content with them, but should consult the whole range of discussion and especially the dialogue in book reviews. The annual *Romantic Movement Bibliography* (nos. 31, 41) has been listing reviews of previous work since 1965 and the *Heine-Jahrbuch* has done so since 1977.

Owing to the great mass of Heine material, some account of the principles of selection needs to be given. The dates are easily defended. The centenary of Heine's death in 1956 brought forth an enormous outpouring of material, not only in East Germany and Eastern Europe, but also in West Germany and abroad. The modern phase of discussion may properly be dated from that year. The 125th anniversary of Heine's death in 1981 will obviously bring another surge and perhaps some signs of a new spirit; 1980 therefore seems a reasonable closure. Only such works that were actually in hand by the end of 1980 are considered. It has been my purpose to include all genuinely scholarly work in the major Western languages; any omissions of that kind are owing to oversight and not to discrimination. There is, to be sure, no little historical continuity in the discussion; in general I have left out earlier work reprinted in this period, though I have admitted some major items, especially those whose influence really belongs to the contemporary phase even though they may have been originally written earlier. Only those editions that have been indispensable to scholarship are listed, though it should be noted that, of the dozens of Heine texts published in collected or individual editions during these twenty-five years, many contain scholarly commentary. A large and representative selection of the general intellectual discussion has been included, and I have tried to bring in everything by prestigious authors and anything that appeared to exhibit some insight. Even here one encounters much conventionality, especially in ideological matters. Outside of these limits much that is written tends to be very much alike, depending upon its geographical or ideological origin. A case in point is the large amount of Japanese material, of which I have given a few representative examples. From what I have been able to learn of it through German versions or abstracts, it is more remarkable for its quantity than its quality. I have excluded:

- unpublished or privately printed dissertations, with the exception of two or three that are important to scholarly discussion;
- the large pedagogical literature on the propagation and teaching of Heine in schools, primarily in the East but latterly in considerable bulk in the West, except in a few cases where it seemed to me significantly symptomatic of ideological concerns;
- exhibition catalogues and commentary in newspapers and popular magazines;
- the vast number of Heine translations into foreign languages, important as they are to an assessment of his world-wide reputation, as well as imitations and parodies;
- the many discussions of Heine in comprehensive literary history or thematic studies;
- Heine as a figure in fiction, a topic that, in my experience, is a little depressing;
- a small amount of utter flapdoodle and rant, as well as some few items that are too difficult of access.

Finally, I have tried to make it a principle not to include anything I have not actually seen, with only a handful of exceptions.

Despite the ambivalence and complexity of Heine's mind and the variety of modes in which he wrote, there is a sense in which his life work is all of a piece, deriving from relatively few strongly felt attitudes and purposes. From the beginning this unity and the consequent fluidity of boundaries in his oeuvre have made it difficult to know how best to structure a collected edition, and they also present the bibliographer with a problem of organization. Experience with Heine bibliography shows that attempting to make fine distinctions by genre, title, and subject leads to much repetition and elaborate cross-referencing. For this reason I have opted for relatively few gross categories. A heading such as VII.6, "Literature, Art, Music, Religion, Philosophy, Politics, Journalism," may seem excessively broad, but in fact all these things are tightly interwoven in Heine's writings. To distinguish, for example, among religion, philosophy, and literature would have meant separating *Zur Geschichte der Religion und Philosophie in Deutschland* from *Die Romantische Schule*, although they were originally conceived as two parts of one book. In fact the distinctions I have made, for example, between lyric and political poetry, or between fiction and journalism, or between general commentary and general criticism, are difficult to maintain, for the secondary literature naturally reflects the exceptional interrelatedness and generic fluidity of Heine's work. For the well-informed student it may be helpful to note the following: I have denominated as "lyric" all the poetry except the mock-epics *Atta Troll* and *Deutschland, ein Wintermärchen* and the *Zeitgedichte* with their middle and late paralipomena. Under "fiction" I have included all the *Reisebilder* (except the obviously reportorial *Englische Fragmente*) and the three novel fragments *Der Rabbi von Bacherach, Schnabelewopski,* and *Florentinische Nächte.* The autobiographical *Geständnisse* and *Memoiren* are treated under the catch-all category VII.6. All knowledgeable persons will recognize these distinctions as devices of convenience only, and in some cases placement has been little more than arbitrary. I have tried to ease this difficulty with thorough indexing.

No student of Heine can be alone in the world, and I owe much to exchanges and debates with others, even when acrimonious. I have too many obligations to colleagues and institutions to list adequately, but several major ones need to be mentioned. One is to the scholars and laborers at the Heinrich Heine–Institut in Düsseldorf, who for many years have been immediately forthcoming and helpful. I am also grateful to the Leo Baeck Institute in New York for prompt aid with genuinely remote items. A further obligation is to the staff of the Interlibrary Loan Department of the Yale University Library, whose efficiency and promptness were especially helpful in the last stages of this project. To the Yale humanities bibliographer George Vrooman, a prince among librarians, I owe an unrepayable debt of many years' standing. I have had helpful assistance with Italian-language items from Susan Jed of Yale and Professor Richard C. Figge of the College of Wooster. The ultimate acknowledgment is to my wife, Dr. Christa Sammons, Curator of the German Literature Collection in the Beinecke Rare Book and Manuscript Library of Yale University, whose support has been more than bibliographical.

New Haven, Connecticut
On the 125th anniversary of Heine's death,
February 17, 1981

ABBREVIATIONS
AND SHORT TITLES

AION *Annali Istituto Universitario Orientale,* Naples, *Sezione Germanica*

AUMLA *Journal of the Australasian Universities Language and Literature Association*

Cahier Heine Michael Werner, ed., *Cahier Heine.* Publications du Centre d'Histoire et d'Analyse de Manuscrits Modernes. Paris: Presses de l'Ecole Normale Supérieure, 1975 (no. 367)

CG *Colloquia Germanica*

CL *Comparative Literature*

DB *Doitsu Bungaku*

DD *Diskussion Deutsch*

DK *Duitse Kroniek*

DU (East) *Deutschunterricht* (Berlin)

DU (West) *Der Deutschunterricht* (Stuttgart)

DVLG *Deutsche Vierteljahrsschrift für Literaturwissenschaft und Geistesgeschichte*

EG *Etudes Germaniques*

ELN *English Language Notes*

GL&L *German Life & Letters*

GN *Germanic Notes*

GQ *German Quarterly*

GR *Germanic Review*

GRM *Germanisch-romanische Monatsschrift*

Heinrich Heine und die Zeitgenossen Akademie der Wissenschaften der DDR, Zentralinstitut für Literaturgeschichte, and Centre National de la Recherche Scientifique, Centre d'Histoire et d'Analyse des Manuscrits Modernes, eds., *Heinrich Heine und die Zeitgenossen: Geschichtliche und literarische Befunde.* Berlin and Weimar: Aufbau Verlag, 1979 (no. 273)

HJ *Heine-Jahrbuch*

Immerwahr and Spencer, eds., *Heinrich Heine* Raymond Immerwahr and Hanna Spencer, eds., *Heinrich Heine: Dimensionen seines Wirkens. Ein internationales Heine-Symposium.* Bonn: Bouvier, 1979 (no. 302)

JDSG   *Jahrbuch der deutschen Schiller-Gesellschaft*
JIG   *Jahrbuch für internationale Germanistik*
KFLQ   *Kentucky Foreign Language Quarterly*
Koopmann, ed., *Heinrich Heine*   Helmut Koopmann, ed., *Heinrich Heine*. Darmstadt: Wissenschaftliche Buchgesellschaft, 1975 (no. 310)
Kuttenkeuler, ed., *Heinrich Heine: Artistik und Engagement*   Wolfgang Kuttenkeuler, ed., *Heinrich Heine: Artistik und Engagement*. Stuttgart: Metzler, 1977 (no. 317)
LiLi   *Zeitschrift für Literaturwissenschaft und Linguistik*
MLN   *Modern Language Notes*
MLQ   *Modern Language Quarterly*
MLR   *Modern Language Review*
Monatshefte   *Monatshefte für deutschen Unterricht, deutsche Sprache und Literatur*
NDH   *Neue deutsche Hefte*
NDL   *Neue deutsche Literatur*
OGS   *Oxford German Studies*
OL   *Orbis Litterarum*
PLL   *Papers on Language and Literature*
PMLA   *Publications of the Modern Language Association of America*
PQ   *Philological Quarterly*
RdA   *Revue d'Allemagne*
RLC   *Revue de Littérature comparée*
RLV   *Revue des Langues vivantes*
SG   *Studi Germanici*
Streitbarer Humanist   Karl Wolfgang Becker, Helmut Brandt, and Siegfried Scheibe, eds., *Heinrich Heine: Streitbarer Humanist und volksverbundener Dichter*. Weimar: Nationale Forschungs- und Gedenkstätten der klassischen deutschen Literatur in Weimar, [1973] (no. 276)
SuF   *Sinn und Form*
TK   *Text + Kritik*
Wadepuhl, *Heine-Studien*   Walter Wadepuhl, *Heine-Studien*. Weimar: Arion, 1956 (no. 362)
WB   *Weimarer Beiträge*
Windfuhr, ed., *Heine-Kongreß*   Manfred Windfuhr, ed., *Internationaler Heine-Kongreß Düsseldorf 1972: Referate und Diskussionen*. Hamburg: Hoffmann und Campe, Heinrich Heine Verlag, 1973 (no. 375)
WuW   *Welt und Wort*
WW   *Wirkendes Wort*
ZDP   *Zeitschrift für deutsche Philologie*

HEINRICH HEINE

I

EDITIONS

1. Complete Editions

1. Briegleb, Klaus, et al., eds. *Sämtliche Werke*. Munich: Hanser.

I. *Buch der Lieder*; *Nachgelesene Gedichte 1812-1827*; *Tragödien*; *Byron-Übersetzungen*; *Zur Literatur (1820-1828)*; *Fragmente erzählender Prosa*. Ed. Klaus Briegleb. 1968. 884 pp.

II. *Briefe über Berlin*; *Über Polen*; *Reisebilder*; *Nachlese*; *Aufsätze aus dem Umkreis der "Reisebilder"*; *Einleitung zu: Kahldorf über den Adel*; *Pariser Vorreden zu den "Reisebildern."* Ed. Günter Häntzschel. 1969. 964 pp.

III. *Vorrede zu Salon I*; *Verschiedenartige Geschichtsauffassung*; *Über Frankreich*; *Über Deutschland*. Ed. Karl Pörnbacher. 1971. 1,038 pp.

IV. *Ludwig Börne*; *Don Quixote*; *Shakespeares Mädchen und Frauen*; *Neue Gedichte*; *Nachgelesene Gedichte 1828-1848*; *Atta Troll*; *Deutschland, Ein Wintermärchen*. Ed. Klaus Briegleb. 1971. 1,062 pp.

V. *Schriftstellernöte 1832-1855*; *Bruchstücke Korrespondenzartikel 1832-1852*; *1844*; *Vor dem Zusammenbruch 1847/48*; *Lutetia*. Ed. Klaus Briegleb and Karl Heinz Stahl, 1974. 1,103 pp.

VI/1. *Romanzero*; *Gedichte 1853 und 1854*; *Bimini*; *Nachgelesene Gedichte 1854-1856*; *Der Doktor Faust*; *Die Götter im Exil*; *Die Göttin Diana*; *De l'Allemagne*; *Geständnisse*; *Bruchstücke nach den Geständnissen*; *Testamente*; *Memoiren*; *Aufzeichnungen*. Ed. Klaus Briegleb and Walter Klaar. 1975. 679 pp.

VI/2. *Kommentar zu Band 6/1. Anhang zur Gesamtausgabe*. Ed. Klaus Briegleb and Walter Klaar. 1976. 886 pp.

From the point of view of Heine's complete text, this edition in the respected Hanser format is the most convenient.

It is sensibly organized, it is for the most part textually
reliable, and it conludes with useful indexes. But the
editorial practices have made the edition questionable. A
huge, opaque, and frequently ill-written commentary of more
than 2,700 pages of small print is difficult to use for
quick reference, packed with ancillary materials reprinted
extensively along with lengthy argumentative essays, and
ideologically very aggressive, bullying the reader into
often debatable judgments; it is also defective or erroneous in many places. The edition is a prime exhibit of the
peculiarities of contemporary Heine scholarship and would
repay study from that perspective alone.

2. Kaufmann, Hans, with Gotthard Erler and Eva Kaufmann, eds.
Werke und Briefe. Berlin: Aufbau-Verlag. Reprinted,
without the letters and with much of the commentary
deleted, as *Sämtliche Werke*. Kindler-Taschenbücher,
1001/2-1027/8. Munich: Kindler, 1964. 14 vols.

I. *Buch der Lieder*; *Neue Gedichte*; *Atta Troll*; *Deutsch-
land. Ein Wintermärchen*. 1961. 587 pp.
II. *Romanzero*; *Gedichte 1853 und 1854*; *Nachlese zu den
Gedichten*; *Almansor*; *William Ratcliff*. 1961. 707 pp.
III. *Reisebilder*. 1961. 783 pp.
IV. *Der Rabbi von Bacherach*; *Aus den Memoiren des Her-
ren von Schnabelewopski*; *Florentinische Nächte*; *Kleine
Schriften 1820-1831*; *Französische Zustände*; *Vorrede zum
ersten Band des "Salon."* 1961. 681 pp.
V. *Die romantische Schule*; *Zur Geschichte der Religion
und Philosophie in Deutschland*; *Elementargeister*; *Kleine
Schriften 1832-1839*; *Shakespeares Mädchen und Frauen.* 1961.
748 pp.
VI. *Über die französische Bühne*; *Ludwig Börne*; *Lutetia*.
1962. 739 pp.
VII. *Der Doktor Faust*; *Die Götter im Exil*; *Die Göttin
Diana*; *Geständnisse*; *Memoiren*; *Kleine Schriften 1840-1856*;
Aphorismen und Fragmente; *Testamente*. 1962. 555 pp.
VIII. *Briefe 1815-1838*. 1961. 696 pp.
IX. *Briefe 1839-1856*. 1962. 804 pp.
X. *Heinrich Heine: Poesie, Vaterland und Menschheit*,
by Hans Kaufmann. *Nachträge*; *Register*. 1964. 452 pp.

The standard East German complete edition is not a critical edition, though it contains major variants and some
informational commentary, as well as a comprehensive essay
by the editor. The text is based upon the critical edition

of Oskar Walzel, et al., *Sämtliche Werke* (Leipzig: Insel, 1910–20); the letters are selected. The West German paperback reprint was not a success and was withdrawn from the market.

3. Nationale Forschungs- und Gedenkstätten der klassischen deutschen Literatur in Weimar and Centre National de la Recherche Scientifique in Paris, eds. *Säkularausgabe*. Berlin and Paris; Akademie Verlag, Editions du CNRS.

I. *Gedichte 1812–1827*. Ed. Hans Böhm and Fritz Mende. 1979. 272 pp.

II. *Gedichte 1827–1844 und Versepen*. Ed. Irmgard Möller, Hans Böhm, Renate Francke, and Fritz Mende. 1979. 384 pp.

V. *Reisebilder I 1824–1828*. Ed. Karl Wolfgang Becker and Fritz Mende. 1970. 214 pp.

VII. *Über Frankreich 1831–1837*. *Berichte über Kunst und Politik*. Ed. Fritz Mende and Karl Heinz Hahn. 1970. 315 pp.

VIII. *Über Deutschland 1833–1836*. *Aufsätze über Kunst und Philosophie*. Ed. Renate Francke and Fritz Mende. 1972. 252 pp.

IX. *Prosa 1836–1840*. Ed. Fritz Mende and Christa Stöcker. 1979. 399 pp.

X. *Pariser Berichte 1840–1848*. Ed. Lucienne Netter and Paul Laveau. 1979. 296 pp.

XI. *Lutezia*. Ed. Lucienne Netter and Paul Laveau. 1974. 263 pp.

XIII. *Poèmes et légendes*. Ed. Pierre Grappin and Paul Laveau. 1978. 456 pp.

XIV. *Tableaux de voyage I*. Ed. Claude David and Paul Laveau. 1978. 320 pp.

XV. *Tableaux de voyage II*. *Italie*. Ed. René Anglade and Paul Laveau. 1979. 230 pp.

XVI. *De l'Allemagne I*. Ed. Claude Pichois and Paul Laveau. 1978. 216 pp.

XVII. *De l'Allemagne II*. Ed. Jean-René Derré and Paul Laveau. 1978. 280 pp.

XVIII. *De la France*. Ed. Fritz Mende and Paul Laveau. 1977. 196 pp.

XIX. *Lutèce*. Ed. Jacques Voisine and Paul Laveau. 1977. 263 pp.

XX. *Briefe 1815–1831*. Ed. Fritz H. Eisner and Fritz Mende. 1970. 445 pp.

XX K. *Briefe 1815–1831 Kommentar*. Ed. Fritz H. Eisner, Fritz Mende, and Christa Stöcker. 1975. 288 pp.

XXI. *Briefe 1831–1841*. Ed. Fritz H. Eisner and Christa Stöcker. 1970. 436 pp.

XXI K. *Briefe 1831-1841 Kommentar.* Ed. Fritz H. Eisner, Christa Stöcker, and Fritz Mende. 1975. 291 pp.

XXII. *Briefe 1842-1848.* Ed. Fritz H. Eisner and Christa Stöcker. 1972. 327 pp.

XXII K. *Briefe 1842-1848 Kommentar.* Ed. Fritz H. Eisner, Christa Stöcker, and Fritz Mende. 1976. 220 pp.

XXIII. *Briefe 1850-1856.* Ed. Fritz H. Eisner and Christa Stöcker. 1972. 495 pp.

XXIII K. *Briefe 1850-1856 Kommentar.* Ed. Fritz H. Eisner, Christa Stöcker, and Fritz Mende. 1976. 280 pp.

XXIV. *Briefe an Heine 1823-1836.* Ed. Renate Francke, Fritz Mende, Nicole Bandet, and Paul Laveau. 1974. 437 pp.

XXIV K. *Briefe an Heine 1823-1836 Kommentar.* Ed. Renate Francke and Fritz Mende. 1978. 340 pp.

XXV. *Briefe an Heine 1837-1841.* Ed. Christa Stöcker, Fritz Mende, Nicole Bandet, and Paul Laveau. 1974. 356 pp.

XXV K. *Briefe an Heine 1837-1841 Kommentar.* Ed. Christa Stöcker and Fritz Mende. 1979. 298 pp.

XXVI. *Briefe an Heine 1842-1851.* Ed. Christa Stöcker, Fritz Mende, Nicole Bandet, and Paul Laveau. 1975. 376 pp.

XXVI K. *Briefe an Heine 1842-1851 Kommentar.* Ed. Christa Stöcker and Fritz Mende. 1979. 347 pp.

XXVII. *Briefe an Heine 1852-1856.* Ed. Winfried Woesler, Christa Stöcker, Nicole Bandet, and Paul Laveau. 1976. 398 pp.

XXVII K. *Briefe an Heine 1852-1856 Kommentar.* Ed. Christa Stöcker and Winfried Woesler. 1980. 323 pp.

The East German critical edition differs from its West German counterpart (see no. 5) in three major aspects: it will not supply a complete variant apparatus but will restrict itself to major variants; instead of treating the French texts as variants of the German ones, it has separated them into a detachable French Heine (Vols. XIII-XIX); and it has reedited Heine's correspondence, including, for the first time, the letters to him. The last of these is its most important and indeed indispensable contribution. Otherwise this bulkiest of Heine editions is something of a disappointment: the commentary so far has been rather sketchy and assiduously avoids confronting problems; the printing has not been as careful as one might wish; and paper and binding do not suggest that the edition is intended to last for the ages.

4. Vordtriede, Werner, Jost Perfahl, and Uwe Schweikert, eds.
   Sämtliche Werke. Munich: Winkler-Verlag.
   I. *Gedichte*. [1969.] 964 pp.
   II. *Dichterische Prosa*. *Dramatisches*. [1969.] 972 pp.
   III. *Schriften zu Literatur und Politik I*. [1972.] 863
   pp.
   IV. *Schriften zu Literatur und Politik II*. *Vermischtes*.
   [1972.] 894 pp.

   This compact edition seems to have been devised in haste
   to meet the lively Heine market. The commentary is random,
   perfunctory, and sometimes unreliable. See also no. 361.

5. Windfuhr, Manfred, ed. *Historisch-kritische Gesamtausgabe
   der Werke*. Hamburg: Hoffmann und Campe.
   I. *Buch der Lieder*. Ed. Pierre Grappin. 1975. 1,306
   pp. in two volumes.
   VI. *Briefe aus Berlin*. *Über Polen*. *Reisebilder I/II*.
   Ed. Jost Hermand. 1973. 922 pp.
   VIII/1. *Zur Geschichte der Religion und Philosophie in
   Deutschland*. *Die Romantische Schule*. *Text*. Ed. Volkmar
   Hansen and Christiane Giesen. 1979. 505 pp.
   XI. *Ludwig Börne, Eine Denkschrift und Kleinere poli-
   tische Schriften*. Ed. Helmut Koopmann. 1978. 951 pp.

   Upon its completion, which is a good many years away, the
   West German critical edition will be the major standard
   edition for modern times. It is a complete variant edition
   with a thorough commentary at the height of contemporary
   scholarship. Its only questionable feature is the restora-
   tion of original texts for which there is no MS. accord-
   ing to Heine's known orthographic habits, which in some
   cases establishes as the most authentic basic text one
   nowhere known to exist.

2. Selected Editions

6. Altenhofer, Norbert, ed. *Heinrich Heine*. Dichter über
   ihre Dichtungen, ed. Rudolf Hirsch and Werner Vordtriede,
   Vol. VIII. Munich: Heimeran, [1971]. 3 vols. 483,
   422, 525 pp.

   The Heine volumes in the familiar series of writers'
   comments on their own works also contains much ancillary
   information. Primarily it is a reference resource for the
   Heine scholar.

7. Atkins, Stuart, et al., eds. *Werke.* Beck's kommentierte
    Klassiker. Munich: C.H. Beck.

    I. *Almansor; Buch der Lieder; Reisebilder.* Ed. Stuart
    Atkins and Oswald Schönberg, 1973. 973 pp.
    II. *Der Salon; Die Romantische Schule; Französische
    Zustände* [excerpts]; *Der Salon III; Lutetia* [excerpts];
    Neue Gedichte [excerpts]; *Atta Troll; Deutschland, ein
    Wintermärchen; Romanzero; Späte Gedichte.* Ed. Stuart
    Atkins and Oliver Boeck. 1978. 1,296 pp.

    This voluminously annotated edition is recommendable as
    a thorough and informative selected introduction to Heine;
    unfortunately it is very expensive. Atkins' part in it
    is of the highest scholarly standard; otherwise Boeck's
    contribution to the second volume is superior to Schönberg's
    to the first.

8. Mann, Michael, ed. *Zeitungsberichte über Musik und Malerei.*
    Frankfurt am Main: Insel Verlag, 1964. 257 pp.

    This edition marks a beginning in the important task of
    separating Heine's original newspaper articles from their
    later revised book versions. The volume is restricted to
    reportage on music and art. See also nos. 703, 704, 705.

9. Mayer, Hans, ed. *Beiträge zur deutschen Ideologie.* Ull-
    stein Buch No. 2822. Frankfurt am Main: Ullstein, 1971.
    518 pp.

    An annotated edition of selected writings on politics
    and ideology.

10. Siegrist, Christoph, et al., eds. *Werke.* Frankfurt am
    Main: Insel Verlag, 1968.

    I. *Gedichte.* Ed. Christoph Siegrist. 555 pp.
    II. *Reisebilder; Erzählende Prosa; Aufsätze.* Ed. Wolf-
    gang Preisendanz. 916 pp.
    III. *Schriften über Frankreich.* Ed. Eberhard Galley.
    729 pp.
    IV. *Schriften über Deutschland.* Ed. Helmut Schanze.
    682 pp.

    Volumes II, III, and IV of this extensive selected edi-
    tion are excellent, with fine introductions and commentary
    by outstanding scholars; a significant essay by Hans Mayer
    opens Volume I (see also no. 329). But the editor of the
    first volume holds the poetry in low regard; the cycles
    are severely cut, leaving out many important poems, and
    the comprehensive essay generally degrades and denigrates

Heine's poetry. The result is that a potentially useful
and recommendable edition was spoiled.

11. Trilse, Christoph, ed. *Über die französische Bühne und
    andere Schriften zum Theater.* Berlin: Henschelverlag
    Kunst und Gesellschaft, 1971. 651 pp.

    A compendium of Heine's writings on theater and drama
    edited and annotated from an East German perspective.

II

BIBLIOGRAPHY AND RESEARCH REPORTS

12. Becker, Eva D. "Denkwürdigkeiten der Heine-Forschung
     im letzten Jahrzehnt. Zu 'Ideen. Das Buch Le Grand'
     und 'Deutschland. Ein Wintermärchen.'" DD 8 (1977):
     333-351.

     Examines criticism on the two works from a literary-
     sociological point of view.

13. ————. "Heinrich Heine: Ein Forschungsbericht 1945-
     1965." DU (West) 18, No. 4 (1966): Supplement, 1-18.
     Reprinted Koopmann, ed., Heinrich Heine, pp. 377-403.

     A reportorial discussion of some of the international
     Heine scholarship for a twenty-year period.

14. Berendsohn, Walter A. Eine erfreuliche Wendung in der
     Heine-Forschung. Moderna språk Monographs, Literature,
     No. 2. Stockholm: P.A. Norstedt & Söner, 1972. 12 pp.

     A critical review of nos. 373, 705, 115, 95, and 345,
     along with some remarks about the East and West critical
     editions.

15. Bergenthal, Hugo. "Heine." "The Romantic Movement: A
     Selective and Critical Bibliography." PQ 35 (1956):
     140. Reprinted p. 958 in The Romantic Movement Bibliog-
     raphy 1936-1970: A Master Cumulation from ELH, Philo-
     logical Quarterly and English Language Notes, ed. A.C.
     Elkins and L.J. Forstner. Vol. III: 1955-1959. Ann
     Arbor: Pierian Press, 1973.

     A short listing, carried on more thoroughly in annual
     installments by others.

16. Cwojdrak, Günther. "Heine in Weimar." Die Weltbühne
     16 (1961): 1462-1466.

     A collective review of the Heine publications of the

Arion Verlag in Weimar, nos. 362, 48, and 747, surprising-
ly frank on the weaknesses of the last.

17. Dresch, J. "Le Centenaire de Heine: Publications heinéennes.
    RLC 30 (1956): 232-236.

    Comment on the events and publications of the centenary,
    particularly skeptical in regard to West Germany.

18. Feudel, Werner. "Positionen und Tendenzen in der Heine-
    Forschung der BRD." Pp. 183-218 in Helmut Bock, et al.,
    eds., *Streitpunkt Vormärz: Beiträge zur Kritik bürger-
    licher und revisionistischer Erbeauffassungen.* Berlin:
    Akademie-Verlag, 1977. 323 pp.

    A strictly orthodox critique of West German Heine scholar-
    ship, measuring everything according to the single correct
    East German line.

19. Finke, Franz. "Heine-Bibliographie 1954/1959." *HJ 1964*,
    pp. 80-94.

    Closes the gap between no. 48 and the beginning of the
    Heine-Jahrbuch.

20. Giese, Gerhard, and Dietrich Mühlberg. "Deutsche Heine-
    Literatur 1945 bis 1954"; "Deutsche Heine-Literatur 1945
    bis 1955. Nachtrag." *NDL* 4, No. 3 (March 1956): 166-
    170; 4, No. 6 (June 1956): 169-171.

    A selected working bibliography for the first post-war
    decade.

21. G[örsch], E[va]. "Überblick über die Veröffentlichungen
    zum Heine-Jahr 1956." *DU* (East) 10, No. 3 (1957): 167-
    171.

    A provisional international bibliography of publications
    in the centenary year.

22. Hagström, Tore. "Nyare Heinelitteratur." *Samlaren* 93
    (1972): 189-199.

    A thoughtful review of nos. 352, 307, 346, 95, 373,
    700, 390, and 694.

23. Hamelau, Karin. "Kommentierte Auswahlbibliographie zu
    Heinrich Heine." *TK*, Nos. 18/19 (1968): 45-49.

    A very selective general bibliography, partly dependent
    upon no. 12, with not always judicious comments.

24. Hay, Louis. "Henri Heine et ses critiques. Travaux
    de bibliographie internationale." *RLC* 35 (1961): 258-
    261.

    International research report on the centennial year.

25. Hermand, Jost. *Streitobjekt Heine: Ein Forschungsbericht
    1945-1975*. Frankfurt am Main: Athenäum Fischer Taschen-
    buch Verlag, 1975. 200 pp.

    Though very thorough and accurate in its coverage of
    thirty years of Heine scholarship, the critical account
    is marked by extreme tendentiousness, acknowledging only
    the most radical viewpoints and consistently hostile to
    any literary criticism, which is said to "degrade" Heine
    to a poet. Argument and analysis are replaced by an in-
    temperate denunciatory rhetoric.

26. Immerwahr, Raymond. "Heine." "The Romantic Movement:
    A Selective and Critical Bibliography." *PQ* 40 (1961):
    233; 41 (1962): 707-708. Reprinted pp. 1457, 1544-
    1545 in *The Romantic Bibliography 1936-1970: A Master
    Cumulation from ELH, Philological Quarterly and English
    Language Notes*, ed. A.C. Elkins and L.J. Forstner. Vol.
    IV: 1960-1964. Ann Arbor: Pierian Press, 1973.

    Continuation of no. 27.

27. Kahn, Robert L. "Heine." "The Romantic Movement: A
    Selective and Critical Bibliography." *PQ* 37 (1958):
    212-213; 38 (1959): 202; 39 (1960): 202. Reprinted
    pp. 1162-1163, 1268, 1363 in *The Romantic Movement
    Bibliography 1936-1970: A Master Cumulation from ELH,
    Philological Quarterly and English Language Notes*, ed.
    A.C. Elkins and L.J. Forstner. Vol. III: 1955-1959.
    Ann Arbor: Pierian Press, 1973.

    Continuation of no. 38.

28. Lischke, Johannes. "Heinrich Heines 'Romanzero' und 'Der
    Doktor Faust' in den deutschen Bibliographien." *Börsen-
    blatt für den deutschen Buchhandel* (Leipzig) 132 (1965):
    382-384.

    Corrects the entries for the first editions of *Romanzero*
    and *Faust* in no. 48.

29. Malycky, Alexander. "A Note on the Writings of Karl Emil
    Franzos on Heinrich Heine." *Studies in Bibliography and*

Booklore 6 (1962/64): 73-74.

Additions to no. 48.

30. Mende, Fritz. "Der lebendige Heine in unserer Zeit. Zu
     einigen neueren einbändigen Heine-Anthologien." *WB* 6
     (1960): 648-662.

     A report on several anthologies in German, English,
     French, and Russian.

31. Nerjes, Günther. "Heine." "The Romantic Movement: A
     Selective and Critical Bibliography." *ELN*, Supplement,
     3 (1965): 103-105; 4 (1966): 101-103; 5 (1967): 95-97;
     6 (1968): 99-100. Reprinted pp. 1854-1856, 2001-2003,
     2128-2130, 2268-2269 in *The Romantic Movement Bibliog-
     raphy 1936-1970: A Master Cumulation from ELH, Philo-
     logical Quarterly and English Language Notes*, ed. A.C.
     Elkins and L.J. Forstner. Vol. IV; 1960-1964, Vol. V;
     1965-1967. Ann Arbor: Pierian Press, 1973.

     Successor to no. 36. In Nerjes' hands the bibliography
     began to become more thorough in coverage, critical com-
     ments, and notation of book reviews.

32. Polak, Léon. "Heinrich Heine in englischer Beleuchtung."
     RLV 22 (1956): 33-54.

     Detailed discussion of the work of Sol Liptzin and
     Barker Fairley.

33. Reeves, Nigel. "Heinrich Heine--Politics or Poetry?
     Hegel or Enfantin? A Review of Some Recent Develop-
     ments in Research." *MLR* 75 (1980): 105-113.

     A review article discussing nos. 764, 324, 562, and 98,
     and continuing a debate with Sternberger (no. 356) over
     the relative priority of Hegel and Saint-Simonianism in
     Heine's thought.

34. Reiss, H.S. "The Criticism of Heine in the 'Heine-Jahr':
     A Survey." *GL&L* N.S. 11 (1957/58): 130-136.

     An account of the Heine work during the centenary year
     of 1956.

35. ————. "The Criticism of Heine Since the War: An Assess-
     ment." *GL&L* N.S. 9 (1955/56): 210-219.

     An overview of Heine studies from the end of World War
     II to the threshold of the contemporary phase.

36.   ————. "Heine." "The Romantic Movement: A Selective
       and Critical Bibliography." *PQ* 42 (1963): 492-494.
       Reprinted pp. 1626-1628 in *The Romantic Bibliography
       1936-1970: A Master Cumulation from ELH, Philological
       Quarterly and English Language Notes*, ed. A.C. Elkins
       and L.J. Forstner. Vol. IV: 1960-1964. Ann Arbor:
       Pierian Press, 1973.

       Continuation of no. 26.

37.   ————. "The Study of Heine: Retrospect and Prospect."
       GQ 32 (1959): 3-10.

       Accomplishment and unsolved problems in biography,
       history, and criticism.

38.   Rose, Ernst. "Heine." "The Romantic Movement: A Selective
       and Critical Bibliography." *PQ* (1957): 154-155. Re-
       printed pp. 1050-1051 in *The Romantic Movement Bibliog-
       raphy 1936-1970: A Master Cumulation from ELH, Philo-
       logical Quarterly and English Language Notes*, ed. A.C.
       Elkins and L.J. Forstner. Vol. III: 1955-1959. Ann
       Arbor: Pierian Press, 1973.

       Continuation of no. 15.

39.   Rose, William. "Studies of Heine Since the War." *OL*
       10 (1956): 166-174.

       Another examination of Heine scholarship before the
       current upsurge.

40.   Sammons, Jeffrey L. "Current Heine Editions." *GQ* 44
       (1971): 628-639.

       A critical examination of available editions and editing
       problems.

41.   ————. "Heine." "The Romantic Movement: A Selective
       and Critical Bibliography." *ELN*, Supplement, 7 (1969):
       101-106; 8 (1970): 102-108; 9 (1971): 128-140; 10 (1972):
       148-155; 11 (1973): 129-140; 12 (1974): 136-144; 13
       (1975): 144-153; 14 (1976): 121-129; 15 (1977): 160-168;
       16 (1978): 157-166; 17 (1979); 200-210; continued pp.
       279-293 in *The Romantic Movement: A Selective and Criti-
       cal Bibliography for 1979*, ed. David V. Erdman, et al.
       New York and London: Garland, 1980. xxviii + 333 pp.
       The first three reprinted pp. 2428-2433, 2588-2594,
       2772-2784 in *The Romantic Movement Bibliography 1936-
       1970: A Master Cumulation from ELH, Philological Quarterly*

and *English Language Notes*, ed. A.C. Elkins and L.J.
Forstner. Vol. VI, 1968–1970. Ann Arbor: Pierian
Press, 1973.

Successor to no. 31. Further expands coverage, critical
comments, and notation of book reviews.

41a. ————. "Phases of Heine Scholarship, 1957–1971." *GQ*
46 (1973): 56–88.

A critical review, divided into philological, interpretive, and ideological phases.

42. Schäfer-Weiss, Dorothea. "Dichter oder Sozialliterat?
Probleme und Problematik der gegenwärtigen Heine-
Forschung." *Göttingsche Gelehrte Anzeigen* 227 (1975):
72–104.

An extensive review article on nos. 278, 807, 101, 694,
469, and 373, containing an acerbic critique of stylistic
and methodological failings and of one-sidedness in the
literary-sociological approach.

43. Seifert, Siegfried. *Heine-Bibliographie 1954–1964*. Berlin and Weimar: Aufbau-Verlag, 1968. xiv + 396 pp.

A bibliographical listing of 3,743 items, striving for
completeness for the eleven years covered. The successor
to no. 48, to which it makes additions and corrections.
Indispensable to the Heine scholar.

44. Stekelenburg, Dick van. "Heine Forschung." *Deutsche
Bücher* (Amsterdam) 5 (1975): 61–67.

A collective review of nos. 7, 469, 729, 694, 101, 161,
and 216.

45. Thomke, Hellmut. "Dichtung und Politik im Werke Heinrich
Heines. Eine kritische Auseinandersetzung mit einigen
Tendenzen in der Heine-Forschung der Nachkriegszeit."
Pp. 205–211 in *Akten des V. Internationalen Germanisten-
Kongresses Cambridge 1975*, ed. Leonard Forster and Hans-
Gert Roloff. (*JIG*, Series A, Vol. 2, Pt. 4.) Bern and
Frankfurt am Main: Lang, 1976. 365 pp.

Complains of one-sidedness in both Marxist and "bourgeois" criticism.

46. Vogel, Carl Ludwig. "Heinrich Heine Year 1972." *Central
Europe Journal* 20 (1972): 141–144.

A brief and not always strictly accurate account of the
situation in 1972.

47. Werner, Michael. "Sozialgeschichtliche Heine-Forschung 1970 bis 1978." *Internationales Archiv für Sozialgeschichte der deutschen Literatur* 5 (1980): 234-250.

   A sensible and well-informed report on recent scholarly work on Heine's biography and social situation, the censorship, and his relations to his publisher, the press, and the public.

48. Wilhelm, Gottfried, and Eberhard Galley. *Heine Bibliographie*. 2 vols. Weimar: Arion Verlag, 1960. 192, 294 pp.

   Lists 2,011 items of primary literature and 4,032 of secondary literature from the beginning through 1953. Indispensable to the Heine scholar.

III

BIOGRAPHICAL STUDIES

49. Bartelt, Frauke. "Zur Entstehungsgeschichte der 'Ver-
    mischten Schriften.' Ein fingierter Brief des Kölner
    Musikverlegers Michael Schloß an Heine vom 22. August
    1853." *HJ 1974*, pp. 53-59.

    Shows how Heine had his composer friend fake a letter
    claiming offers from other publishers to bring pressure
    on his own publisher.

50. Becker, Heinz. *Der Fall Heine-Meyerbeer: Neue Dokumente
    revidieren ein Geschichtsurteil*. Berlin: De Gruyter,
    1958. 149 pp.

    A documented re-examination of Heine's opaque relations
    with Giacomo Meyerbeer, in general vindicating Meyerbeer.
    Important.

51. Benda, Gisela. "'Dem Dichter war so wohl daheime....'
    Heines verhaltene Deutschlandliebe." *HJ 1972*, pp.
    117-125.

    Shows that Heine was deeply attached to his German
    homeland.

52. Bianquis, Geneviève. "Heine et George Sand." *EG* 11 (1956):
    114-121.

    Combats the legend of Heine as George Sand's lover.

53. Brand, Jean-Jacques. "Heinrich Heine in Frankreich."
    NDL 4, No. 2 (February 1956): 41-46.

    Casual observations on Heine's life and connections
    in France.

54. Briegleb, Klaus. "Der 'Geist der Gewalthaber' über Wolf-
    gang Menzel: Zur Dialektik des denunziatorischen Prinzips
    in der neuen Literatur 1827/28-1835/36. Mit einem

19

Neudruck aus dem preußischen Auftragspamphlet 'Heinrich
Heine und Ein Blick auf unsere Zeit' (1834)." Pp. 117-
150 in *Demokratisch-revolutionäre Literatur in Deutschland: Vormärz*, ed. Gert Mattenklott and Klaus R. Scherpe.
Literatur im historischen Prozess 3/2. Kronberg: Scriptor Verlag, 1975. 263 pp.

An argument that Menzel's reactionary position grew out
of his liberalism, and that Heine had always been ideologically superior to him. Contains the introduction of
a pamphlet commissioned by the Prussian government recom-
mending that Heine be imprisoned or killed.

55.   ———. "Schriftstellernöte und literarische Produktivi-
      tät. Zum Exempel Heinrich Heine." Pp. 121-159 in
      Neue Ansichten zu einer künftigen Germanistik, ed.
      Jürgen Kolbe. Munich: Hanser, 1973. 357 pp.

Presents in more discursive form the thesis spread out
through Briegleb's edition (no. 1) that Heine's difficulties with the censorship, his public, and his publisher
were a process of learning the impossibility of his emancipatory purposes as a writer in his social and political
situation.

56.   Brinitzer, Carl. *Heinrich Heine: Roman seines Lebens*.
      Hamburg: Hoffmann und Campe, 1960. 594 pp.

A popular, in many places fictionalized biography, not
without intelligent insight, but subject to legend and
speculation owing to its lack of scholarly control.

57.   ———. *Das streitbare Leben des Verlegers Julius Campe*.
      Hamburg: Hoffmann und Campe, 1962. 352 pp.

A biography of Heine's publisher, less fictionalized
than the foregoing item, but subject to similar limitations
owing to the lack of documentation. Nevertheless, the
best account of Campe's life and career before the appear-
ance of the study by Ziegler (no. 169).

58.   Brod, Leo. "Heinrich Heine und Prag." *HJ 1970*, pp. 99-
      109.

Deals primarily with Heine's ill-fated investment in the
Prague gas company "Iris."

59.   Brod, Max. *Heinrich Heine: The Artist in Revolt*. London:
      Vallentine, Mitchell, 1956. x + 355 pp. Republished
      New York: New York University Press, 1957, and New

York: Collier Books, 1962. 381 pp. Original German
as *Heinrich Heine*. Berlin-Grünewald: Non Stop Bücherei,
1956, 238 pp.

Although this is a slightly revised version of a book
that first appeared in 1934, it is listed here because
of its considerable influence around 1956. Though the
scholarship is not reliable, the work contains many thoughtful insights from the sensibility of an accomplished writer.
The Zionist perspective, however, attempts to remove Heine
from the history of German literature and place him in a
separate sequence of Jewish literature, a view that cannot
stand up to scrutiny.

60. Bühler, Hans-Eugen. "Die Wasenmeisterfamilie Edel aus
Düsseldorf. Historisch genealogische Hintergründe der
Begegnung Heinrich Heines mit Josepha Edel." *Genealogie*
15, No. 2 (February 1980): 33-43.

The genealogical facts concerning dishonorable executioners' and knackers' families in the Düsseldorf area
in support of the identification argued in no. 61 below.

61. ————, and Gregor Hövelmann. "Harry Heine und Josepha
Edel. Zum Wirklichkeitsgehalt von Heines 'Memoiren.'"
HJ 1978, pp. 218-223.

An attempt to suggest the real existence of the executioner's daughter Heine claimed in his memoirs to have
loved as a boy.

62. Butler, E.M. "Fragments of a Great Confession." *University of Toronto Quarterly* 25 (1955/56): 109-120.

Considerations on Heine's autobiographical writings,
with special attention to the fragmentary memoirs.

63. ————. *Heinrich Heine: A Biography*. London: Hogarth
Press, 1956. xii + 291 pp.

One of the liveliest of the major Heine biographies,
with much scholarly experience behind it, but rather
susceptible to legend, especially in regard to Heine's
love life.

64. Cheval, René. *Heinrich Heine zwischen Deutschland und
Frankreich*. Schriften der Heinrich Heine-Gesellschaft,
Düsseldorf, 4. Düsseldorf: Heinrich Heine-Gesellschaft,
1969. 19 pp.

In contrast to the usual sentimental view of Heine as
a mediator between France and Germany, Cheval stresses

aspects of his isolation in French exile and the negative
opinions of him among contemporary French intellectuals.

65. Cuby, Louis. "Die theologische Revision in Heines Spät-
    zeit." Windfuhr, ed., *Heine-Kongreß*, pp. 336-342.

    Closely analyzes the texts of Heine's religious "return."

66. Dirrigl, Michael. "Heinrich Heine." Pp. 393-426 in Dir-
    rigl, *Residenz der Musen. München: Magnet für Musiker
    Dichter und Denker. Studien zur Kultur- und Geistes-
    geschichte Münchens.* Munich: Bruckmann, 1968. 768 pp.

    A popular account of Heine's half year in Munich.

67. Dresch, Joseph. *Heine à Paris (1831-1856) d'après sa
    correspondance et les témoignages de ses contemporains.*
    Paris: Didier, 1956. 177 pp.

    A documentary study of Heine's connections and influence
    in Paris. While some of the information has since been
    superseded, its cautious judgments might well have been
    imitated by other scholars.

68. Eisner, Fritz H. "Einige Rätsel in Heines Leben." *HJ
    1968*, pp. 32-38.

    A review of several unsolved biographical riddles.

69. Finke, Franz. "Gustav Hugos Laudatio auf Heine." *HJ
    1968*, pp. 12-17.

    Gives the text of Professor Hugo's Latin laudation upon
    the award of Heine's doctoral degree, praising him little
    as a law student but strongly as a poet.

70. Fränkel, Jonas. "Heine, der Jude." *Israelitisches
    Wochenblatt für die Schweiz.* February 17, 1956.
    Special supplement, unpaged.

    Stresses that Heine was a German poet and that he saw
    his apostasy to Judaism as treason.

71. Galley, Eberhard. "Harry Heine als Benutzer der Landes-
    bibliothek in Düsseldorf." *HJ 1971*, pp. 30-42.

    Shows that Heine as a boy was very bookish and a con-
    stant borrower of library books. Includes a list of the
    books he borrowed.

72. ————. "Heine." Pp. 285-291 in *Neue Deutsche Biographie.*
    VIII (Berlin: Duncker & Humblot, 1969). xvi + 784 pp.

    A general account in a major biographical compendium.

73. ————. "Heine im literarischen Streit mit Gutzkow. Mit
    unbekannten Manuskripten aus Heines Nachlaß." *HJ 1966*,
    pp. 3-40. Reprinted in Koopmann, ed., *Heinrich Heine*,
    pp. 164-206.

    A detailed scholarly account of the quarrelsome rela-
    tions between Heine and Karl Gutzkow.

74. ————. "Heine und der Kölner Dom." *DVLG* 32 (1958):
    99-110.

    Shows that Heine, though he satirized the project to
    resume construction of the Cologne Cathedral, was a
    member of a Paris committee collecting funds for it.

75. ————. "Heine und die Burschenschaft. Ein Kapitel aus
    Heines politischem Werdegang zwischen 1819 und 1830."
    HJ 1972, pp. 66-95.

    Reviews the facts and historical background of Heine's
    connection with a student fraternity, and argues that
    his expulsion occurred not on grounds of unchastity,
    as tradition reports, but out of anti-Semitic policy.

76. ————. *Heinrich Heine.* Sammlung Metzler, M 30. Stutt-
    gart: Metzler, 1973. vi + 82 pp. 4th rev. ed., 1976.

    A basic, primary reference source for anyone learning
    about Heine.

77. ————. *Heinrich Heine: Lebensbericht mit Bildern und
    Dokumenten.* Kassel: Georg Wenderoth Verlag, 1973.
    168 pp.

    A handsome, profusely illustrated account of Heine's
    life and times.

78. ————. "Heinrich Heines Privatbibliothek." *HJ 1962*,
    pp. 96-116.

    A detailed description of the remnant of Heine's private
    library preserved in Düsseldorf. Important for scholar-
    ship.

79. ————. "Das rote Sefchen und ihr Lied von der Otilje.
    Ein Kapitel Dichtung und Wahrheit in Heines 'Memoiren.'"
    HJ 1975, pp. 77-92.

    Speculations on Heine's alleged youthful love for the
    executioner's daughter.

80. Gössmann, Wilhelm. "Die theologische Revision Heines in
    der Spätzeit." Windfuhr, ed., *Heine-Kongreß*, pp. 320-
    335.

    An analysis of the context and terms of Heine's reli-
    gious return.

81. Grabowska, Maria. "Heine und Polen--die erste Begegnung."
    Windfuhr, ed., *Heine-Kongreß*, pp. 349-369.

    An account of the circumstances of Heine's visit to
    Poland, detailed but covering familiar ground.

82. Grandjonc, Jacques. "Die deutschen Emigranten in Paris.
    Ihr Verhältnis zu Heinrich Heine." Windfuhr, ed.,
    Heine-Kongreß, pp. 165-177.

    A thorough student of the German refugee community in
    Paris in the 1830s and 1840s examines Heine's relations
    with it.

83. Grupe, Walter. "Goethes ehemaliger Sekretär John als
    Zensor Heinrich Heines." *DU* (East) 9 (1956): 623-627.

    Karl Ernst John became a Prussian censorship official
    after Goethe dismissed him. The article discusses his
    reports on Heine's introduction to *Don Quixote*, the
    second edition of *Buch der Lieder*, *Über den Denunzianten*,
    and the third edition of the *Reisebilder*.

84. ────. "'Ein Scheusal von Schrift...' Heine-Akten
    im ehemaligen Preußischen Staatsarchiv zu Merseburg."
    NDL 4, No. 9 (September 1956): 157-160.

    Traces the response to *Reisebilder IV* by the Prussian
    censorship, showing which passages were objected to.

85. ────. "Der Treibjagd der preußischen Junker auf Hein-
    rich Heine im Jahre 1844." *DU* (East) 9 (1956): 731-
    733.

    On the efforts of the Prussian government to have Heine
    expelled from France.

86. Guichard, Léon. "Berlioz et Heine." *RLC* 41 (1967):
    5-23.

    A thorough investigation of Heine's cordial relation-
    ship with Berlioz, showing that there is much more mater-
    ial than had been previously realized.

87. Heim, Harro. "Freiligrath über Heine. Eine Anekdote."
    HJ 1965, pp. 48-50.

    An anecdote by Freiligrath in English relating to a
    visit to Heine by Alexander von Humboldt.

88. Heinegg, Peter. "Heine's Conversion and the Critics."
    GL&L N.S. 30 (1976/77): 45-51.

    Argues the sincerity of Heine's late religious "return."

89. Heinemann, Gerd. *Die Beziehungen des jungen Heine zu
    Zeitschriften im Rheinland und in Westfalen: Unter-
    suchungen zum literarischen Leben der Restaurationszeit.*
    Geschichtliche Arbeiten zur Meinungsbildung und zu
    den Kommunikationsmitteln in Westfalen, Vol. I. Münster:
    Aschendorff, 1974. xii + 289 pp.

    A learned and informative if somewhat labored study of
    Heine's relations to six of fifty Rhenish and Westphalian
    periodicals in which he published in the earliest part
    of his career.

90. ————. "Heine und Cotta. Zu Problemen des freien
    Schriftstellers in der Restaurationzeit." Kuttenkeuler,
    ed., *Heinrich Heine: Artistik und Engagement*, pp. 256-266.

    Problems in Heine's relationship to the powerful pub-
    lisher Baron Cotta.

91. Hess, John A. "Heine's Return to Religion: Two Catholic
    Factors." *KFLQ* 5 (1958): 88-94.

    A rather pointless inquiry as to whether Heine lacked
    the courage to join the Catholic Church.

92. Heymann, Fritz. "Der Chevalier von Geldern." Pp. 245-
    359 in Heymann, *Der Chevalier von Geldern: Eine Chronik
    der Abenteuer der Juden.* Cologne: Melzer, 1963. xvi
    + 480 pp.

    Originally published in 1937, this is the first exten-
    sive, popular but informative account of Heine's adventurous
    great-uncle Simon van Geldern.

93. Hilscher, Eberhard. "Heinrich Heine und Richard Wagner."
    NDL 4, No. 12 (December 1956): 107-112.

    Heine's relations with and influence on Wagner.

94. Hirsch, Helmut. "Karl Ludwig Bernays. Heines Kampf-
    gefährte aus den vierziger Jahren." *HJ 1974*, pp. 85-
    102.

    Heine's connections to one of his radical acquaintances.

95. Hultberg, Helge. *Heine: Levned, Meninger, Bøger.* Copen-
    hagen: Munksgaard, 1969. 235 pp. Tr. as *Heine: Leben,
    Ansichten, Bücher.* Kopenhagener germanistische Studien,
    Vol. 4. Copenhagen: Akademisk Forlag, 1974. 210 pp.

    A combination of biography and comprehensive criticism
    that stresses Heine's artistry and aesthetic attitude
    toward life; the argument denies importance to Heine's
    extrinsic commitments, devalues the poetry, and is
    marred by careless reading and factual imprecision.

96. Johnston, Otto W. "Miszelle. Heinrich Heine and the
    Thirteenth of December." *CG* [6], 1972: 196-202.

    Suggests that Heine might have picked December 13, 1799,
    as his birthdate because that was the date of the comple-
    tion of the Napoleonic constitution that emancipated the
    Jews.

97. Kanowsky, Walter. "Heine als Benutzer der Bibliotheken
    in Bonn and Göttingen." *HJ 1973*, pp. 129-153.

    Shows that Heine was an exceptionally frequent borrower
    of books as a student.

98. ————. *Vernunft und Geschichte: Heinrich Heines Studium
    als Grundlegung seiner Welt- und Kunstanschauung.*
    Abhandlungen zur Kunst-, Musik- und Literaturwissenschaft,
    Vol. 150. Bonn: Bouvier, 1975. [viii] + 434 pp.

    A richly informative examination of Heine's university
    professors and their possible influence on him; less
    valuable in respect to Hegel and the other well-known
    figures than to the lesser professors.

99. Krueger, Joachim. *Heine und Berlin.* Berlin: Berliner
    Heine-Komitee, 1956. 31 pp.

    Describes Heine's personal contacts in Berlin in the
    1820s.

100. Kruse, Joseph A. *Heines Hamburger Zeit.* Heine-Studien,
     ed. Manfred Windfuhr. Hamburg: Hoffmann und Campe,
     Heinrich Heine Verlag, 1972. 372 pp.

     A dry but extremely detailed study of Heine's experiences

in Hamburg, the Hamburg environment as it related to
Heine, and the reflex of Hamburg in his works.

101. Kryzwon, Ernst Josef. *Heinrich Heine und Polen.* Cologne
      and Vienna: Böhlau Verlag, 1972. 376 pp.

      A detailed study of Heine's visit to and writings on
      Poland and his connections to Polish persons.

102. ————. "Heinrich Heine und Polen: Modell für eine
      deutsch-polnische Verständigung?" *Stimmen der Zeit*
      190 (1972): 373-388.

      Reviews the theme of the preceding book and weighs
      its value for international understanding.

103. Kuttenkeuler, Wolfgang. "Heinrich Heine und Karl L.
      Immermann. Produktivität eines wechselseitigen
      Mißverständnisses." *ZDP* 91 (1972), Special Issue
      Heine und seine Zeit: 90-110.

      Points out the worthwhile aspects of Heine's relation-
      ship with Immermann despite incongruities between them.

104. Lefebvre, Jean-Pierre. "Heine à Boulogne-sur-mer." *RLC*
      47 (1973): 196-224.

      Discusses the details and circumstances of all of
      Heine's visits to Boulogne.

105. Lehrmann, Cuno Ch. *Heinrich Heine: Kämpfer und Dichter.*
      Bern: Francke, 1957. 220 pp.

      An undocumented, "intuitive," confidently written
      biography, with quotations from Heine woven in. While
      the book is not without perceptive judgment, the method
      is vulnerable to legend and impressionism.

106. Leonhardt, Rudolf Walter. *Das Weib, das ich geliebet
      hab: Heines Mädchen und Frauen.* Hamburg: Hoffmann
      und Campe, 1975. 184 pp.

      An occasionally perceptive, not always accurate, and
      sometimes mildly sensationalized account of Heine's
      relations with women.

107. Lilge, Herbert. *Heinrich Heine: Biographie und Auswahl.*
      Hanover: Verlag für Literatur und Zeitgeschehen, 1960.
      64 pp.

      A brief popular biography with exemplary texts, stres-
      sing Heine as a political writer.

108. Liptzin, Sol. "Heinrich Heine's Homecoming." *Jewish Book Annual* 13 (1955/56): 55-57.

      A sketchy argument making Heine's religious "return" paradigmatic for Jews who renounce assimilation.

109. Lüth, Erich. *Der Bankier und der Dichter: Zur Ehrenrettung des grossen Salomon Heine.* Tambour-Bücherei, No. 1. Hamburg-Altona: Verlag "Der gute Tambour," [1964]. 46 pp.

      A brief popular account of Uncle Salomon Heine.

110. ————. *Hamburgs Juden in der Heine-Zeit.* Hamburg: Hoffmann und Campe, [1961]. 27 pp.

      Sketches of Jewish personalities in Heine's Hamburg environment.

111. Maché, Ulrich. "Der junge Heine und Goethe. Eine Revision der Auffassung von Heines Verhältnis zu Goethe vor dem Besuch in Weimar (1824)." *HJ 1965*, pp. 42-47. Reprinted Koopmann, ed., *Heinrich Heine*, pp. 156-163.

      An important reconsideration of young Heine's attitude to Goethe.

112. Marcuse, Ludwig. *Heinrich Heine in Selbstzeugnissen und Bilddokumenten.* rowohlts monographien, No. 41. Reinbek bei Hamburg: Rowohlt Taschenbuch Verlag, 1960. 178 pp.

      Since this is a version of a book originally published in German and English in the 1930s, it is the longest-lived of books on Heine, here in the familiar illustrated Rowohlt format. Observant and intelligent, though not up to scholarly standards. See also no. 113.

113. ————. *Heine: Melancholiker, Streiter in Marx, Epikureer.* Rothenburg ob der Tauber: Verlag J.P. Peter, Gebr. Holstein, 1970. 467 pp.

      A revised and expanded version of no. 112.

114. Mayer, Hans. "Rothschild und Heine." Pp. 350-366 in Mayer, *Aussenseiter.* Frankfurt am Main: Suhrkamp, 1975. 511 pp.

      A thoughtful and witty examination of Heine's curious relations with the Rothschild family.

115. Mende, Fritz. *Heine Chronik: Daten zu Leben und Werk*.
     Munich: Hanser, 1975. 278 pp.

     A new version of no. 116. Although some of the errors
     have been corrected, the material has been abridged and
     the ancillary information deleted, so that the earlier
     version is still the more recommendable to the scholar.

116. ————. *Heinrich Heine: Chronik seines Lebens und
     Werkes*. Berlin: Akademie-Verlag, 1970. xvi + 418 pp.

     A day-by-day chronicle of all of Heine's known and
     suspected activities along with much ancillary informa-
     tion. Despite an occasional inaccuracy, indispensable
     to the Heine scholar.

117. Monz, Heinz. "Karl Marx und Heinrich Heine verwandt?"
     Jahrbuch des Instituts für deutsche Geschichte (Tel
     Aviv) 2 (1973): 199-207.

     A tenuous genealogical argument suggesting that Heine
     and Karl Marx may have been distantly related.

118. Na'aman, Shlomo. "Heine und Lassalle. Ihre Beziehungen
     im Zeichen der Dämonie des Geldes." *Archiv für Sozial-
     geschichte* 4 (1964): 45-86.

     On the problems in Heine's relations with Ferdinand
     Lassalle.

119. ————. "Heinrich Heine als zentrales Problem einer
     Lassalle-Biographie." *HJ 1968*, pp. 18-31.

     Deals with the same subject as the preceding item.

120. Netter, Lucienne. "Une campagne de presse contre Heine."
     EG 27 (1972): 80-86.

     Proves that Heine's enemy Salomon Strauss, in the wake
     of the *Börne* affair, planted paid items disguised as news
     reports against Heine in Parisian newspapers.

121. ————. "Heine, Thiers et la presse parisienne en 1840."
     RdA 4 (1972): 113-153.

     Describes what is known about Heine's unclear relations
     with Adolphe Thiers and shows that, despite his criti-
     cisms, he generally supported Thiers's policies in his
     journalism.

122. Paraf, Pierre. "Henri Heine et Hans-Christian Andersen."
      Europe, Nos. 125/126 (May-June 1956): 67-71.

      A sentimentalized and somewhat fictionalized account
      of Heine's first meeting with Andersen in 1833.

123. Porcell, Claude. "Genèse d'un silence. Henri Heine
      et ses 'Aveux.'" *Littérature*, No. 28 (December 1977):
      63-76.

      A "deconstructionist" approach to Heine's reticence
      concerning Napoleon in the German and French drafts of
      the *Geständnisse*.

124. Prawer, S.S. "Heine's Return." *GL&L* N.S. 9 (1955/56):
      171-180.

      A rather skeptical view of Heine's religious "return."

125. ———. "Heines Stimme." *HJ 1964*, pp. 56-62.

      On the quality of Heine's speaking voice, deduced from
      the phonetics of his poetry.

126. Raddatz, Fritz J. *Heine: Ein deutsches Märchen. Essay.*
      Hamburg: Hoffmann und Campe, 1977. 204 pp.

      A biographical impromptu, arguing that Heine's main
      allegiance was to unfettered artistry. Extremely care-
      less in fact and judgment; not recommended.

127. Radlik, Ute. "Heine in der Zensur der Restaurations-
      epoche." Pp. 460-489 in *Zur Literatur der Restaura-
      tionsepoche 1815-1848: Forschungsreferate und Aufsätze*,
      ed. Jost Hermand and Manfred Windfuhr. Stuttgart:
      Metzler, 1970. viii + 599 pp.

      A scholarly and historical examination of Heine's rela-
      tions with the censorship.

128. Raphael, J[akob]. "Die Hamburger Familie Gumpel und
      der Dichter Heinrich Heine." *Zeitschrift für die
      Geschichte der Juden* 6 (1969): 33-38.

      On the banking family of Gumpel, one of whom may have
      been the model for Gumpelino in *Die Bäder von Lucca*.

129. ———. "Die Preßburger Verwandtschaft Heinrich Heines."
      Zeitschrift für die Geschichte der Juden 4 (1967):
      151-154.

      Family and marriage of Heine's maternal great-grandmother.

130. Reeves, Nigel. "Heine and the Young Marx." *OGS* 7 (1972/
      73): 44-97.

      A rational review of Heine's relations with Marx, sug-
      gesting that Heine may have influenced some of the young
      Marx's thinking. Subsequently included in no. 342.

131. Ros, Guido. "Heinrich Heine und die 'Pariser Zeitung'
      von 1838. Ein Beitrag zur Geschichte der deutschen
      Emigrantenpresse in Paris 1830-1848." *Publizistik*
      15 (1970): 216-228.

      A discussion of Heine's plan to found a German news-
      paper in Paris; contains no new information not to be
      found in Heine's letters and Hirth's commentary to them.

132. Rosenthal, Ludwig. "Die Beziehungen des 'Chevalier van
      Geldern' zu regierenden Fürstenhäusern, hohen Staats-
      beamten und anderen Standespersonen." *HJ 1975*, pp.
      115-149.

      MS. materials on the high social connections of Heine's
      great-uncle Simon van Geldern.

133. ————. *Heinrich Heines Großoheim Simon von Geldern:*
      Ein historischer Bericht mit dem bisher meist unver-
      öffentlichten Quellenmaterial. Veröffentlichungen
      des Heinrich Heine-Instituts Düsseldorf, ed. Joseph
      A. Kruse. Kastellaun: Aloys Henn, 1978. 210 pp.

      Materials and results of Rosenthal's extensive researches
      into the life of Heine's great-uncle; the definitive
      study of the subject.

134. ————. "Neue Einblicke in das Leben und die Persön-
      lichkeit von Heines Großoheim Simon van Geldern (Sein
      Addressenverzeichnis)." *HJ 1973*, pp. 154-199.

      Results of researches into Simon van Geldern's address
      book.

135. Roth, Nathan, M.D. "The Porphyria of Heinrich Heine."
      Comprehensive Psychiatry 10, No. 2 (March 1969): 90-
      106. Reprinted, without reference notes, as "The
      Porphyria of Heinrich Heine." *Elmcrest Classic of*
      the Month, Vol. III, No. 3. Portland, Connecticut:
      Elmcrest Psychiatric Institute, 1978.

      Argues that Heine's disease was not venereal but was
      a case of acute intermittent porphyria. Weakened by
      ill-informed psychological speculations.

136.   Rümmler, Else. "Düsseldorf zur Zeit Heinrich Heines."
       Düsseldorf (1972, No. 3): 21-24.

       Illustrated description of Düsseldorf in Heine's boy-
       hood.

137.   Sammons, Jeffrey L. "Dilemmas of Literary Biography:
       The Case of Heine." Immerwahr and Spencer, eds.,
       Heinrich Heine, pp. 9-22.

       Considerations on general and specific problems of
       literary biography drawn from the experience of compos-
       ing no. 138.

138.   ————. *Heinrich Heine: A Modern Biography*. Princeton:
       Princeton University Press, 1979. xviii + 425 pp.

       A fully documented biography based on modern scholar-
       ship.

139.   Schmidt, Wolff A. von. "Heine und Marx." *Archiv für
       Kulturgeschichte* 54 (1972): 143-152.

       Attacks non-Marxist scholars for minimizing the rela-
       tionship, but agrees that Heine was not a follower of
       Marx and argues correctly that Heine influenced Marx
       more than vice-versa.

140.   Schneider, Manfred. "Die Angst des Revolutionärs vor
       der Revolution. Zur Genese und Struktur des politischen
       Diskurses bei Heine." *HJ 1980*, pp. 9-48. Expanded
       and somewhat revised pp. 27-86 in Schneider, *Die kranke
       schöne Seele der Revolution: Heine, Börne, das "Junge
       Deutschland," Marx und Engels*. Frankfurt am Main:
       Syndikat, 1980. 314 pp. Published in part as "'...
       Die Liebe für schöne Frauen und die Liebe für die
       französische Revolution...' Anmerkungen zum romanti-
       schen Spracherwerb und zur Ikonographie des politischen
       Diskurses bei Heine." Pp. 158-193 in *Perspektiven
       psychoanalytischer Literaturkritik*, ed. Sebastian
       Goeppert. Freiburg im Breisgau: Rombach, 1978. 276
       pp.

       The most significant and probing psychoanalytic treat-
       ment of Heine, convincingly tracing the peculiarities
       of his personality and conduct to his mother's repression
       of his imaginative and emotional faculties.

141.   Schoeps, Hans-Joachim. "Ein unbekannter Agentenbericht
       über Heinrich Heine." *HJ 1967*, pp. 67-80.

       An 1833 report to the Berlin court on Heine by a

secret agent, probably the Oriental scholar, H.J. Klaproth.

142. Schulte, Klaus H.S. "Das letzte Jahrzehnt von Heinrich
     Heines Vater in Düsseldorf. Notariatsurkunden über
     Samson Heines Geschäfte (1808-1821)." *HJ 1974*, pp.
     105-131.

     Documentary research yields very interesting and
     illuminating information on the bankruptcy of Heine's
     father and Heine's own business failure.

143. Steinhauer, Harry. "Heine and Cécile Furtado: A Re-
     consideration." *MLN* 89 (1974): 422-447.

     A demythifying examination of Heine's relations and
     difficulties with Cousin Carl Heine's wife, Cécile, and
     her family.

144. Stern, Arthur. "Heinrich Heines Krankheit und seine
     Ärzte." *HJ 1964*, pp. 63-79. Original version in
     Schweizer Rundschau für Medizin 45 (1956): 357-364.

     The most recent scientific study of Heine's illness
     and treatment.

145. Stöcker, Hans. "Heines rheinische Zeitgenossen." *HJ
     1972*, pp. 96-109.

     Information on the friends and acquaintances of Heine's
     youth.

146. Thomas, Marcel. "Heine Franc-Maçon." Windfuhr, ed.,
     Heine-Kongreß, pp. 155-164.

     Heine's possible connection to Freemasonry in Paris.

147. Uhlmann, A.M. *Heinrich Heine: Sein Leben in Bildern.*
     Leipzig: VEB Bibliographisches Institut, 1964. 63
     pp. + 48 plates with 97 illustrations.

     An unanalytical, orthodox, and flat biographical
     sketch accompanied by a useful collection of illustra-
     tions with not always accurate captions.

148. Veit, Philipp F. "Heine and his Cousins. A Reconsider-
     ation." *GR* 47 (1972): 20-40.

     Endeavors to reconstruct the probabilities in the
     relationship between Heine and his cousins Amalie and
     Therese by extrapolating from the sociology of Jewish
     marriage at the time; concludes that Heine's interest
     in them was pecuniary and as a resource for poetry.

149. ————. "Heine: The Marrano Pose." *Monatshefte* 66
     (1974): 145-156.

     Argues that Heine imagined himself to be of Spanish
     Marrano descent, pretending to an aristocratic Jewish
     heritage.

150. ————. "Heine's Birth: Illegitimate or Legitimate?"
     GR 33 (1958): 276-284. See also "Two Corrections,"
     GR 34 (1959): 241.

     Examines the problems surrounding the mystery of Heine's
     birthdate, and establishes the marriage date of his par-
     ents, thus proving he was not illegitimate.

151. ————. "Heine's Birthday." *GR* 36 (1961): 35-39.

     Reconsideration of the evidence leads to a hypothesis
     that Heine was born in February 1798 and that the birth-
     dates of his siblings need also to be readjusted.

152. ————. "Heinrich Heine und David Friedländer." *HJ*
     1980, pp. 227-234.

     Heine's opposition to the views of the extreme Jewish
     assimilationist David Friedländer, a great-uncle of
     Cousin Amalie's husband, whom Veit connects to Hyacinth
     Hirsch in *Die Bäder von Lucca*.

153. ————. "Die Rätsel um Heines Geburt." *HJ 1962*, pp.
     5-25.

     A revised and translated version of nos. 150 and 151.

154. Vontin, Walther. "Heinrich Heine und Hebbels 'Judith.'"
     HJ 1963, pp. 43-59.

     Discusses Heine's relations with Hebbel and suggests
     that Heine's account of Vernet's painting of *Judith*
     might have influenced Hebbel's tragedy.

155. Vordtriede, Werner. "Der Berliner Saint-Simonismus."
     HJ 1975, pp. 93-110.

     Heine's possible acquaintance with Saint-Simonianism
     in Berlin through Varnhagen.

156. Wadepuhl, Walter. "Heine auf dem Düsseldorfer Lyceum
     und Gymnasium." Wadepuhl, *Heine-Studien*, pp. 33-38.

     Researches into Heine's schooling.

157. ————. "Heine's Geburtsjahr." Wadepuhl, *Heine-Studien*,
      pp. 9-32. Originally published in *PMLA* 61 (1946):
      126-156.

      Discussion of Heine's birthdate, arguing illegitimacy.
      Since superseded.

158. ————. "Heines Memoiren." Wadepuhl, *Heine-Studien*,
      pp. 152-173.

      History and fate of the text of Heine's *Memoiren*.
      Since superseded.

159. ————. "Heine und Campe, Dichter und Verleger."
      Wadepuhl, *Heine-Studien*, pp. 61-85.

      Sympathetic examination of the publisher Campe's side
      of the relationship. Since superseded by the publica-
      tion of Campe's correspondence with Heine and other
      studies.

160. ————. "Heine und Friedrich Merckel." Wadepuhl,
      Heine-Studien, pp. 47-60.

      Heine's relations with Campe's editorial assistant
      Merckel.

161. ————. *Heinrich Heine: Sein Leben und seine Werke.*
      Cologne and Vienna: Böhlau Verlag, 1974. xvi + 451
      pp. Republished in paperback: Heyne-Biographie, 38.
      Munich: Heyne, 1977. 474 pp.

      A full-length biography, the bulk of which was un-
      doubtedly written many years ago; untouched by the
      last four decades of Heine scholarship. Many errors
      and misapprehensions. Argues that Heine's opinions
      were corrupted by the Rothschild interest. Undocumented;
      not recommended.

162. Weiss, Gerhard. "Heines Englandaufenthalt (1827)."
      HJ 1963, pp. 3-32.

      Researches Heine's visit to England.

163. Werner, Michael, ed. *Begegnungen mit Heine: Berichte
      der Zeitgenossen, in Fortführung von H.H. Houbens
      "Gespräche mit Heine."* Hamburg: Hoffmann und Campe,
      1973. Vol. I: *1797-1846*; 629 pp. Vol. II: *1847-
      1856*; 740 pp.

      A complete revision and reediting of Houben's long-
      standard edition of Heine's conversations, with an

informative and judicious commentary. An outstanding
achievement, indispensable to the Heine scholar.

164. ————. *Genius und Geldsack: Zum Problem des Schrift-
      stellerberufs bei Heinrich Heine*. Heine-Studien, ed.
      Manfred Windfuhr. Hamburg: Hoffmann und Campe, Hein-
      rich Heine Verlag, 1978. 164 pp.

      The first thorough and reliable examination of Heine's
      finances and income, showing him to have been much more
      prosperous than commonly believed.

165. ————. "Heine's französische Staatspension." *HJ 1977*,
      pp. 134-142.

      Redates the beginning of Heine's French pension to
      1840, showing that Prime Minister Thiers probably had
      some political purpose in granting it.

166. ————. "Imagepflege. Heines Presselenkung zur Propa-
      gierung seines Persönlichkeitsbildes." Kuttenkeuler,
      ed., *Heinrich Heine: Artistik und Engagement*, pp. 267-283.

      A study of Heine's techniques of self-advertisement.

167. Wille, François. "Erinnerungen an Heinrich Heine," ed.
      Eberhard Galley, *HJ 1967*, pp. 3-20.

      An interesting unpublished memoir by one of Heine's
      acquaintances.

168. Wolf, Ruth. *Heinrich Heine: schrijver in ballingschap*.
      [Amsterdam]: Kosmos, 1976. 131 pp.

      A general account for a Dutch audience from a Jewish
      point of view. Contains thoughtful perceptions but
      also many errors; out of touch with contemporary scholar-
      ship.

169. Ziegler, Edda. *Julius Campe: Der Verleger Heinrich
      Heines*. Heine-Studien, ed. Manfred Windfuhr.
      Hamburg: Hoffmann und Campe, Heinrich Heine Verlag,
      1976. 383 pp.

      The most thorough study yet undertaken of Heine's
      relations with his publisher Campe. Exceptional histor-
      ical significance; although some of the factual details
      have been challenged, one of the most interesting and
      informative books on Heine of recent years.

IV

PHILOLOGICAL STUDIES

170. Atkins, Stuart. "The First Draft of Heine's Newsletter from Paris, May 30, 1840." *Harvard Library Bulletin* 15 (1967): 353-367.

A diplomatic transcription of the draft, concerning the decision to return Napoleon's remains to Paris (corresponds to *Lutezia* X), with commentary on the circumstances and Heine's stylistic revisions.

170a. Baum, Wilhelm. "Ein Heinrich-Heine-Manuskript im Besitz von Ludwig von Pastor." *HJ 1971*, pp. 26-29.

MS. of a satire on King Frederick William IV found in the Vatican.

171. Beissner, Friedrich. "Lesbare Varianten. Die Entstehung einiger Verse in Heines 'Atta Troll.'" Pp. 15-23 in *Festschrift Josef Quint, anläßlich seines 65. Geburtstages überreicht*, ed. Hugo Moser, Rudolf Schützeichel, and Karl Stackmann. Bonn: Semmel, 1964. 306 pp.

The experienced Hölderlin editor enters the discussion on how to produce a legible variant apparatus for a critical edition of Heine.

172. Bockelkamp, Marianne. "Ein unbekannter Entwurf zu Heines 'Ideen. Das Buch Le Grand.'" *HJ 1973*, pp. 34-40.

A new MS draft to *Buch Le Grand*.

173. Booss, Rutger. "Dialekteigentümlichkeiten bei Heine." Windfuhr, ed., *Heine-Kongreß*, pp. 514-526.

Heine's increasingly self-conscious employment of Rhenish and Yiddish dialect elements.

174. Carlssohn, Erich. "Erinnerung an bedeutende Sammler (VIII). 'Heinrich Heine--Sammlung Meyer,' Düsseldorf."

Börsenblatt für den deutschen Buchhandel (Frankfurt)
3 (1957): 578-581.

Describes how the important Düsseldorf collection was
accumulated and preserved through the Nazi years.

175. Dyck, Joachim. "Heines Neujahrsglückwunsch für seine
      Kusine Fanny in E.T.A. Hoffmanns 'Elixiere des
      Teufels.'" *HJ 1979*, pp. 202-205.

      A dedication copy to Fanny Heine.

176. Eisner, F.H. "Echtes, Unechtes und Zweifelhaftes in
      Heines Werken. Ergebnisse der Heine-Philologie seit
      1924." *HJ 1962*, pp. 50-69.

      Problems of attribution of questionable Heine texts.

177. ————. "Neues zu 'Heine und die Politischen Annalen.'"
      WB 5 (1959): 425-427.

      Authorship of two articles obtained by Heine for
      publication in the *Politische Annalen*.

178. ————. "Notwendigkeit und Probleme einer definitiven
      Heine-Ausgabe." *WB* 3 (1957): 283-290.

      Some specific philological problems confronting a
      new edition.

179. ————. "Unbekannte Beiträge Heines zum 'Morgenblatt'
      und zur 'Allgemeinen Zeitung.'" *WB* 4 (1958): 72-87.

      New material on music and French politics found in
      the archives of the publisher Cotta.

180. ————. "Vier Manuskriptseiten von Heines 'Ludwig
      Börne.'" *HJ 1973*, pp. 71-74.

      A close MS. examination showing Heine's way of working
      and possible censorship difficulties.

181. Finke, Franz. "Bestandsverzeichnis der Düsseldorfer
      Heine-Autographen. I. Gedichtmanuskripte." *HJ 1968*,
      pp. 75-101.

      First installment of a catalogue of the Düsseldorf MS.
      holdings. See also nos. 196, 208, 209.

182. Francke, Renate, and Fritz Mende. "Aus dem Briefwechsel
      Julius Campes mit der Hofbuchdruckerei in Altenburg:
      Materialien zur Entstehungs- und Druckgeschichte von

Heinrich Heines Werken 1829-1837." Pp. 351-387 in
*Impulse: Aufsätze, Quellen, Berichte zur deutschen
Klassik und Romantik*, Vol. II, ed. Walter Dietze and
Peter Goldammer. Berlin and Weimar: Aufbau-Verlag,
1979. 420 pp.

Excerpts from Campe's correspondence with his printer
are useful documents for the genesis of Heine's works
of the 1830s and the struggle with the censorship.

183. Galley, Eberhard. "Das Düsseldorfer Heine-Archiv.
Geschichte und Aufgabe." *HJ 1968*, pp. 58-74.

Historical account of the archival material in Düsseldorf.

184. ————. "Die Düsseldorfer Heine-Sammlung." *WB* 3 (1957):
278-282.

Similar to no. 183 above.

185. ————. "Heines 'Briefe über Deutschland' und die
'Geständnisse.' Eine Textgeschichte an Hand der
Manuskripte des Heine-Archivs." *HJ 1963*, pp. 60-
84.

Shows how Heine's text and French versions were revised with an eye to the intended public in each case.

186. ————. "Der 'Neunte Artikel' von Heines Werk 'Zur
Geschichte der neueren schönen Literatur in Deutsch-
land. Eine ungedruckte Vorarbeit zur 'Romantischen
Schule.'" *HJ 1964*, pp. 17-36.

An unpublished pre-study to *Die Romantische Schule*.

187. ————. "Problematik der zwei historisch-kritischen
Heineausgaben." *ZDP* 91 (1972), Special Issue *Heine
und seine Zeit*: 205-216.

Describes the differences in concept between the
East and West German critical editions.

188. Germann, Dietrich. "Die Vorbereitungsarbeiten an der
Heine-Säkularausgabe." *Forschungen und Fortschritte*
39 (1965): 273-278.

A description of the complex philological preparations
for the East German critical edition, with some comments
on the inadequacies of previous editions.

189. Grappin, Pierre. "Comment seront éditées les oeuvres
     complètes de Henri Heine." *OGS* 7 (1972/73): 34-43.

     A discussion of the differences between the East and
     West German critical edition by a scholar connected
     with both.

190. Grésillon, Almuth, and Barbara Geiger. "Les brouillons
     allemands de la préface à 'Lutèce.' Histoire textuelle,
     classement et datation des manuscrits." *Cahier Heine*,
     pp. 9-41.

     Textual genesis of the controversial preface criticiz-
     ing Communism.

191. Hahn, Karl-Heinz. "Die Heine-Säkularausgabe: Anliegen
     und Probleme der wissenschaftlichen Edition neuzeit-
     licher poetischer Texte." *Streitbarer Humanist*, pp.
     277-299.

     Defense of the editorial practices of the East German
     critical edition.

192. Hansen, Volkmar. "Hermeneutischer Realkommentar. Über-
     legungen aus Anlaß von Klaus Brieglebs 'Heine-Ausgabe.'"
     HJ 1978, pp. 239-250.

     Critical discussion of the editorial practices in no.
     1.

193. Hay, Louis. "Heine-Handschriften und Heine-Forschung in
     Paris." *JIG* 3 (1971): 331-334.

     Brief description of the Heine materials acquired by
     the Bibliothèque Nationale and the team working on them.

194. Heinemann, Gerd. "Heine und August Gebauer. Eine un-
     bekannte Heine-Strophe." *HJ 1972*, pp. 110-116.

     Discovery in a Rhenish newspaper of previously unknown
     stanzas in Heine's poem to Eugen von Breza.

195. ————. "Zur Entstehungsgeschichte und Datierung der
     'Memoiren' Heinrich Heines." *EG* 32 (1977): 441-444.

     Makes probable that the large gap in the *Memoiren*
     was excised by Heine himself for use in his *Geständnisse*.

196. Hermstrüver, Inge. "Bestandsverzeichnis der Düsseldorfer
     Heine-Autographen. Neuerwerbungen: 1968-1975." *HJ*
     1976, pp. 166-175.

     Continues no. 209.

197. ———, and Joseph A. Kruse. "Bisher unbekannte oder verschollene Briefe, Wechsel und Albumblätter Heinrich Heines aus Privatbesitz sowie im Heine-Archiv." *HJ 1978*, pp. 224-232.

Recent MS. discoveries.

198. Höltgen, Karl Joseph. "'Shakespeares Mädchen und Frauen.' Eine Fehlzuschreibung." *HJ 1975*, pp. 47-49.

The text in the pirated Amsterdam edition of 1854-1861 is not by Heine at all.

199. Holtzhauer, Helmut. "Zur Säkularausgabe von Heines Werken. Briefwechsel und Lebenszeugnissen." *WB* 3 (1957): 266-277.

Guiding principles of the East German critical edition (which at the time was still intended to be a cooperative East-West venture).

200. Kruse, Joseph A. "Die Überlieferung literarisch-kulturhistorischer Quellen. Goethe, Schiller und Heine als Bildner von Literaturarchiven." *HJ 1978*, pp. 186-210.

A justification of the principle of archival preservation, to which is appended a history of the Heinrich Heine-Institut.

201. ———. "Ein Widmungsgedicht Heines an Carl Brunner?" *HJ 1973*, pp. 75-82.

Discovery of a dedicatory poem.

202. Lebrave, Jean-Louis. "La Fréquence des nominalisations chez Heine." *Cahier Heine*, pp. 66-86. Tr. as "Die Frequenz der Nominalisierungen bei Heine." Pp. 108-126 in *Heinrich Heine und die Zeitgenossen*.

A rather inconsequential examination of Heine's employment of substantivized verbs.

203. Mann, Michael. "Heine-Handschriften als Quellenmaterial zu einem biographischen Revisionsbericht. Heines Musikberichte in der 'Allgemeinen Zeitung' und in der 'Lutezia.'" *HJ 1963*, pp. 85-101.

Commentary on the philological work associated with Mann's edition, no. 8.

204. Mende, Fritz. "Der gegenwärtige Stand der Arbeiten an
     der Heine-Säkularausgabe." *Forschungen und Fortschritte*
     41 (1967): 153-156.

     Progress report on the East German critical edition.

205. Moenkemeyer, Heinz. "Die deutschen Erstdrucke von
     Heines 'Doktor Faust.'" *HJ 1966*, pp. 58-67.

     Detailed discussion of the differences between the
     two printings of Heine's *Faust* and their probable chrono-
     logy.

206. Netter, Lucienne. "De nouveaux documents sur Heine et
     ses contemporains à la disposition des chercheurs."
     EG 25 (1970): 135-136.

     Description of the valuable documentary material
     assembled by Friedrich Hirth, now sorted and available
     for use at the Bibliothèque Nationale.

207. Noethlich, Werner. "Was geschah mit Heines Nachlaß?"
     HJ 1966, pp. 107-120.

     The best information to that date on the dispersal
     and fate of Heine's posthumous papers.

208. Radlik, Ute. "Bestandsverzeichnis der Düsseldorfer
     Heine-Autographen II. Epen und Prosa." *HJ 1969*,
     pp. 108-127.

     Continues no. 181.

209. ―――. "Bestandsverzeichnis des Heine-Archivs, Düssel-
     dorf. Autographen. III. Briefe von Heine. VI [*sic*
     for IV]. Briefe an Heine." *HJ 1971*, pp. 90-119.

     Continues nos. 181 and 208.

210. Rendleman, Neal, and Bruce L. Ehrmann. "Is this an
     Unknown Heine Poem?" *GR* 51 (1976): 190-191.

     A trivial satirical verse that might be by Heine.

211. Stöcker, Christa. "Verwirrende Daten in der Druckge-
     schichte von Heines 'Salon,' Ein Beitrag zur Ge-
     schichte der Zensur im 19. Jahrhundert." *WB* 26
     (1980): 158-164.

     A fascinating sidelight on the censorship situation:
     two letters from Campe to his printer that appear to
     order the printing of *Salon I* in 1832 rather than 1833

seem to have been forged and predated by Campe to help
the printer out of threatening difficulties with the
censorship.

212. Vordtriede, Werner. "Drei Heine-Miszellen." *DVLG* 50
      (1976): 537-544.

      Suggests, not equally convincingly, sources for Heine's
      description of Madame de Staël, one of his verse fables,
      and a couple of verse passages.

213. Wadepuhl, Walter. "Steinmanns Heinefälschungen." Wade-
      puhl, *Heine-Studien*, pp. 39-46.

      Discusses the philologically confusing forgeries of
      Heine's quondam friend Friedrich Steinmann.

214. Weber, Gerhard W. "Einigung in Sachen Heine?" *TK*, No.
      21/22 (1968): 81-82.

      History and a brief description of the important
      Schocken Collection of Heine MSS., acquired by the
      Bibliothèque Nationale in 1967.

215. Weidl, Erhard. "Das Elend der Editionstechnik." *LiLi*,
      No. 19/20 (1975): 191-199.

      Excessively polemical discussion of editorial practices.

216. ────. *Heinrich Heines Arbeitsweise: Kreativität der
      Veränderung*. Heine-Studien, ed. Manfred Windfuhr.
      Hamburg: Hoffmann und Campe, Heinrich Heine Verlag,
      1974. 145 pp.

      Close examination of Heine's habits of revision in
      connection with the construction of a variant apparatus
      as well as with Heine's creative habits. Not uninter-
      esting, though poorly written in an ill temper.

217. Weiss, Gerhard. "Niederdeutsche Laute und rheinisches
      Wortgut bei Heinrich Heine." *HJ 1962*, pp. 39-49.

      Dialect elements in Heine's style.

218. Weiss, Wisso. "Papier und Wasserzeichen zu Heine-
      Autographen. Ein Verzeichnis der in der DDR vor-
      handenen Manuskripte." *HJ 1972*, pp. 170-217.

      Detailed examples of the dry but philologically im-
      portant topic of paper types and watermarks.

219. Windfuhr, Manfred, Ute Radlik, and Helga Weidmann, "Die
      Düsseldorfer Heine-Ausgabe." *HJ 1970*, pp. 3–40. Ex-
      panded and revised in *JIG* 3 (1971): 271–330.

      Description and defense of the editorial practices of
      the West German critical edition.

220. Windfuhr, Manfred. "'Ritter Olaf.' Editorische Aspekte
      einer Romanze von Heine." *HJ 1978*, pp. 95–125.

      Exhibits the complex variant problems involved in edit-
      ing even a relatively simple poem.

221. ————. "Zu einer kritischen Gesamtausgabe von Heines
      Werken. Auswertung der Sammlung Strauß." *HJ 1962*,
      pp. 70–95.

      Explanation and defense of the principles of the West
      German critical edition.

222. Zinke, Jochen. "Die Arbeiten am Heine-Index." Wind-
      fuhr, ed., *Heine-Kongreß*, pp. 497–513.

      Report on the work on the word-index to Heine's works.

223. ————. *Autortext und Fremdeingriff: Die Schreibkon-
      ventionen der Heine-Zeit und die Textgeschichte des
      'Buches der Lieder.'* Heine-Studien, ed. Manfred Wind-
      fuhr. Hamburg: Hoffmann und Campe, Heinrich Heine
      Verlag, 1974. 316 pp.

      A study of Heine's idiosyncratic and rather old-fashioned
      orthographic habits and their relevance for philology
      and editing practice.

224. ————, and Gerd Heinemann. "Bericht über den Heine-
      Index." *HJ 1971*, pp. 76–89.

      An earlier report on the word-index.

V

LETTERS

225. Atkins, Stuart. "The French Text of Eleven Letters from Heine to his Wife (1844)." *Harvard Library Bulletin* 18 (1970): 267-281.

> The original French of Heine's letters to his wife correctly published for the first time.

226. ———. "Heine and the Wreck of the *Amphitrite*." *Harvard Library Bulletin* 14 (1960): 395-399.

> Heine's private letter to *Le Temps* on the terrible shipwreck of August 1833 at Boulogne.

227. ———. "Heine's Letter to Bocage, September 11, 1855." *MLQ* 20 (1959): 74-76.

> First complete transcription of the letter to the actor and friend of George Sand, explaining its hidden allusions.

228. ———. "The Unpublished Passages of Heine's Letter to Charlotte Embden, July 11, 1844." *MLN* 76 (1961): 824-826.

> Corrections and repair of lacunae.

229. Eisner, Fritz H. "Four Heine Letters." *Year Book of the Leo Baeck Institute* 6 (1961): 280-284.

> Facsimiles and transcriptions of letters to Merckel, Dolorès Roger, Heine's sister, and Dr. Sichel.

230. ———. "Heine's Letters: A New Edition." *GL&L* N.S. 9 (1955/56): 220-225. Also as "Heines Briefe: Eine Neuausgabe." *WB* 2 (1956): 365-372.

> Criticism of Volumes I-II of the edition of Friedrich Hirth.

231.   —————. "Verschollene Briefe an Heine. Ein neuer Fund."
        HJ 1966, pp. 68-89.

        An important discovery, consisting primarily of letters
        to Heine of Uncle Salomon, Cousin Carl, Carl's wife, and
        her family.

232.   Elema, Hans. "Jan van Gent, Justus van Gent and John
        of Gaunt. Zu Heines Brief vom 1. Januar 1827." *HJ
        1978*, pp. 237-238.

        Clarification of a previously obscure allusion in a
        letter to Merckel.

233.   Estermann, Alfred. "Die Gesamtausgabe des Heine-Brief-
        wechsels. Zu den Bänden 20-27 der Heine-Säkularaus-
        gabe." *HJ 1978*, pp. 251-259.

        Criticism of and corrections to the text volumes of
        Heine's letters in the East German edition.

234.   Guichard, L. "Une lettre inédite de Heine à Berlioz."
        RLC 42 (1968): 570-571.

        Text of Heine's letter to Berlioz of December 18 or
        19, 1854.

235.   Knibiehler, Yvonne, and Lucienne Netter. "Heine und
        die Prinzessin Belgiojoso. Ein unbekannter Brief
        Heines." *HJ 1975*, pp. 111-114.

        Previously unpublished letter to Princess Belgiojoso
        of August 26, 1835.

236.   Kruse, Joseph A. "Noch einmal 'Berlioz und Heine.'
        Ein unbekannter Brief Heines an den Komponisten."
        HJ 1979, pp. 206-208.

        Previously unpublished note to Berlioz dated in the
        mid-1840s.

237.   Laveau, Paul. "Julius Campe als Briefpartner Heines."
        Streitbarer Humanist, pp. 301-319.

        One of the editors of Campe's correspondence with
        Heine in the East German edition makes some observa-
        tions on the character of Campe and his letters.

238.   Mathes, Jürg. "'Adieu Romantik.' Ein unbekannter
        Brief Heines an August Meyer." *DVLG* 52 (1978):
        469-475.

        Previously unknown letter of February 25, 1824.

239. Mende, Fritz. "Aus Heines journalistischer Werkstatt. Ein Brief an 'Le Constitutionnel' im Juni 1840." *SG* N.S. 6 (1968): 41-55.

    Contains an important discussion of Heine's relations with Adolphe Thiers.

240. ———. "Heine und Ewerbeck. Zwei unveröffentlichte Briefe an Heine." Pp. 281-290 in *Goethe-Almanach auf das Jahr 1969*, ed. Helmut Holtzhauer and Hans Henning. Berlin and Weimar: Aufbau-Verlag, 1968.

    Detailed commentary on letters from the Communist League representative in Paris.

241. Reissner, Hanns G. "Heinrich Heine und Eduard Gans: 'Quand même...' Bemerkungen zu einem kürzlich gefundenen Heine-Brief." *Zeitschrift für Religions- und Geistesgeschichte* 10 (1956): 44-50.

    Correct text and commentary on the letter in which Heine made deeply ironic reference to his and Gans's baptism.

242. Stöcker, Christa. "'... Ihr Erbfeind v. Arnim.' Zur Identifizierung und Datierung eines Briefes an Heinrich Heine." *HJ 1978*, pp. 233-236.

    Identifies Bettine von Arnim's son Siegmund as author of a letter of 1832.

243. Weigand, Hermann J. "Heine in Paris: Friedrich Hirth's Commentary on the Letters 1831-44." *OL* 11 (1956): 175-193.

    An annihilating but just critique of Vol. V of Hirth's edition of Heine's correspondence.

244. Woesler, Winfried. "Miszelle zum Briefwechsel Berlioz-Heine." *HJ 1974*, pp. 103-104.

    Dating of two letters from Berlioz.

245. ———. "Zum Briefwechsel Heinrich Heine--Gustav Kolb." *HJ 1970*, pp. 110-133.

    Calendars all extant and lost letters and provides significant information on the relationship to the editor of the Augsburg *Allgemeine Zeitung*.

VI

GENERAL EXPOSITIONS AND COMMENTARY

246. Abraham, Pierre. "Pourquoi Heine?" *Europe*, Nos. 125/
126 (May–June 1956): 3–11.

     Complaint about ignorance of Heine in West Germany.

247. Abusch, Alexander. "Mit Heine leben." *SuF* 24 (1972):
1125–1135.

     A claim that only East Germany preserves Heine's
     memory faithfully, with a violent and inaccurate attack
     on the Düsseldorf Heine Conference.

248. Bein, Alex. "Heinrich Heine, der 'Schamlose.'" *HJ
1978*, pp. 152–174.

     Sympathetic but imprecise discussion of Heine's posi-
     tion as a Jew in the emancipation period.

249. Bernhard, Hans Joachim. "Heinrich Heines Modernität."
*Wissenschaftliche Zeitschrift der Universität Rostock.
Gesellschafts- und Sprachwissenschaftliche Reihe* 22
(1973): 415–421.

     A propaganda piece claiming Heine for the spirit of
     Communism and East Germany on the basis of the poem
     "Doktrin."

250. Biermann-Ratjen, H.H. *"Festrede--Heine nach 100 Jahren."
Gedenkfeier aus Anlaß des 100. Todestages von Heinrich
Heine.* Hamburg: Kulturbehörde, 1956. Unpaged. Re-
printed and expanded pp. 107-120 in Hans Harder Biermann-
Ratjen, *Kultur und Staat: Reden und Schriften aus den
Jahren 1945-1959*, ed. W. Gramberg, C.G. Heise, and J.
Staubesand. 237 pp.

     A critical survey of the monuments of Heine to the
     present time.

251. Boucher, Maurice. "Heine parmi nous." *EG* 11 (1956):
     98-104.

     An eloquent eulogy delivered at the Sorbonne on the
     occasion of the centenary.

252. Colleville, Maurice. "Heinrich Heine in Paris: seine
     Mittlerrolle zwischen Deutschland und Frankreich."
     Pp. 143-157 in *Beiträge zur vergleichenden Literatur-
     geschichte: Festschrift für Kurt Wais zum 65. Geburtstag*,
     ed. Johannes Hösle and Wolfgang Eitel. Tübingen:
     Niemeyer, 1972. x + 406 pp.

     A somewhat dilettantish discussion of Heine's role as
     a mediator between Germany and France.

253. Eggert, Jens. *Mit lachender Träne: In memoriam Heinrich
     Heine*. Schriften der Heinrich Heine-Gesellschaft
     Düsseldorf, 3. Düsseldorf: Heinrich Heine-Gesellschaft,
     1965. 39 pp.

     A loosely organized cento of Heine quotations inter-
     spersed with meditations on his historical fate and sig-
     nificance.

254. Flake, Otto. "Heine." Pp. 274-281 in Flake, *Die Verur-
     teilung des Sokrates: Biographische Essays aus sechs
     Jahrhunderten*. Heidelberg: Lambert Schneider, 1970.
     351 pp.

     An appreciation of Heine by an older conservative
     writer.

255. François-Poncet, André. "Discours prononcé à Paris le
     17 février 1956." *Allemagne d'aujourd'hui* (March-
     April 1956): 84-86.

     Centenary address of the French ambassador to West
     Germany.

256. Geis, Robert. "Heinrich Heine. Die jüdische Bestimmung
     eines deutschen Dichters." *Frankfurter Hefte* 11 (1956):
     277-280. Also as "Heinrich Heines jüdische Bestimmung."
     Pp. 239-246 in *Littera Judaica: In memoriam Edwin Gug-
     genheim*, ed. Paul Jacob and Ernst Ludwig Ehrlich.
     [Frankfurt am Main]: Europäische Verlagsanstalt, [1964].
     308 pp.

     Argues that Heine's Jewish rootedness was more profound
     than was common among Western Jews, and that much can be
     explained out of the Jewish situation of his life.

257. Heinemann, Gustav. "Heinrich Heine." *HJ 1974*, pp. 5-9.

A pleasant statement of allegiance to Heine by the president of West Germany.

258. Hermlin, Stephan. "Über Heine." *SuF* 8 (1956): 78-90.
      Reprinted pp. 233-248 in Hermlin, *Begegnungen: 1954-
      1959*. Berlin: Aufbau-Verlag, 1960. 304 pp.; pp.
      549-564 in *Mit der Zukunft im Bunde: Klassisches Erbe
      deutscher Dichtung im Urteil unseres Jahrhunderts.
      Eine Anthologie*, ed. Peter Goldammer. Berlin and
      Weimar: Aufbau Verlag, 1965. 599 pp.; as "Sur Henri
      Heine." *Europe* Nos. 125/126 (May-June 1956): 33-46.

Argues that Heine was appreciated only by the proletariat and that his aspirations have become social reality
in East Germany.

259. Huder, Walter. "Rückblick auf Heine." *WuW* 28 (1973):
      26-32.

A sympathetic if somewhat vague appreciation, not
always reliable in details.

260. Karst, Roman. "Über Heine." *SuF* 8 (1956): 836-866.

An essay, apparently aimed at a general audience, on
Heine's paradoxes and his political and artistic commit-
ments.

261. Kesten, Hermann. "Heinrich Heine. Der Witz im Exil."
      Pp. 279-291 in Kesten, *Lauter Literaten: Porträts,
      Erinnerungen*. Vienna, Munich, and Basel: Kurt Desch,
      1963. 457 pp.

An appreciation of the wit in Heine's lyrics by a
writer who has lived with Heine from earliest childhood.

262. Kohn, Hans. *Heinrich Heine: The Man and the Myth*. The
      Leo Baeck Memorial Lecture, 2. New York: Leo Baeck
      Institute, 1959. 24 pp.

Heine is presented as a Romantic and aristocratic poet
of modern tendencies prefiguring Nietzsche, and as spe-
cifically German; it is argued that he lacked the integrity and selflessness to be a credible democrat or
emancipator.

263. ————. "Heinrich Heine--Poet and Patriot." Pp. 99-
      127 in Kohn, *The Mind of Germany--The Education of
      a Nation*. New York: Scribner, 1960. 370 pp. Reprinted
      as "Heinrich Heine: Dichter und Patriot." Pp. 104-134
      in Kohn, *Wege und Irrwege: Vom Geist des deutschen
      Bürgertums*. Düsseldorf: Droste, 1962. 395 pp.

Heine in the context of German intellectual history,
much in the spirit of the preceding item.

264. Leonhardt, Rudolf Walter, ed. *Heinrich Heine 1797-1856.*
     Hamburg: Hoffmann und Campe, 1972. 63 pp.

     A picture book with commentary designed for interna-
     tional distribution.

265. ———. "Heinrich Heine—der erste Jude in der deutschen
     Literatur." Pp. 37-56 in *Porträts deutsch-jüdischer
     Geistesgeschichte*, ed. Thilo Koch. Cologne: M. Du
     Mont Schauberg, 1961. 281 pp.

     A popularly written potpourri of citations, opinions,
     and historical observations contributing to the topic
     of Heine as a Jew in German literature.

266. Leschnitzer, Adolf. "Vom Dichtermärtyrtum zur politischen
     Dichtung: Heines Weg zur Demokratie." Pp. 665-693 in
     *Zur Geschichte und Problematik der Demokratie: Fest-
     gabe für Hans Herzfeld*, ed. Wilhelm Berges and Carl
     Hinrichs. Berlin: Duncker & Humblot, 1958. 693 pp.

     Heine's political development seen from a Jewish stand-
     point.

267. Mann, Golo. "Heine, wem gehört er?" Windfuhr, ed.,
     Heine-Kongreß, pp. 13-22. Reprinted in *Neue Rundschau*
     83 (1972): 650-659; pp. 281-292 in Mann, *Zwölf Versuche.*
     Frankfurt am Main: S. Fischer, 1973. 334 pp. Tr. as
     "Who Owns Heine?" *Encounter* 40, No. 6 (June 1973):
     31-36.

     A subsequently controversial assessment of Heine by a
     conservative historian.

268. Rappaport, S. "Heinrich Heine." Pp. 186-195 in Rappa-
     port, *Jewish Horizons.* Johannesburg: B'nai B'rith,
     1959. x + 264 + 41 pp.

     A conventional Jewish appreciation.

269. Schmid, Carlo. *"Denk ich an Deutschland in der Nacht":
     Eine Heinrich-Heine-Rede.* Berlin: Arani, 1956. 22
     pp. Reprinted pp. 53-70 in Schmid, *Tätiger Geist:
     Gestalten aus Geschichte und Politik.* Hanover: Dietz,
     1964. 214 pp. Tr. in excerpt as "Discours prononcé
     à Francfort par M. Carlo Schmid, vice-président du
     Bundestag." *Allemagne d'aujourd'hui* (March-April
     1956): 87-89.

     A centenary meditation by one of the most venerable
     and respected of Germany's political thinkers.

270. Süskind, W.K. "Heinrich Heine nach hundert Jahren."
      NDH 2 (1955/56): 862-866.

      An appreciation by an older conservative writer.

271. Werner, Alfred. "Heinrich Heine: Jewish Nationalist."
      Judaism 5 (1956): 76-84.

      A Zionist perspective.

VII

CRITICISM

1. General

272. Abels, Kurt. "Zum Scharfrichtermotiv im Werk Heinrich
Heines." *HJ 1973*, pp. 99-117.

Discusses the executioner as a pariah figure, relating
it to Heine's Jewish feeling.

273. Akademie der Wissenschaften der DDR, Zentralinstitut
für Literaturgeschichte, and Centre National de la
Recherche Scientifique, Centre d'Histoire et d'Analyse
des Manuscrits Modernes, eds. *Heinrich Heine und die
Zeitgenossen: Geschichtliche und literarische Befunde.*
Berlin and Weimar: Aufbau-Verlag, 1979. 328 pp.

The anonymously edited volume is meant to illustrate
the cooperation between the Heine scholars in Weimar and
the Heine team in the Bibliothèque Nationale in Paris.
The relevant items are listed separately in this bibliography.

274. Alker, Ernst. "Heine-Probleme: Randnotizen." *OL* 11
(1956): 138-149.

Argues that Heine belongs in Jewish rather than German
literary history.

275. Altenhofer, Norbert. "Chiffre, Hieroglyphe, Palimpsest.
Vorformen tiefenhermeneutischer und intertextueller
Interpretation im Werk Heines." Pp. 149-193 in *Text-
hermeneutik: Aktualität, Geschichte, Kritik*, ed. Ulrich
Nassen. Uni-Tachenbücher, 961. Paderborn, Munich,
Vienna, and Zurich: Schöningh, 1979. 226 pp.

Some of Heine's habits of interpreting historical and
literary tradition are pre-modern, but he is also aware

of neurotic, antagonistic compromises requiring a depth
analysis that prefigures Freud. The observant, highly
intelligent study draws on nos. 551 and 789.

276. Becker, Karl Wolfgang, Helmut Brandt, and Siegfried
     Scheibe, eds. *Heinrich Heine: Streitbarer Humanist
     und volksverbundener Dichter*. Weimar: Nationale
     Forschungs- und Gedenkstätten der klassischen deutschen
     Literatur in Weimar, [1973]. 511 pp.

     Collected papers of the East German Heine conference
     in December 1972. The individual items are listed sep-
     arately in this bibliography.

277. Behal, Michael, Martin Bollacher, Jürgen Brummack, Bern-
     hard Mann, and Jürgen Walter. *Heinrich Heine: Epoche
     --Werk--Wirkung*, ed. Jürgen Brummack. Beck'sche Ele-
     mentarbücher: Arbeitsbücher für den literaturgeschicht-
     lichen Unterricht, ed. Wilfried Barner and Günter Grimm.
     Munich: Beck, 1980. 366 pp.

     An effort to extract from the mass of contemporary
     Heine scholarship a basic contemporary introduction use-
     ful to students and others is largely successful owing
     to clarity, good sense, and a certain independence from
     Heine's own views. Unusually professional and perspica-
     cious review of the political and social environment.

278. Betz, Albrecht. *Ästhetik und Politik: Heinrich Heines
     Prosa*. Munich: Hanser, 1971. 175 pp.

     A lively and ingenious, but also distortive and re-
     ductive analysis of Heine's modernity from the perspec-
     tive of the far Left.

279. Broicher-Stöcker, Ursula. "Studien zum Stil Heines."
     HJ 1972, pp. 3-30.

     The fragmentary apprehension of the world is supple-
     mented by the privileged poetic imagination.

280. Brokerhoff, Karl Heinz. "Der tapfere Soldat..." Pp.
     114-139 in *Tradition und Gegenwart: Festschrift zur
     125-Jahrfeier des Städt. Humboldt-Gymnasiums, Düssel-
     dorf*, ed. H.W. Erdbrügger. Düsseldorf: Muth, 1963.
     393 pp. Reprinted as *Über die Ironie bei Heinrich
     Heine*. Schriften der Heinrich Heine-Gesellschaft, 1.
     Düsseldorf: [Heinrich Heine-Gesellschaft], 1964. 30
     pp. Excerpted as "Zu Heinrich Heines Ironie." *HJ
     1964*, pp. 37-55.

A loosely argued discussion of the generation of irony
from Heine's ambiguity, which gives way to an ultimate
seriousness.

281. Brummack, Jürgen. "Heinrich Heine." Pp. 130-196 in
      Brummack, *Satirische Dichtung: Studien zu Friedrich
      Schlegel, Tieck, Jean Paul und Heine.* Theorie und
      Geschichte der Literatur und der schönen Künste,
      Texte und Abhandlungen, Vol. 53. Munich: Fink, 1979.
      239 pp.

      A mature, stimulating, and balanced analysis argues
      that in Heine's satire his self-awareness as a poet
      draws on Romantic and idealist resources; in the *Reise-
      bilder* there is a postulated identity of the poet's
      subjectivity with the progressive dynamic of the histor-
      ical situation; in the verse epics this unity has become
      more problematic.

282. Bürger, Peter. *Der Essay bei Heinrich Heine.* Munich:
      Steinbauer u. Hagemann, 1959. 142 pp.

      A subsequently much neglected or maligned study of
      Heine's art of the essay.

283. Chiarini, Paolo. "Dolore e grandezza di Heinrich Heine."
      Belfagor 13 (1958): 21-40. Reprinted pp. 5-32 in
      Chiarini, *Romanticismo e realismo nella letteratura
      tedesca.* Padua: Liviana Editrice, 1961. viii + 293 pp.

      An analysis of Heine's career, showing that he came to
      a balance between bourgeois aesthetic values and progres-
      sive social ones. Partly identical with no. 284.

284. ————. "Per una biografia spirituale di Heinrich Heine.
      Appunti e proposte." Pp. 165-188 in Chiarini, *Lette-
      ratura e società: Studi sulla cultura tedesca da Lessing
      a Heine.* Bari: Adriatica Editrice, 1959. 188 pp.

      Describes and analyzes Heine's career, concluding with
      an analogic contrast between Rossini and Meyerbeer, the
      tension Heine felt between delicate sentiment and the
      grandiose embrace of all humanity.

285. Debluë, Vera. *Anima naturaliter ironica--Die Ironie in
      Wesen und Werk Heinrich Heines.* Europäische Hoch-
      schulschriften, Series I, Vol. 26. Bern: Herbert Lang,
      1970. 98 pp.

      An unfocused and Romanticized effort to distinguish
      irony from satire in Heine.

286. Djordjević, Miloš. "Heine und die Tiefe." Pp. 284-288
      in *Akten des V. Internationalen Germanisten-Kongresses
      Cambridge 1975*, ed. Leonard Forster and Hans-Gert Roloff
      (*JIG*, Series A, 2, part 3.) Bern and Frankfurt: Lang,
      1976. 482 pp.

      A thin effort to demonstrate that Heine was "deep."

287. Ederer, Hannelore. "Heinrich Heine." Pp. 12-115 in
      Ederer, *Die literarische Mimesis entfremdeter Sprache:
      Zur sprachkritischen Literatur von Heinrich Heine bis
      Karl Kraus*. Cologne: Pahl-Rugenstein, 1979. iv + 434
      pp.

      In a study primarily conceived as an explication and
      defense of Kraus, Ederer applies to Heine's critical
      relationship to language strict Marxist assumptions
      about the alienation and reification of language under
      capitalism, the market economy, and bourgeois ideology.
      Her view of Heine is conventional, nearly uncritical,
      derivative, and naive.

288. Fairley, Barker. *Heinrich Heine: Eine Interpretation*.
      Stuttgart: Metzler, 1965. 185 pp.

      German translation of Fairley's sensitive major study,
      first published in 1954 by the Oxford University Press.

289. ————. "Himmel und Hölle." Koopmann, ed., *Heinrich
      Heine*, pp. 56-81.

      A chapter of no. 288 above, following the motifs of
      heaven and hell in Heine's works.

290. Fingerhut, Karl-Heinz. *Standortbestimmungen: Vier
      Untersuchungen zu Heinrich Heine*. Heidenheim (Brenz):
      Heidenheimer Verlagsanstalt, 1971. 197 pp.

      Thoughtful and perspicacious essays on Heine's poeto-
      logical poems, his concept of progress, the conflict
      between poesy and public commitment, and his self-repre-
      sentation.

291. Fränkel, Jonas. *Heinrich Heine: Ein Vortrag*. Biel:
      Vorstadtpresse, 1960. 23 pp.

      Reflective lecture by the elderly scholar who edited
      Heine's poetry around World War I.

292. Fuerst, Norbert. "The Age of Heine?" Pp. 75-100 in
      Fuerst, *The Victorian Age of German Literature: Eight*

> *Essays*. University Park: Pennsylvania State University
> Press, 1966. 206 pp.

A generally unsympathetic and somewhat superficial deni-
gration--with faint praise--of Heine as a nihilist writer
and poet.

293. Goranow, Kristo. "Kunst und Gesellschaft vor dem Richter-
spruch Heinrich Heines." *Streitbarer Humanist*, pp.
335-340.

A diffuse and conventional version of the official
Eastern European position on Heine.

294. Hamburger, Michael. "Heinrich Heine." Pp. 147-175 in
Hamburger, *Reason and Energy: Studies in German Literature*. London: Routledge & Paul; New York: Grove Press,
1957. 319 pp. Reprinted as pp. 140-169 in Hamburger,
Contraries: Studies in German Literature. New York:
Dutton, 1970. x + 367 pp. Tr. pp. 30-57 in Hamburger,
*Vernunft und Rebellion: Aufsätze zur Gesellschaftskritik
in der deutschen Literatur*. Munich: Hanser, 1969. 236
pp.

A sometimes perceptive though rather sour view of Heine's
weaknesses.

295. Hatfield, Henry. "Heine and the Gods." Pp. 12-42 in
Hatfield, *Clashing Myths in German Literature from
Heine to Rilke*. Cambridge, Mass.: Harvard University
Press, 1974. 222 pp.

An overview for the uninformed reader of Heine's treatment of the Greek gods and the question of Hellenism
versus Nazarenism.

296. Hecht, Wolfgang. "Wandlungen von Heines Antikebild."
Streitbarer Humanist, pp. 132-143.

A conventional Marxist view of Heine's attitude to
Classical antiquity.

297. Hess, John A. "Heine as a Prophet of Modern Europe."
KFLQ 6 (1959): 103-111.

Valueless discussion of Heine as a prophet of the
West European alliance.

298. Höllerer, Walter. "Heinrich Heine." Pp. 58-99, 403-
418 in Höllerer, *Zwischen Klassik und Moderne: Lachen
und Weinen in der Dichtung der Übergangszeit*. Stuttgart:

Klett, 1958. 503 pp.

Heine's modernity is exhibited in the ironic combina-
tion of feeling with realistic wakefulness.

299. Hofrichter, Laura. "Heines Kampf gegen die Tradition."
      MLN 70 (1960): 507-514. Reprinted Koopmann, ed.,
      Heinrich Heine, pp. 97-105.

      Heine's rebellion against Romanticism consisted in
      the depersonalization of individual emotion.

300. ————. *Heinrich Heine*. Tr. by Barker Fairley. Oxford:
      Clarendon Press, 1963. xvi + 174 pp. Original text
      published as *Heinrich Heine: Biographie seiner Dichtung*.
      Kleine Vandenhoeck-Reihe 230 S. Göttingen: Vandenhoeck
      & Ruprecht, 1966. 190 pp.

      One of the most stimulating if often debatable studies
      of modern times sees Heine's whole career as a difficult
      process of escape from Romantic lyricism.

301. Hueppe, Frederick E. *Unity and Synthesis in the Work of
      Heinrich Heine*. European University Studies, Series I,
      Vol. 289. Bern, Frankfurt am Main, and Las Vegas:
      Peter Lang, 1979. 68 pp.

      An uncritically paraphrasing presentation argues the
      unity of Heine's middle period in the doctrine of sensual-
      ism versus spiritualism; well below the acceptable level
      of contemporary scholarship.

302. Immerwahr, Raymond, and Hanna Spencer, eds. *Heinrich
      Heine: Dimensionen seines Wirkens. Ein internationales
      Heine-Symposium*. Studien zur Literatur der Moderne,
      ed. Helmut Koopmann, Vol. 8. Bonn: Bouvier, 1979.
      113 pp.

      The papers of the Heine symposium held at the University
      of Western Ontario in May 1978 are listed separately in
      this bibliography.

303. Jennings, Lee B. "Heine: The Demon Rampant." Pp. 28-
      49 in Jennings, *The Ludicrous Demon: Aspects of the
      Grotesque in German Post-Romantic Prose*. University
      of California Publications in Modern Philology, Vol.
      LXXI. Berkeley and Los Angeles: University of California
      Press, 1963. x + 214 pp.

      An examination of Heine in the context of the theme of
      the grotesque, with many thoughtful observations.

304. ———. "Heine's Psycho-political Image Matrices." Pp.
       32-43 in *El pensamiento de Ludwig Klages en la ciencia
       contemporánea: Homanje a su biógrapho Hans-Eggert
       Schröder*, ed. Walter Reinso Sánchez Moreno and Anibal
       Sánchez Díaz. Trujillo, Peru: Universidad Nacional
       de Trujillo, 1976.

       A Jungian analysis of the recurring images of the
       threatening or avenging mother in Heine's work.

305. Kadt, J. d. "Heine in onze tijd? Opmerkingen bij een
       biographie." *Tirade* (October 1968): 433-442.

       A principled and detailed critique of no. 351 below.

306. Karger, Irmingard. *Heinrich Heine: Literarische Aufklä-
       rung und wirkbetonte Textstruktur. Untersuchungen zum
       Tierbild*. Göppinger Arbeiten zur Germanistik, No. 91.
       Göppingen: Kümmerle, 1975. 247 pp.

       Heine's animal imagery is examined in a methodological
       framework of semiotics and communication theory; it is
       a question whether the complex procedure yields anything
       not accessible to careful critical reading; it does not
       protect against misinterpretations and distortions.

307. Kaufmann, Hans. *Heinrich Heine: Geistige Entwicklung
       und künstlerisches Werk*. Berlin and Weimar: Aufbau-
       Verlag, [1967]. 288 pp.

       An expanded version of the essay appended to Kaufmann's
       edition, no. 2. Knowledgeable and lucidly written, it is
       clearly the best East German monograph on Heine, and also
       the last one of any importance.

308. ———. "Heinrich Heines literaturgeschichtliche Stel-
       lung." *WB* 19 (1973): 10-34. Reprinted pp. 32-60 in
       Kaufmann, *Analysen, Argumente, Anregungen: Literatur
       und Gesellschaft*. Berlin: Akademie-Verlag, 1973. 216
       pp.; and in *Streitbarer Humanist*, pp. 18-39.

       The thoughtful if complacent keynote address to the
       East German Heine conference of 1972.

309. Koelwel, Eduard. "Die Diktion Heinrich Heines." Pp.
       76-110 in Koelwel, *Von der Art zu schreiben: Essays
       über dichterische Ausdrucksmittel*. Halle: VEB Verlag
       Sprache und Literatur, 1962. 221 pp.

       A study of Heine's style to show its modern and endur-
       ing quality.

310. Koopmann, Helmut, ed. *Heinrich Heine.* Wege der Forschung,
     Vol. CCLXXXIX. Darmstadt: Wissenschaftliche Buchgesell-
     schaft, 1975. xvi + 424 pp.

     Reprints of representative studies from 1911 to the
     threshold of the current development. Items published
     1956 and after are noted separately in this bibliography.

311. ———. "Heinrich Heine." Pp. 149–173 in *Deutsche
     Dichter des 19. Jahrhunderts: Ihr Leben und Werk,* ed.
     Benno von Wiese. Berlin: Erich Schmidt Verlag, 1969.
     600 pp.

     A detailed general assessment by a major student of
     the period of moderate views.

312. ———. "Heinrich Heines Selbstverständnis." Pp. 205–
     214 in *Beiträge zur Theorie der Künste im 19. Jahr-
     hundert,* ed. Helmut Koopmann and J. Adolph Schmoll
     gen. Eisenwerth, Vol. I. Studien zur Philosophie
     und Literatur des neunzehnten Jahrhunderts, Vol. 12/1.
     Frankfurt am Main: Vittorio Klostermann, 1971. 373 +
     lxxi pp.

     An important effort to see Heine less as an innovator
     than as a writer in critical reaction to his immediate
     past.

313. Korstadt, Carl. "Die Individualisierung der Prosa Hein-
     rich Heines in Sprache und Stil durch französische
     Sprachelemente." *HJ 1974,* pp. 60–84.

     The study of the influence of French lexicon and syn-
     tax on Heine's style by a since deceased schoolteacher
     is instructive but reads as though it might be part of
     a dissertation of some decades ago.

314. Kraft, Werner. "Zur Heine-Deutung. Hommage à Dolf
     Sternberger zum 70. Geburtstag (28.7.77)." *NDH* 24
     (1977): 472–483.

     A critical view of no. 356, in a style rather difficult
     to follow.

315. Kurz, Paul Konrad. *Künstler Tribun Apostel: Heinrich
     Heines Auffassung vom Beruf des Dichters.* Munich:
     Fink, 1967. 249 pp.

     A perceptive and thoroughly documented study by a
     Jesuit priest of Heine's sense of poetic vocation.
     Worth reading and valuable for reference.

316. Kuttenkeuler, Wolfgang. "Skepsis und Engagement. Zur
      'Misere' Heinrich Heines." Kuttenkeuler, ed., *Heinrich
      Heine: Artistik und Engagement*, pp. 187-206.

      A careful discussion of Heine's repudiation of meta-
      physical doctrine while retaining a commitment to action,
      to the present, and to the welfare of the individual.

317. ———, ed. *Heinrich Heine: Artistik und Engagement*.
      Stuttgart: Metzler, 1977. x + 332 pp.

      The papers in this collection are listed separately
      in this bibliography.

318. Lahy-Hollebecque, Marie. "L'humour lyrique." *Europe*,
      Nos. 125/126 (May-June 1956): 92-114.

      Distinguishes humor from the other forms of Heine's
      wit and identifies a lyric quality turned from personal
      love lament to wider public issues. The examples, though
      apposite, are presented without regard to context or
      chronology.

319. Lehmann, Ursula. *Popularisierung und Ironie im Werk
      Heinrich Heines: Die Bedeutung der textimmanenten
      Kontrastierung für den Rezeptionsprozess*. Europäische
      Hochschulschriften, Series I, Vol. 164. Frankfurt am
      Main: Peter Lang; Bern: Herbert Lang, 1976. 261 pp.

      A semiotic search for textual elements that indicate
      accommodation to the reader's horizon of expectation
      and those presupposing a more intellectual reader sensi-
      tive to irony. Both methodologically elegant and rational,
      but says little about Heine's actual, generally poor,
      relation to his public.

320. Lehrmann, Cuno Ch. "Heinrich Heine, ein deutscher,
      französischer oder jüdischer Dichter?" *Bulletin des
      Leo Baeck Instituts* 11 (1968): 225-247.

      Endeavors to illustrate Heine's three allegiances with
      reference to a folkloric, a Napoleonic, and a Biblical
      poem. Well-meant but light fare.

321. Lévy, Madeleine. *Victoire du poète: Essai sur Henri
      Heine*. Paris and Geneva: Jeheber, 1960. 210 pp.

      An amiably written, moderately well-informed presenta-
      tion, with liberal paraphrase and quotation based largely
      on the French edition. There are detailed excursions on
      Heine's relationship to Schumann and to Judaism.

322. Loeb, Ernst. "Das gute wollen weil es schön ist--zur
     Frage der Einheit in Heines Werk." *Emuna* 4 (1969):
     151-160.

     Included in no. 324 below.

323. ———. "Heinrich Heine: Engagement und 'Pathos der
     Distanz.' Anläßlich seines 175. Geburtstages." *Emuna*
     7 (1972): 282-291.

     Included in no. 324 below.

324. ———. *Heinrich Heine: Weltbild und geistige Gestalt.*
     Studien zur Germanistik, Anglistik und Komparatistik,
     Vol. 31. Bonn: Bouvier, 1975. 87 pp.

     Essays on the aesthetic unity of the Nazarene-Hellene
     dichotomy, the nuances of Heine's socio-political views,
     Heine's picture of Luther and Napoleon, and the religious
     character of the *Geständnisse.* Written from a modern
     religious standpoint, the essays are thoughtful and
     sympathetic, though not always searching, and the style
     can be somewhat strained.

325. ———. "Zweispältige Einheit: Heines Luther- und
     Napoleonbild." *HJ 1973*, pp. 118-128.

     Included in no. 324 above.

326. Mackensen, Lutz. "Heines Beitrag zur Muttersprache.
     Ein Vortrag zum 17. 2. 1956." *Muttersprache*, No. 4
     (April 1956): 121-132.

     Derives Heine's grammatical and stylistic peculiarities
     from lonely isolation and aristocratic temper, and
     argues that his stylistic innovations were vulgarized
     by posterity.

327. Maliniemi, Irja. "Über rhythmische Satzkadenzen in
     Heinrich Heines Prosaschriften." *HJ 1965*, pp. 33-37.

     A brief consideration of Heine's sentence rhythms to
     illustrate his stylistic superiority.

328. Mandelkow, Karl Robert. "Heinrich Heine und die deutsche
     Klassik." Pp. 63-85 in Mandelkow, *Orpheus und Maschine:
     Acht literaturgeschichtliche Arbeiten.* Poesie und
     Wissenschaft, IX. Heidelberg: Stiehm, 1976. 175 pp.

     Observations on Goethe's importance for Heine and his
     unresolved dilemma between art and political activism

implicitly undermine conventional claims for Heine's alleged decision for politics against art.

329. Mayer, Hans. "Die Ausnahme Heinrich Heine." Pp. 273–296 in Mayer, *Von Lessing bis Thomas Mann*. Pfullingen: Neske, 1959. 414 pp. Reprinted as the introduction to Vol. I of no. 10, pp. 7–26, and pp. 323–341 in *Marxistische Literaturkritik*, ed. Viktor Žmegač. Bad Homburg: Athenäum, 1970. 441 pp.

A lively, acute, if not always accurate argument for Heine as an Enlightenment figure between the fronts and a German scandal.

330. ————. "Heinrich Heine, German Ideology, and German Ideologists." *New German Critique* 1, No. 1 (Winter 1973): 2–18.

Similar to the above with some added strictures, not always judicious, on current scholarship and the Düsseldorf conference of 1972.

331. Mende, Fritz. *Heinrich Heine im Literaturunterricht.* Berlin: Volk und Wissen, 1962. 152 pp.

A basic text for examining East German cultural politics in regard to Heine at the school level.

332. ————. "Heinrich Heine--Künstler und Tribun." *SG* N.S. 10 (1972): 591–618.

More a ceremonial address than a study; Mende gives a list of quotations presenting Heine as an ally of the proletariat who has transcended bourgeois notions of reason, humanity, and freedom.

333. ————. "Heinrich Heines literarisches Persönlichkeitsideal." *HJ 1965*, pp. 3–16.

Discusses Heine's personal models in his effort to combine public, progressive effectiveness with high poetic aspirations.

334. Möller, Dierk. *Heinrich Heine: Episodik und Werkeinheit.* Wiesbaden and Frankfurt am Main: Humanitas Verlag, 1973. x + 477 pp.

An important study based on the methods of the Russian formalists that rightly discovers patterns of rational disposition and cohesion despite the disparateness and apparent free associativeness of Heine's texts.

335. Neubert, Werner. "Die Rezensionen des Heinrich Heine."
     NDL 20, No. 10 (October 1972): 62-78.

     An East German Heine Prize winner and editor of *NDL*
     discusses Heine's autobiographical account for a French
     newspaper, the dispute with Börne, the introduction to
     Don Quixote, and his radical phase. All these can only
     be understood by Marxism.

336. Paucker, Henri Roger. *Heinrich Heine: Mensch und Dichter
     zwischen Deutschland und Frankreich*. Europäische Hoch-
     schulschriften, Series I, No. 4. Bern: Herbert Lang,
     1967. 95 pp.

     Most of the monograph is devoted to a compact analysis
     of Heine's manner of expression; the remainder to his
     thematic treatment of the contrast between Germany and
     France.

337. Prawer, S.S. "Heines 'Doppelgänger.'" *Publications of
     the English Goethe Society* N.S. 31 (1960/61): 60-81.

     Traces the motif of the "double" through Heine's works.
     Materials employed in Prawer's book, no. 448.

338. Preisendanz, Wolfgang. "Heinrich Heines Dichtertum."
     Ruperto-Carola 8, Vol. 19 (June 1956): 70-74.

     An appreciation delivered in the anniversary year.
     Included in no. 341 below.

399. ⸺. "Ironie bei Heine." Pp. 85-112 in *Ironie und
     Dichtung: Sechs Essays von Beda Allemann, Ernst Zinn,
     Hans-Egon Hass, Wolfgang Preisendanz, Fritz Martini
     und Paul Böckmann*, ed. Albert Schaefer. Beck'sche
     Schwarze Reihe, Vol. 66. Munich: Beck, 1970. 175 pp.

     Irony is not a subjective gesture but reflects the
     radical dissonance of the world in its political, social,
     and ideological processes.

340. ⸺. "Der Funktionsübergang von Dichtung und Pub-
     lizistik bei Heine." Pp. 343-374 in *Die nicht mehr
     schönen Künste: Grenzphänomene des Ästhetischen*, ed.
     H.R. Jauss. Poetik und Hermeneutik, III. Munich:
     Fink, 1968. 735 pp.

     One of the most famous and often-cited modern papers
     on Heine discusses with exceptional subtlety the fluid
     boundary between fictional and expository prose, stres-
     sing not only the expository element in the fiction but
     the literary aspects of the non-fiction. Included in
     no. 341 below.

341. ———. *Heinrich Heine: Werkstrukturen und Epochenbe-*
      züge. Uni-Taschenbücher, 206. Munich: Fink, 1973.
      130 pp.

      Contains nos. 338, 340, 735, and 450.

342. Reeves, Nigel. *Heinrich Heine: Poetry and Politics.*
      Oxford Modern Languages and Literature Monographs.
      Oxford: Oxford University Press, 1974. [iv] + 209 pp.

      An outstanding, well-written book that describes the
      development and crisis of Heine's historical eschatology,
      while exhibiting sensitive, precise interpretations,
      many observant details, and effective employment of past
      scholarship.

343. Roos, Carl. "Nordische Elemente im Werk Heinrich Heines."
      OL 11 (1956): 150-165.

      Originally published in Danish in 1952, the article
      rather speculatively points to Scandinavian influences
      in Heine's works.

344. Salinger, Herman. "Heinrich Heine: The Child in the Man."
      Pp. 129-135 in *Vistas and Vectors: Essays Honoring*
      the Memory of Helmut Rehder, ed. Lee B. Jennings and
      George Schulz-Behrend. Austin: Department of Germanic
      Languages, University of Texas, 1979. 214 pp.

      A ramble through a few texts purports to show how
      Heine retained childlike elements of memory overlaid
      with adult satire.

345. Sammons, Jeffrey L. *Heinrich Heine: The Elusive Poet.*
      Yale Germanic Studies, 3. New Haven and London: Yale
      University Press, 1969. xiv + 542 pp.

      A comprehensive study based on Heine's employment of
      a fictive persona of his own self. Extensive bibliography.

346. Sandor, A.I. *The Exile of Gods: Interpretation of a*
      Theme, a Theory and a Technique in the Work of Heinrich
      Heine. Anglica Germanica: British Studies in Germanic
      Languages and Literature, IX. The Hague and Paris:
      Mouton, 1967. 192 pp.

      The main theme is Heine's poetic identification of
      himself with personae of ideal power who have somehow
      been rendered powerless. Though marked by questionable
      individual interpretations, one of the most imaginative
      and probing Heine studies in modern times.

347. Santoli, Vittorio. "Der Neubarock Heinrich Heines."
     Pp. 133-151 in Santoli, *Philologie und Kritik:*
     Forschungen und Aufsätze. Bern and Munich: Francke,
     1971. 239 pp.

     The late dean of Italian Germanists denominates as
     "Neo-Baroque" the mannered use of rhetorical devices
     in Heine's style.

348. Scheiffele, Eberhard. "Heine als Rhetor." *HJ 1979*,
     pp. 9-26.

     A detailed though uncritical account of Heine's use
     of rhetorical figures.

349. Sengle, Friedrich. "Heinrich Heine." Pp. 468-591 in
     Sengle, *Biedermeierzeit: Deutsche Literatur im Span-*
     nungsfeld zwischen Restauration und Revolution 1815-
     1848. Vol. III: *Die Dichter.* Stuttgart: Metzler,
     1980. xvi + 1,162 pp.

     Sengle stresses Heine's relationship to the literary
     context and traditions of his age, especially in regard
     to the mixture of stylistic levels and the dexterous
     employment of rhetorical tones. He rightly minimizes
     Heine's breach with the alleged *Kunstperiode*, stressing
     his rootedness in the eighteenth century and his links
     to Romantic and idealist traditions. Sengle does pug-
     nacious battle with the short-sightedness of much con-
     temporary scholarship, although some of his own views
     are highly debatable. They will demand study and at-
     tention.

350. Simon, Ernst. "Heine und die Romantik." Pp. 135-156
     in Simon, *Brücken: Gesammelte Aufsätze.* Heidelberg:
     Schneider, 1965. 531 pp.

     Follows Heine's use of the term Romanticism and argues
     that all modern Romantic theory leads back to Heine.

351. Snethlage, J.L. *Heinrich Heine 1797-1856: Voorloper*
     van existentialisme en oecumenisch christendom.
     Amsterdam: Scheltema & Holkema NV, 1968. 320 pp.

     An ill-tempered and factually exceptionally inaccurate
     attempt to make Heine responsible for existentialism
     and ecumenism, of both of which the author disapproves.
     For a very severe criticism of this worthless book, see
     no. 305.

352. Spann, Meno. *Heine.* Studies in Modern Literature and

Thought, ed. Erich Heller and Anthony Thorlby. London: Bowes and Bowes, 1966. 111 pp.

A basic essay with an appended history of Heine criticism. Spann denies that Heine can be judged by literary criteria and argues that all statements about him are partisan.

353. Spencer, Hanna. *Dichter, Denker, Journalist: Studien zum Werk Heinrich Heines*. Bern, Frankfurt am Main, and Las Vegas: Peter Lang, 1977. 149 pp.

Contains five previously published papers (nos. 354, 757, 464, 755, 756) and a new one, a close reading of the first poem of *Lyrisches Intermezzo*.

354. ———. "Heinrich Heine: Dichter, Essayist und Journalist." *JIG* 7 (1975): 71-87.

On Heine's essayistic style, with numerous references to current scholarship. Included in no. 353.

355. Stern, J.P. "History and Prophecy: Heine." Pp. 208-238 in Stern, *Re-Interpretations: Seven Studies in Nineteenth-Century German Literature*. New York: Basic Books, 1964. x + 370 pp.

Discusses Heine's relationship to history and nationalism, arguing that his "unique achievement" is that of a political poet.

356. Sternberger, Dolf. *Heinrich Heine und die Abschaffung der Sünde*. Hamburg and Düsseldorf: Claassen, 1972. 408 pp. Reprinted as Suhrkamp Taschenbuch 308. Frankfurt am Main: Suhrkamp, 1976. 441 pp.

In one of the most important and provocative modern books on Heine, a political scientist takes a conservative and rather skeptical view of Heine, denying that he had political views in the strict sense. Its main contribution is a thorough reexamination of Heine's relationship to Saint-Simonianism. The second edition contains replies to Sternberger's critics, many of whom oppose his downgrading of Hegel's influence.

357. ———. "Rede über Heinrich Heine." *Gestalt und Gedanke* 4 (1957): 148-170.

An early presentation of Sternberger's views on Heine.

358. Stockhammer, Morris. "Heinrich Heine als Pessimist."

Schopenhauer-Jahrbuch 43 (1962): 111-116.

With a cento of quotations taken out of context and chronology, Stockhammer generalizes Heine's undeniable pessimistic side, and argues that he protested against death because he was childless.

359. Tarnói, László. "Heine und die deutsche Romantik." *Annales Universitatis Scientiarum Budapestinensis de Rolando Eötvös Nominate. Sectio Philologica Moderna* 5 (1974): 11-20.

Warns against seeing Heine in the light of orthodox Marxist rejection of Romanticism.

360. Überling, Wolf. "Der Dichter des kolossalen Epigramms." *TK* 18/19 (1968): 1-6.

A general appreciation, stressing Heine's spirit of criticism and love of freedom.

361. Vordtriede, Werner, and Uwe Schweikert. *Heine-Kommentar:* I. *Zu den Dichtungen*; II. *Zu den Schriften zur Literatur und Politik.* Munich: Winkler, 1970. 146, 192 pp.

Essentially the commentary to the Winkler edition (no. 4) with the page numbers removed; therefore not always easy to use.

362. Wadepuhl, Walter. *Heine-Studien.* Beiträge zur deutschen Klassik, ed. Nationale Forschungs- und Gedenkstätten der klassischen deutschen Literatur in Weimar, Abhandlungen, Vol. 4. Weimar: Arion, 1956. 207 pp.

The papers are listed separately in this bibliography.

363. Weinberg, Kurt. "Die Entsublimierung des Unheimlichen im Werk Heines." Immerwahr and Spencer, eds., *Heinrich Heine*, pp. 84-95.

Applies a Freudian analysis to Heine's "desublimation of the eerie."

364. Weiss, Walter. "Heines, Lenaus and Immermanns Kritik am Pantheismus. Zur Krise des Pantheismus in der Dichtung der Restaurationszeit." *Innsbrucker Beiträge zur Kulturwissenschaft* 6 (1959): 191-221.

A brief version of the following item.

365. ————. "Heinrich Heine." Pp. 157-194 in Weiss, *Ent-*
      täuschter Pantheismus: Zur Weltgestaltung der Dichtung
      in der Restaurationszeit. Gesetz und Wandel: Inns-
      brucker literarhistorische Arbeiten, Vol. III. Dorn-
      birn: Vorarlberger Verlagsanstalt, 1962. 336 pp.

      Sees Heine's comedy as hovering over an abyss, and his
      irony as a defense against chaos and meaninglessness.
      Contains a good treatment of Heine's religious concern.

366. Werner, Hans Georg. "Der junge Heine." *Német Filológia*
      Tanulmányok: Arbeiten zur deutschen Philologie 7 (1973):
      17-34.

      An elementary Marxist presentation, apparently for an
      uninformed audience.

367. Werner, Michael, ed. *Cahier Heine.* Publications du
      Centre d'Histoire d'Analyse des Manuscrits Modernes.
      Paris: Presses de l'Ecole Normale Supérieure, 1975.
      149 pp.

      The articles are listed separately in this bibliography.

368. ————. "Rollenspiel oder Ichbezogenheit? Zum Problem
      der Selbstdarstellung in Heines Werk." *HJ 1979*, pp.
      99-117.

      A subtle if arguable discussion of the tension between
      Heine's public self-representations and private reticence.

369. Wiese, Benno von. "Goethe und Heine als Europäer." Pp.
      295-315 in *Teilnahme und Spiegelung: Festschrift für*
      Horst Rüdiger, ed. Beda Allemann, et al. Berlin and
      New York: De Gruyter, 1975. viii + 680 pp.

      While Goethe saw Europe as a cosmopolitan community of
      the cultured, Heine saw the nations individually as con-
      texts for his own self-understanding. A chapter of no.
      371.

370. ————. "Heine und Schiller." *JDSG* 20 (1976): 448-463.

      Reviews Heine's attentive, differentiated response to
      Schiller.

371. ————. *Signaturen: Zu Heinrich Heine und seinem Werk.*
      Berlin: Erich Schmidt Verlag, 1976. 251 pp.

      In a currently unusual effort to read Heine in literary-
      critical terms, von Wiese devotes several essays to Heine's

effort to interpret the sign system of the world and
apprehend essences. An animating contribution, though
not always secure in details.

372. Wilhelm, Friedrich. "Das Indienbild Heinrich Heines."
     Saeculum 10 (1959): 208-212.

     Heine's reception and critique of the Romantic en-
     thusiasm for India.

373. Windfuhr, Manfred. *Heinrich Heine: Revolution und Re-
     flexion.* Stuttgart: Metzler, 1969. x + 300 pp. 2nd
     rev. ed. Stuttgart: Metzler, 1976. ix + 310 pp.

     The first full-length comprehensive monograph on Heine
     by a West German scholar. It is exceptionally knowledge-
     able and pleasantly written, and contains some fine
     judgments, but it regularly avoids difficult problems
     and probing analysis.

374. ————. "Heinrich Heines Modernität: Ein Vortrag." Pp.
     441-459 in *Zur Literatur der Restaurationsepoche 1815-
     1848: Forschungsreferate und Aufsätze,* ed. Jost Hermand
     and Manfred Windfuhr. Stuttgart: Metzler, 1970. viii
     + 599 pp.

     A homily locating Heine's modernity in his democratic
     commitment.

375. ————, ed. *Internationale Heine-Kongreß Düsseldorf
     1972. Referate und Diskussionen.* Hamburg: Hoffmann
     und Campe, Heinrich Heine Verlag, 1973. 532 pp.

     The conference papers are listed separately in this
     bibliography.

376. Wülfing, Wulf. "Skandalöser 'Witz.' Untersuchungen zu
     Heines Rhetorik." Kuttenkeuler, ed., *Heinrich Heine:
     Artistik und Engagement,* pp. 43-65.

     Puts Heine's wit and criticism of wit into rhetorical
     categories and considers Heine's relationship to the
     rhetorical tradition.

377. Zepf, Irmgard. "Exilschilderungen in Heines Prosaschrif-
     ten." *Emuna* 10 (1975): 129-134.

     A compendium of Heine's feelings about exile, with
     special attention to his reaction to mistreatment of
     Jews.

2. Lyric Poetry

378. Adorno, Theodor W. "Die Wunde Heine." *Texte und Zeichen* 2 (1956): 291–295. Reprinted pp. 144–152 in Adorno, *Noten zur Literatur* I (Frankfurt am Main: Suhrkamp, 1958). 193 pp.

Argues that Heine's poetry reflected mass-production and gave expression to man's homelessness under capitalism.

379. Anglade, René. "Eine Begegnung, die nicht stattfand. Heines 'Der weisse Elefant': Eine Interpretation." *JDSG* 20 (1976): 464–491.

Allegorizes Heine's comic poem into a parable on despotism and Catholicism. Improbable and insufficiently informed.

380. Arbogast, Hubert. "'Ein erblindender Adler.' Bemerkungen zu einem unbekannten Manuskript Heines." *JDSG* 13 (1969): 47–61. Reprinted Koopmann, ed., *Heinrich Heine*, pp. 288–306.

An early version of "Aus einem Briefe" in *Neue Gedichte* shows more explicit reference to both the state of Heine's health and the political environment of 1841.

381. ————. "Marginalien zu der 'Marginalie zu einem Aufsatz.'" *JDSG* 16 (1972): 478–482.

Reply to no. 409, criticism of no. 380 above.

382. Arendt, Dieter. "Heinrich Heine: '...Ein Märchen aus alten Zeiten....' Dichtung zwischen Märchen und Wirklichkeit." *HJ 1969*, pp. 3–20.

An effort to make our understanding of the Loreley poem more precise, but somewhat rambling in pursuit of implications.

383. Atkins, Stuart. "The Evaluation of Heine's *Neue Gedichte*." Pp. 99–107 in *Wächter und Hüter: Festschrift für Hermann J. Weigand zum 17. November 1957*, ed. Curt von Faber du Faur, Konstantin Reichardt, and Heinz Bluhm. New Haven: Department of Germanic Languages, Yale University, 1957. 176 pp.

Important as one of the first thoughtful modern interpretations of Heine's traditionally least regarded collection of poetry.

384.   ———. "The First Draft of Heine's 'Für die Mouche.'"
        Harvard Library Bulletin 13 (1959): 415-443.

        A description of the MS. of one of Heine's most im-
        portant and most imperfectly transmitted poems.

385.   ———. "The Function of the Exotic in Heine's Later
        Poetry." Pp. 119-130 in *Connaissance de l'étranger:
        Mélanges offerts à la mémoire de Jean-Marie Carré*, ed.
        Marcel Bataillon et al. Paris: Didier, 1964. xx +
        527 pp.

        The artistic importance of the exoticism of the pas-
        sionflower in "Für die Mouche" and exotic elements drawn
        from late French Romanticism in *Romanzero*.

386.   Ayrault, Roger. "Le Symbolisme du décor dans le *Lyrisches
        Intermezzo*." *EG* 11 (1956): 105-113.

        Analyzes the abstract, mental universe of nature imagery
        in *Lyrisches Intermezzo* and compares it to the nature
        imagery in Runge's paintings.

387.   Bayerdörfer, Hans-Peter. "Heine: Karl I." Pp. 109-117
        in *Geschichte im Gedicht: Texte und Interpretationen.
        Protestlied, Bänkelsang, Ballade, Chronik*, ed. Walter
        Hinck. Edition Suhrkamp, 721. Frankfurt am Main:
        Suhrkamp, 1979. 308 pp.

        Bayerdörfer shows the exact balance of history and
        present relevance in "Karl I.," but does not say much
        about the poem's elegiac dimension.

388.   ———. "'Politische Ballade.' Zu den Historien in
        Heines 'Romanzero.'" *DVLG* 46 (1972): 435-468.

        A sound and precise contribution on the balancing of
        aesthetic and political values in the late poetry, con-
        centrating on "Karl I."

389.   Berendsohn, Walter A. "Heines 'Buch der Lieder.' Struk-
        tur- und Stilstudie." *HJ 1962*, pp. 26-38.

        Tries to separate *Buch der Lieder* from autobiographical
        detail but argues that it gives insight into Heine's in-
        ner history. Well-intended but not strong interpretively.

390.   ———. *Die künstlerische Entwicklung Heines im Buch
        der Lieder: Struktur- und Stilstudien.* Stockholmer
        Germanistische Forschungen, 7. Stockholm: Almqvist &
        Wiksell, 1970. 209 pp.

Some worthwhile observations on the inner history of
the poet and his increasing realism, but atomized, burdened by paraphrase and lists of quoted passages, and
seriously out of touch with modern scholarship.

391. Bloch, Ernst. "Ponce de Léon, Bimini und der Quell."
Pp. 226-231 in Bloch, *Verfremdungen*, I. Bibliothek
Suhrkamp, Vol. 85. Frankfurt am Main: Suhrkamp, 1968.
233 pp.

Fits "Bimini" into Bloch's theme of utopian hopefulness.

392. Boie, Bernhild. "Am Fenster der Wirklichkeit. Verflech-
tungen von Wirklichem und Imaginärem in Heinrich Heines
später Lyrik." *DVLG* 48 (1974): 342-353. Reprinted pp.
163-177 in *Heinrich Heine und die Zeitgenossen*.

Points to the difference between poesy, as a realm of
the imagination, and poetry, which gives access to it,
and argues Heine's current relevance.

393. Brandt, Helmut. "Geschichtsbewußtsein und Poesie. Zum
literarhistorischen Charakter der Lyrik Heinrich Heines."
Streitbarer Humanist, pp. 78-108.

While rather short on critical methodology, interesting
because orthodox Marxists had tended to avoid Heine's
lyric poetry and play down his Romantic heritage.

394. Brate, Gertrud. "Heinrich Heines 'Ich grolle nicht'
-Trilogie." *HJ 1972*, pp. 31-37.

Interpretation of *Lyrisches Intermezzo* 17, 18, and 19.

395. Brummack, Jürgen. "Heines Entwicklung zum satirischen
Dichter." *DVLG* 41 (1967): 98-116.

In the search for a unifying principle in Heine's
poetic career, Brummack finds the folksong elements of
Buch der Lieder to be the positive pole of a strain between a lost poetic world and the depressing present;
as Heine proceeds to satire, which establishes its own
values by negation, the folk element is no longer neces-
sary. Interesting and valuable.

396. Buchheit, Gert. "'Ich weiß nicht, was soll es bedeuten
....' Eine Studie über die Lorelei-Sage." *Muttersprache*, No. 4 (April 1956): 143-145.

Discusses the etymology of "Loreley" and endeavors to
show that the original legend concerned a mountain spirit,
not a water spirit.

397. Christmann, Helmut. "Heinrich Heine: Belsazar." Pp.
     261-266 in *Wege zum Gedicht*, ed. Rupert Hirschenauer
     and Albrecht Weber. Vol. II. Munich and Zurich:
     Schnell und Steiner, 1963. 574 pp.

     An interpretation primarily useful as a guide to class-
     room presentation.

398. Destro, Alberto. "L'attesa contradetta. La svolta
     finale nelle liriche del 'Buch der Lieder' di Heinrich
     Heine." *AION* 20, No. 1 (1977): 7-127.

     A fairly strict technical examination of ironical de-
     vices and contradicted expectations in Heine's poems.

399. Dmitrejew, Alexander Sergejewitsch. "Die Beziehungen
     zwischen dem Schaffen des jungen Heine und dem ästhet-
     ischen Programm der Jenaer Romantik." *Streitbarer
     Humanist*, pp. 172-189.

     The chief interest of the essay is the evidence that
     a Soviet critic has much less difficulty accepting
     Heine's Romantic origins than German Marxists do.

400. Dück, Hans-Udo. "Heinrich Heine: Die Wallfahrt nach
     Kevlaar." Pp. 270-277 in *Wege zum Gedicht*, ed. Rupert
     Hirschenauer and Albrecht Weber. Vol. II. Munich and
     Zurich: Schnell und Steiner, 1963. 574 pp.

     Purpose similar to no. 397 above.

401. Ezergailis, Inta. "On Musicality in Poetry: The Case of
     Heine." *HJ 1977*, pp. 20-48.

     The vexed question of "musicality" in Heine's poetry
     is resolved by reference to the harsh sounds of modern
     music. Unconventional argument, possibly to the point
     of eccentricity.

402. Feise, Ernst. "Heine's 'Unterwelt.'" *GR* 31 (1956): 276-
     278.

     The outstanding student of Heine's metrics shows how
     his citation of a poem of Schiller's in one of his own
     parodistically alters Schiller's tone despite the same
     basic meter.

403. Fendri, Mounir. "'Fröhliche Mahle' oder Heine und die
     'Moallakat.'" *HJ 1977*, pp. 129-133.

     Shows that Heine paraphrased from a collection of
     Arabic poetry that was important to Goethe.

404. Feuerlicht, Ignace. "Heines 'Es war ein alter König.'"
     HJ 1976, pp. 67-74.

     A close reading showing that the poem is not as simple
     as it appears at first sight.

405. ────. "Heine's 'Lorelei': Legend, Literature, Life."
     GQ 53 (1980): 82-94.

     A critical review of the scholarship on the background
     of the Lorelei legend and an examination of the poem's
     enigmas concludes that it expresses the dangerous con-
     trast between beauty and the everyday.

406. Fingerhut, Karlheinz. "Strukturale Interpretation und
     die Tätigkeit des Rezipienten. Untersuchungen zu Hein-
     rich Heines 'Das Sklavenschiff.'" *DD* 8 (1977): 281-
     304.

     Application of semiotic reception theory burdens what
     is not a very abstruse poem while failing to account for
     significant features.

407. Finke, Franz. "Heinrich Heine als Lyriker des Übergangs."
     HJ 1963, pp. 33-42. Reprinted in Koopmann, ed., *Hein-
     rich Heine*, pp. 106-116.

     Examines Heine's transitional position between tradi-
     tional and modern poetry and asks whether he was not more
     influential in the future than commonly assumed.

408. Gebhard, Hella. *Interpretation der "Historien" aus
     Heines "Romanzero."* Munich: Fotodruck, 1957. 135 +
     vii pp.

     This Erlangen dissertation is included here as an ex-
     ception because of its pioneering importance in the in-
     terpretation of *Romanzero* in Germany.

409. Gebhardt, Christoph. "Marginalie zu einem Aufsatz."
     JDSG 16 (1972): 477-478.

     A methodological critique of no. 380 above.

410. Gishdëu, S. "Die lyrischen Zyklen Heinrich Heines."
     Kunst und Literatur 20 (1972): 1192-1202. Reprinted
     as Sergej Pawlowitsch Gishdeu, "Das Private, Empirische
     und Zufällige in der Lyrik von Heinrich Heine." *Streit-
     barer Humanist*, pp. 322-334.

     Observations on the realistic account of the web of

feeling among the high points of emotion and mythopoeic
constructions showing the poet shut out from the cosmos.
Another example of a Soviet critic more sympathetic to
Heine's poetry than German Marxists.

411. Grappin, Pierre. "Heines lyrische Anfänge." Windfuhr,
      ed., *Heine-Kongreß*, pp. 50-78.

      A thoughtful discussion of Heine's lyrical beginnings
      by the editor of *Buch der Lieder* in the Düsseldorf edition.

412. Hammerich, Louis L. "Trochäen bei Heinrich Heine. Zu-
      gleich ein Beitrag zum Werdegang eines alten Germanisten.
      Pp. 393-409 in *Formenwandel: Festschrift zum 65. Geburts-
      tag von Paul Böckmann*, ed. Walter Müller-Seidel and
      Wolfgang Preisendanz. Hamburg: Hoffmann und Campe, 1964.
      520 pp.

      Interpretations of several of Heine's shorter trochaic
      poems.

413. Hart-Nibbrig, Christiaan L. "Heinrich Heines 'Verwaistes
      Lied.'" *WW* 22 (1972): 392-400.

      Heine's lack of lyric directness and genuineness, his
      suspicion of the world of poetic images, and the gap be-
      tween the dream-world and the day-world are evidence of
      seeking for truth.

414. Heissenbüttel, Helmut. "Materialismus und Phantasmagorie
      im Gedicht. Anmerkungen zur Lyrik Heinrich Heines."
      Pp. 56-69 in Heissenbüttel, *Zur Tradition der Moderne:
      Aufsätze und Anmerkungen 1969-1971*. Neuwied and Berlin:
      Luchterhand, 1972. 394 pp.

      A radio address criticizing Adorno's view of Heine as
      dependent upon traditional aesthetic canons and indicating
      how the questionableness of lyrical language became a
      theme of the poetry; useful in countering Adorno's prej-
      udices, but excessively modernizes Heine.

415. Hermand, Jost. "Erotik im Juste Milieu. Heines 'Ver-
      schiedene.'" Kuttenkeuler, ed., *Heinrich Heine: Artis-
      tik und Engagement*, pp. 86-104.

      Makes the *Verschiedene* more emancipatory and expressive
      of erotic libertinage than they are.

416. Hinck, Walter. "Exil als Zuflucht der Resignation. Der
      Herrscher-Dichter-Konflikt in der Firdusi-Romanze und

die Ästhetik des späten Heine." Pp. 37-59 in Hinck,
Von Heine zu Brecht: Lyrik im Geschichtsprozeß. suhrkamp taschenbuch, 481. Frankfurt am Main: Suhrkamp,
1978. 156 pp.

The refusal of the poet to accept the Shah's silver
instead of the gold he expected in "Der Dichter Firdusi"
is related to the new awareness of the poet's dependence
upon material income, while the gesture of contempt
toward the ruler is an assertion of the rebellious autonomy of poetry.

417. ————. "Heinrich Heine." Pp. 48-69 in Hinck, *Die
deutsche Ballade von Bürger bis Brecht: Kritik und
Versuch einer Neuorientierung.* Kleine Vandenhoeck-
Reihe, 273 S. Göttingen: Vandenhoeck & Ruprecht, 1968.
153 pp.

In his contrastive scheme categorizing the German ballad, Hinck identifies Heine's ballads as "legendary"
rather than "Nordic."

418. ————. "Metamorphosen eines Wiegenliedes: H.L. Wagner,
Heine, G. Hauptmann, Toller, Brecht." Pp. 290-306 in
*Zeiten und Formen in Sprache und Dichtung: Festschrift
für Fritz Tschirch zum 70. Geburtstag,* ed. Karl-Heinz
Schirmer and Bernhard Sowinski. Cologne and Vienna:
Böhlau, 1972. Pp. viii + 460. Reprinted pp. 83-104
in Hinck, *Von Heine zu Brecht: Lyrik im Geschichts-
prozeß.* suhrkamp taschenbuch, 481. Frankfurt am Main:
Suhrkamp, 1978. 156 pp.

Traces the history of the lullaby form in tragic settings with respect to Heine's "Karl I."

419. Höllerer, Walter. "Heine als ein Beginn." *Akzente* 3
(1956): 116-129.

A thoughtful and perceptive essay on the modern quality
of Heine's break with the Romantic pathetic fallacy.

420. Jacobs, Jürgen. "Der späte Heine und die Utopie--zu
'Bimini.'" *EG* 22 (1967): 511-516.

Heine treats the utopian hope of overcoming mortality
with skeptical irony but also with sympathy for human
suffering. A precise and helpful little essay.

421. Jaspersen, Ursula. "Heinrich Heine. 'Abenddämmerung.'"
Pp. 134-143 in *Die deutsche Lyrik: Form und Geschichte,*

ed. Benno von Wiese, Vol. II. Düsseldorf: August Bagel
Verlag, 1964. 512 pp.

An exemplary interpretation of the *Nordsee* poems illustrating anxiety before the closed heaven and the va-
cuum of existence.

422.   ———. "Heinrich Heine. 'Das Fräulein stand am Meere.'"
        Pp. 144-149 in *Die deutsche Lyrik: Form und Geschichte*,
        ed. Benno von Wiese, Vol. II. Düsseldorf: August
        Bagel Verlag, 1964. 512 pp.

Despite Heine's dislike of reality, his recognition
of the illusions of Romanticism obliges an acknowledgment of the real world.

423.   ———. "Heinrich Heine. 'Ich weiß nicht, was soll es
        bedeuten....'" Pp. 128-133 in *Die deutsche Lyrik:
        Form und Geschichte*, ed. Benno von Wiese, Vol. II.
        Düsseldorf: August Bagel Verlag, 1964. 512 pp.

Sublimation of autobiographical sentiment into yearning
for a no longer credible Romanticism.

424.   Kaufmann, Hans. "Zum 'Empfindungsgedicht' bei Heine."
        SuF 15 (1963): 914-935.

Heine's sentimentalism is a complaint about his inability
to reconcile himself with the condition of the world and
his irony an effort to transcend the complaint.

425.   Killy, Walther. "An der Schwelle. Über Heinrich Heine."
        Tribüne: Zeitschrift zum Verständnis des Judenproblems
        1 (1962): 192-197. Reprint of the epilogue to *Buch der
        Lieder*. Exempla classica, No. 106. Frankfurt am Main:
        Fischer, 1961. 192 pp.

Considerations on the decline of the reputation of
Buch der Lieder and on the artificiality of the poems as
a device for coping with a crisis of meaning in literature.

426.   ———. "Mein Pferd für'n gutes Bild. Heine und Geibel."
        Pp. 73-94 in Killy, *Wandlungen des lyrischen Bildes*.
        Göttingen: Vandenhoeck & Ruprecht, 1956. Kleine Vanden-
        hoeck-Reihe, 22/23. Pp. 94-115 in 2nd ed., 1958; 3rd.
        ed., 1961; 4th ed., 1964. 140 pp.

Heine suffers from a worn-out language that destroys
confidence in words and images.

427. Klusen, Ernst. "Heinrich Heine und der Volkston." *Zeit-
     schrift für Volkskunde* 69 (1973): 43-60.

     Heine moves from the folksong understood in Romantic
     terms through folksong as a modern poem that attains
     popularity to the political and social-critical folksong.

428. Klussmann, Paul Gerhard. "Die Deformation des romantischen
     Traummotivs in Heines früher Lyrik." Pp. 259-285 in
     *Untersuchungen zur Literatur als Geschichte: Festschrift
     für Benno von Wiese*, ed. Vincent J. Günther, Helmut
     Koopmann, Peter Pütz, and Hans Joachim Schrimpf. Ber-
     lin: Erich Schmidt Verlag, 1973. 598 pp.

     Shows that the *Traumbilder* cite Romantic, Goethean,
     and popular elements, making them strange through mixed
     style levels.

429. Knüfermann, Volker. "Symbolistische Aspekte Heinischer
     Lyrik." *EG* 27 (1972): 379-387.

     Shows some links between Heine and modern poetry.

430. Koopmann, Helmut. "Heines 'Romanzero': Thematik und
     Struktur." *ZDP* 97 (1978): Special Issue *Studien zur
     deutschen Literaturgeschichte und Gattungspoetik: Fest-
     gabe für Benno von Wiese*: 51-76.

     Sees much of *Romanzero* as a meditation less on the poet's
     personal situation than on the decline of Romantic poesy
     and its illusions, and as a failed effort to achieve a
     a new post-Romantic poetry.

431. Korell, Dieter. *Heinrich Heines 'Letzte Gedichte' als
     Spiegel seines Wesensbildes*. Bonner Schriften zur
     deutschen Literatur. Bonn: Wegener, 1972. 45 pp.

     An old-fashioned, imprecise discussion of the late
     poems of no scholarly importance.

432. Kraft, Werner. "Ein Lied von Heine." Pp. 125-129 in
     Kraft, *Augenblicke der Dichtung: Kritische Betrach-
     tungen*. Munich: Kösel, 1964. 314 pp.

     Interpretation of "Der Tod, das ist die kühle Nacht."

433. ———. "Heine und die Hiobsfrage." Pp. 41-45 in Kraft,
     Augenblicke der Dichtung: Kritische Betrachtungen.
     Munich: Kösel, 1964. 314 pp.

     Interpretation of "Laß die heil'gen Parabolen."

434. Krogmann, Willy. "Lorelei. Geburt einer Sage." *Rhei-
      nisch-westfälische Zeitschrift für Volkskunde* 3 (1956):
      170-196.

      Thorough discussion of the legendary and literary
      background of Heine's "Loreley."

435. Künzel, Horst. "Lyrik als Herrschaftskritik: Zu drei
      Gedichten Heinrich Heines." *HJ 1973*, pp. 83-98.

      Interprets the critique of political power in "Marie
      Antoinette," "1649--1793--????," and "Karl I."

436. Lefebvre, Jean-Pierre. "Le Syllogisme de l'histoire
      dans le 'Romanzero.'" *Cahier Heine*, pp. 116-131.
      Tr. as "Die Stellung der Geschichte im Syllogismus
      des 'Romanzero.'" *Heinrich Heine und die Zeitgenossen*,
      pp. 142-162.

      Imposes a Hegelian scheme of dialectical history upon
      Romanzero.

437. Leja, Alfred E. "Christian Elements in Heine's 'Du
      bist wie eine Blume.'" *American Benedictine Review*
      24 (1973): 124-126.

      Insignificant.

438. Lüdi, Rolf. *Heinrich Heines Buch der Lieder: Poetische
      Strategien und deren Bedeutung.* Europäische Hoch-
      schulschriften, Series I, Vol. 307. Frankfurt am
      Main, Bern, and Las Vegas: Peter Lang, 1979. 209 pp.

      With a methodology derived from Roland Barthes and a
      dry structuralist idiom, *Buch der Lieder* is analyzed
      as a coherent whole and found to be a set of variations
      on the theme of incurable pain derived from love. But
      there is no question of real feeling and experience;
      the poetry is made up of prefabricated parts and exhibits
      the destruction of its own system. This rather conven-
      tional view in up-to-date theoretical dress has serious
      drawbacks and misses many of the nuances of *Buch der
      Lieder*, but the study also makes many worthwhile system-
      atic observations and is welcome as one of the few de-
      tailed analyses of Heine's most famous poetry in modern
      German criticism.

439. Mann, Golo. "Über Heines Gedichte." *Deutsche Rundschau*
      82 (1956): 1300-1309.

      In expiation of the embarrassment that when asked to

name his favorite poems, none of Heine's occurred to
him, Golo Mann prints eleven poems and the last caput
of *Deutschland, Ein Wintermärchen.*

440. Meyer, Raymond. "Inhaltskonstruktion und Verständlich-
keit: Zur Integration der Gedichte 1-11 von Heines
'Lyrisches Intermezzo." *DVLG* 52 (1978): 257-270.

Observations on the static passivity of the fictive
beloved. Mainly discusses only *Lyrisches Intermezzo*
4 and 10.

441. Mommsen, Katharina. "Heines lyrische Anfänge im Schatten
der Karlsbader Beschlüsse." Pp. 453-473 in *Wissen aus
Erfahrungen: Werkbegriff und Interpretation heute.
Festschrift für Herman Meyer zum 65. Geburtstag*, ed.
Alexander von Bormann, et al. Tübingen: Niemeyer,
1976. xi + 958 pp.

Some helpful and some speculative evidence that Heine's
early poetry contains Aesopian language for forbidden
political dissidence.

442. Müller, Joachim. "Heines Nordseegedichte. Eine Sprach-
und Stilanalyse des ersten Teils." *Wissenschaftliche
Zeitschrift der Friedrich-Schiller-Universität Jena:
Gesellschafts- und Sprachwissenschaftliche Reihe* 6
(1956/57): 191-212. Reprinted pp. 492-580 in Müller,
Von Schiller bis Heine. Halle: Niemeyer, 1972. 610
pp.

Explication of text of *Nordsee I* to show that Heine
wanted not to destroy values but to call up renewing
forces without Romanticism or sentimentality.

443. ————. "Romanze und Ballade. Die Frage ihrer Struk-
turen, an zwei Gedichten von Heinrich Heine dargelegt."
*Wissenschaftliche Zeitschrift der Friedrich-Schiller-
Universität Jena: Gesellschafts- und Sprachwissen-
schaftliche Reihe* 7 (1957/58): 377-385. Reprinted
GRM N.S. 9 (1959): 140-156.

A perhaps futile effort to distinguish romance and
ballad by comparing "König Harald Harfagar" and "Schlachtfeld bei Hastings."

444. Pazi, Margarita. "Die biblischen und jüdischen Einflüsse
in Heines 'Nordsee-Gedichten.'" *HJ 1973*, pp. 3-19.

A quite doubtful argument claiming Jewish influence
on the *Nordsee* poems.

445. Peters, George F. "*Neue Gedichte*: Heine's 'Buch des
     Unmuts.'" *Monatshefte* 68 (1976): 248-256.

     A lively and attentive analysis of the connection
     between *Neue Gedichte* and Goethe's *Divan*.

446. Politzer, Heinz. "Um einen Heine von innen bittend."
     GQ 34 (1961): 422-430.

     Stresses Heine's cold and calculated artistry.

447. Prawer, S.S. *Heine: Buch der Lieder*. Studies in German
     Literature, No. 1. London: Edward Arnold, 1960. 64
     pp.

     A relatively brief study of *Buch der Lieder*, with out-
     standingly sensitive interpretations.

448. ⸻. *Heine the Tragic Satirist: A Study of the Later
     Poetry 1827-1856*. Cambridge, Eng.: University Press,
     1961. xii + 315 pp.

     Possibly the finest book of criticism written on Heine
     in modern times, it has yet to find an equal in compre-
     hensive interpretation of the mature poetry.

449. ⸻. "Heine's *Romanzero*." *GR* 31 (1956): 293-306.

     The recovery in the late poetry of a sense of sin and
     evil in history. Prawer traces the line of development
     and concludes with an interpretation of "Schelm von
     Bergen."

450. Preisendanz, Wolfgang. "Die Gedichte aus der Matratzen-
     gruft." Pp. 99-130 in Preisendanz, *Heinrich Heine:
     Werkstrukturen und Epochenbezüge*. Munich: Fink, 1973.
     130 pp.

     Examines the deviation from normal audience expecta-
     tions in the late poetry.

451. Puppe, Heinz W. "Heinrich Heine's 'Tannhäuser.'"
     Monatshefte 66 (1974): 345-354.

     Interprets the poem as a parodistic arrangement of
     traditional conventions in order to coax the public
     into political and social concern.

452. Reeves, Nigel. "The Art of Simplicity: Heinrich Heine
     and Wilhelm Müller." *OGS* 5 (1970): 48-66.

     An important paper showing that Heine's model Müller

was not the naive, unspoiled folk poet Heine took him
to be. Included in no. 342.

453. Rose, Margaret A. *Die Parodie: Eine Funktion der bib-*
      lischen Sprache in Heines Lyrik. Deutschen Studien,
      Vol. 27. Meisenheim am Glan: Hain, 1976. [xii] +
      138 pp.

      A very learned, labored, and sporadically instructive
      study of Heine's use of Biblical quotations and allusions
      in terms of a general theory of parody.

454. Rose, William. "Ein biographischer Beitrag zu Heines
      Leben und Werk." *WB* 3 (1957): 586-597.

      Introduces the argument of the following item.

455. —————. *The Early Love Poetry of Heinrich Heine: An*
      Inquiry into Poetic Inspiration. Oxford: Clarendon
      Press, 1962. xiv + 89 pp.

      One of the most influential Heine studies of modern
      times convincingly cuts the link of the early poetry to
      traditional speculations about Heine's youthful love
      affairs.

456. Salinger, Herman. "Heine's 'Valkyren' Reexamined."
      MLN 90 (1975): 673-677.

      A close reading detects foresight in the poem's
      pessimistic historical outlook.

457. —————. "Helping Heinrich Heine Explain his Archetypal
      'Night Journey' Poem." *Literature and Psychology* 13
      (1963): 30-36.

      A Jungian attempt to explain Heine's most obscure
      short poem, "Nächtliche Fahrt."

458. Sauder, Gerhard. "Blasphemisch-religiöse Körperwelt.
      Heines 'Hebräische Melodien.'" Kuttenkeuler, ed.,
      Heinrich Heine: Artistik und Engagement, pp. 118-143.

      Connects the *Hebräische Melodien* with constant themes
      in Heine's career.

459. Schlein, Rena. "Ein Gedicht aus dem 'Lazarus' und seine
      Quellen." *HJ 1974*, pp. 47-52.

      Possible sources of the brothers Sleep and Death in
      "Morphine."

460. Schlüer, Klaus Dieter. "Zu dem Gedicht 'Erinnerung.'"
     TK 18/19 (1968): 41-42.

     A close reading of Heine's retrospective poem on the
     drowning of a boyhood friend.

461. Schnell, Josef. "Heines Lyrik der emanzipatorischen
     Subjektivität. Zur Funktionsbestimmung der Kunst
     nach dem 'Ende der Kunstperiode.'" *DU* (West) 31
     (1979): 31-46.

     Defines Heine's modernity in terms of a subjectivity
     reflecting a realistic sense of a world that should be
     changed. Conventional, short-sighted reading despite
     a complicated critical idiom.

462. Sieburg, Friedrich. "Beschwörung und Mitteilung. Zur
     Lyrik Heinrich Heines." *Jahresring* 3 (1956/57): 56-
     73.

     An examination of the limitations of Heine's poetic
     language and its bad influence on subsequent verse.

463. Siegrist, Christoph. "Heines Traumbilder: Versuch einer
     Gliederung." *HJ 1965*, pp. 17-25.

     In Heine's dream poems, dreams are refunctioned into
     rational reflection.

464. Spencer, Hanna. "Heinrich Heines *Karl I.*" *GRM* N.S. 22
     (1972): 377-389.

     A close reading showing the primacy of the idea of
     the poem over its epic treatment. Reprinted in no. 353.

465. Stauffacher, Werner. "Le Principe de rupture dans la
     poésie heinéenne." *Etudes de Lettres*, Series III, 10,
     No. 4 (October-December 1977): 55-67.

     Comparisons to Mörike, Eichendorff, and Lenau to show
     Heine's greater realism and the breakdown of pathetic
     fallacy in nature imagery.

466. Stein, Ernst. "Der spröde Klang. Zur Besonderheit der
     Lyrik Heines." *Aufbau* 12 (1956): 118-121.

     An attack on West German criticism for re-Romanticizing
     Heine and for condemning his activist purpose.

467. ———. "Zugang zu Heinrich Heines Gedicht." *DU* (East)
     9 (1956): 133-140, 205-209, 437-443.

A series of exemplary explications, beginning with the early poetry and culminating in a discussion of "Die schlesischen Weber."

468. Stern, J.P. "Heinrich Heine's Contentious Muse." Pp. 53-75 in Stern, *Idylls & Realities: Studies in Nineteenth-Century German Literature*. London: Methuen, 1971. 232 pp.

Sprightly and fluent observations on some elements in Heine's poetry, weakened by lack of close acquaintance with the subject.

469. Storz, Gerhard. *Heinrich Heines lyrische Dichtung*. Stuttgart: Klett, 1971. 258 pp.

The first general book on Heine's poetry to have appeared in Germany in many years contains judicious individual interpretations and thoughtful meditations, but also some bafflement and considerable scholarly carelessness.

470. Swales, Martin. "Nostalgia as Conciliation: A Note on Eichendorff's *Aus dem Leben eines Taugenichts* and Heine's *Der Doppelgänger*." *GL&L* N.S. 30 (1976/77): 36-45.

Argues that Heine, unlike Eichendorff, sees no reconciliation of the self with history, but Swales removes Heine's poem too much from the context of *Buch der Lieder*.

471. Tischer, Heinz. *Ironie und Resignation in der Lyrik Heinrich Heines*. Analysen und Reflexionen, Vol. 1. Hollfeld: Beyer, 1973. 112 pp.

A Marxist interpretation, intended for pedagogical use, of Heine's poems as artificial, reproducible, and commercial; despite an occasional aperçu, uneven and obtuse.

472. Veit, Philipp. F. "Fichtenbaum und Palme." *GR* 51 (1976): 13-27.

A more detailed and delicate reexamination of the familiar view that *Lyrisches Intermezzo* 33 is an allegory of Heine's longing for the Jewish orient.

473. ———. "Lore-ley and Apollogott." Pp. 228-246 in *Analecta Helvetica et Germanica: Eine Festschrift zu Ehren von Hermann Böschenstein*, ed. A. Arnold, H.

Eichner, E. Heier, and S. Hoefert. Studien zur
Germanistik, Anglistik und Komparatistik, 85. Bonn:
Bouvier, 1979. 393 + 9 pp.

Recognizing that the "Apollogott" poem reverses the
"Loreley" situation, Veit suggests that the earlier poem
is also in part a meditation on Heine's Jewish situation.

474. Wagner, Maria. "Heines 'Schlachtfeld bei Hastings'
eine Balladen-Parodie." *HJ 1974*, pp. 34-46.

An unconvincing argument that the poem parodies the
ballad form.

475. Waseem, Gertrud. *Das kontrollierte Herz: Die Darstellung
der Liebe in Heinrich Heines "Buch der Lieder."* Studi-
en zur Germanistik, Anglistik und Komparatistik, 46.
Bonn: Bouvier, 1976. 219 pp.

An analysis of the diction and expressive techniques
of love in Heine's early poetry, consisting almost entirely of a sequence of paraphrasing explications very
derivative of previous criticism.

476. Weber, Dietrich. "'Gesetze des Standpunkts' in Heines
Lyrik." *Jahrbuch des Freien Deutschen Hochstifts*
(1965): 369-399.

A detailed theoretical study of perspective in analogy
to the study of narrative perspective is attentive to
the fictive persona as speaker in Heine's poems and
stresses the realistic rather than Romantic imagery.

477. Weber, Werner. "Heinrich Heine: Die Grenadiere." Pp.
267-269 in *Wege zum Gedicht*, ed. Rupert Hirschenauer
and Albrecht Weber, Vol. II. Munich and Zurich: 1963.
574 pp. Originally as "Suite zur Gegenwart. Heinrich
Heine." Pp. 176-182 in Weber, *Zeit ohne Zeit: Aufsätze
zur Literatur*. Zurich: Manesse, 1959. 237 pp.

An exemplary interpretation for pedagogical purposes.

478. Werner, Michael, and Eva Werner. "Zur Praxis der Hand-
schrifteninterpretation am Beispiel von Heines *Karl I.*
und *An die Jungen*." *Cahier Heine*, pp. 87-115. Reprinted in *Heinrich Heine und die Zeitgenossen*, pp.
78-107.

Examples of the contributions of MS. study to interpretation, perceptive though not as novel as the authors
believe.

479. Westra, P. "Heinrich Heines sogenannte '*Josepha-Lieder*.'"
Neophilologus 40 (1956): 117-128.

Sterile juggling with biographical speculation.

480. Wetzel, Heinz. "Heinrich Heines *Lorelei*: Stimmungszauber
oder Bewußtseinsbildung?" *GRM* N.S. 20 (1970): 42-54.

A close analysis of the levels of ironic distance in
the poem and the ambivalent relationship to Romantic
evocation of mood.

481. Wiese, Benno von. "Mythos und Historie in Heines später
Lyrik. Ein Beitrag zum dichterischen Selbstverständnis."
Windfuhr, ed., *Heine-Kongreß*, pp. 121-146.

Myth and history examined with special reference to
"Der Apollogott," *Atta Troll*, and "Bimini."

482. ————. "Mythos und Mythentravestie in Heines Lyrik."
Pp. 146-174 in von Wiese, *Perspektiven I: Studien zur
deutschen Literatur und Literaturwissenschaft*. Berlin:
Erich Schmidt Verlag, 1978. xv + 224 pp.

Travesties of myth examined in the *Nordsee* poems,
"Unterwelt," and "Der Apollogott"; especially good on
the last.

483. Wikoff, Jerold. *Heinrich Heine: A Study of "Neue Gedichte."*
Stanford German Studies, Vol. 7. Bern: Herbert Lang,
Frankfurt am Main: Peter Lang, 1975. 90 pp.

Attempts to see *Neue Gedichte* as a genuine cycle with
the *Zeitgedichte* as the actual "new poems"; while the
main thesis may not be convincing, the study contains
a number of attentive observations.

484. Windfuhr, Manfred. "Heine und der Petrarkismus." *JDSG*
10 (1966): 266-285. Reprinted Koopmann, ed., *Heinrich
Heine*, pp. 207-231.

An identification, taken also into Windfuhr's general
book on Heine (no. 373) and now common coin in criticism,
of Heine's early poetry with Petrarchism. Useful in
cutting the link from naive biographism, though exagger-
ated if it suggests that Heine's poems were no more than
calculated play with conventional materials.

485. Wolf, Ruth. "Versuch über Heines 'Jehuda ben Halevy.'"
HJ 1979, pp. 84-98.

Traces the impulse of the poem to Heine's activity in

the Jewish *Verein* and provides interesting information
on Jehuda but barely touches upon the complexities of
the poem itself.

486. Zagari, Luciano. "La *Pomare* di Heine e la crisi del
      linguaggio 'lirico.'" *SG* N.S. 3 (1965): 5-38. Re-
      printed pp. 121-154 in Zagari, *Studi di letteratura
      tedesca dell' ottocento*. Rome: Ateneo, 1965. 239 pp.

      A very thorough analysis of "Pomare" to show its rela-
      tion to reality, its construction and destruction of a
      myth of urban eros, and a crisis of lyrical language.

MUSICAL SETTINGS

487. Betz, Albrecht. "Komm! ins Offene, Freund! Zum Ver-
      hältnis von Text und Musik in Kompositionen von Ge-
      dichten Hölderlins und Heines--Thema und Variationen."
      RdA 5 (1973): 649-669.

      Tries to show that a Schumann setting is bourgeois,
      imposing sentiment on Heine, while a Hanns Eisler set-
      ting of Hölderlin brings out the political contradictions
      of the text.

488. Brody, Elaine, and Robert A. Fowkes. *The German Lied
      and Its Poetry*. New York: New York University Press,
      1971. viii + 316 pp.

      Although this is a general and somewhat elementary
      book on the German *Lied*, it is included here owing to
      many references to Heine, including a section on Schu-
      mann's settings on pp. 101-127.

489. Eckhoff, Annemarie. *Dichterliebe: Heinrich Heine im
      Lied. Ein Verzeichnis der Vertonungen von Gedichten
      Heinrich Heines zum 175. Geburtstag des Dichters*.
      Hamburg: Musikbücherei, 1972. 87 pp.

      A catalogue prepared for an exhibition contains one
      of the most thorough listings of settings yet compiled.

490. Miller, Philip L. "Heine." Pp. 96-124 in Miller, *The
      Ring of Words: An Anthology of Song Texts*. Garden
      City, N.Y.: Anchor Books, 1966. xxviii + 518 pp.
      Originally published Garden City, N.Y.: Doubleday,
      1963. 200 pp.

      The value of this anthology, apart from information

on dates, opus numbers, etc., is that by comparison with
the original texts it shows the revisions that composers
made.

491. Mühlhäuser, Siegfried. "'... Kaum wage ich das Bekennt-
     nis--ich verstehe keine Note....' Ein bisher unge-
     druckter Brief Heinrich Heines an Eduard Marxsen: Ein
     Beitrag zur Frage der Vertonung Heinescher Gedichte."
     Die Musikforschung 26 (1973): 63-69.

     Contains some information on compositions of Heine
     songs by Marxsen, Josef Klein, and Schubert.

492. Pfrimmer, Alfred. "Henri Heine et les musiciens roman-
     tiques allemands." *Europe*, Nos. 125/126 (May-June
     1956): 115-120.

     Praises the settings of Schubert and Schumann as par-
     ticularly congenial.

493. Porter, E.G. "Der Doppelgänger." *Music Review* 21 (1960):
     16-18.

     Shows how Schubert's highly praised setting of *Die
     Heimkehr* 20 brings out the compressed emotional force
     of the poem.

494. Robert, Frédéric. "Heine et ses musiciens." *Europe*,
     Nos. 125/126 (May-June 1956): 121-124.

     A partial listing of settings by German, Russian,
     Hungarian, and French composers.

495. Schneider, Frank. "Franz Schuberts Heine-Lieder."
     SuF 31 (1979): 1059-1064.

     Schneider doubts that Schubert had intended to join
     Rellstab's songs to the *Schwanengesang* cycle and argues
     that the title and arrangement were posthumously inspired
     by commercial considerations. As a result posterity
     has sentimentalized the innovative energy, bitter irony,
     and collective rather than private spirit of Schubert's
     Heine settings.

496. Stein, Jack M. "Schubert's Heine Songs." *Journal of
     Aesthetics and Art Criticism* 24 (1965/66): 559-566.
     Reprinted substantially revised pp. 80-91 in Stein,
     *Poem and Music in the German Lied from Gluck to Hugo
     Wolf*. Cambridge: Mass.: Harvard University Press,
     1971. 238 pp.

     Defends the integrity of Heine's poems against the

alternations in tonality to which *Lieder* settings subject them. The book version of the controversial argument contains numerous other references to Heine settings.

497. Truding, Lona. "Des Musikers Verhältnis zum Wort. Schumann und Heine zum 100. Todestag 1856-1956." *Das
Goetheanum: Wochenschrift für Anthroposophie* 35 (1956):
341-342.

Claims a complete harmony of music and poetry in Schumann's Heine settings and also mentions admiringly Luigi
Dallapiccola's cantata of 1955 based on Heine's poems
to his wife.

3. Epic and Political Poetry

498. Atkinson, Ross. "Irony and Commitment in Heine's
Deutschland. Ein Wintermärchen." *GR* 50 (1975):
184-202.

An observant and essential interpretive effort yield-
ing the result that the poet-narrator's solutions are
no solutions at all.

499. Bark, Joachim. "Heine im Vormärz: Radikalisierung oder
Verweigerung? Eine Untersuchung der Versepen." *DU*
(West) 31 (1979): 47-60.

Sees *Atta Troll* and the *Wintermärchen* as complementary
expressions of a consistent political attitude.

500. Bayerdörfer, Hans-Peter. "Fürstenpreis im Jahre 48:
Heine und die Tradition der vaterländischen Panegyrik.
Dargestellt an Gedichten auf den Reichsverweser Johann
von Österreich." *ZDP* 91 (1972), Special Issue *Heine
und seine Zeit*: 163-205.

An effort to show how formal criteria can be brought
to bear on the description and evaluation of political
poetry of the 1840s, with "Hans ohne Land" as the standard of evaluation.

501. ———. "Laudatio auf einen Nachtwächter. Marginalien
zum Verhältnis von Heine und Dingelstedt." *HJ 1976*,
pp. 75-95.

Argues that Dingelstedt's mildly satirical verse sup-
plied the impetus for Heine's style of political poetry.

502. Freund, Winfried. "Heinrich Heine: Die Wanderratten--Zeitgeschichtlicher aspekt und dichterische autonomie." *WW* 26 (1976): 122-132.

Interprets Heine's position in the poem as nonpartisan, defending human values, but the argument that such a poem yields information and cognition is less convincing.

503. ———. "Das Zeitgedicht bei Heinrich Heine: Zum Verhältnis von Dialektik und didaktischer Funktion." *DD* 8 (1977): 271-280.

Heine's political verse seen as a didactic possibility for arousing schoolchildren from their torpor when confronted with poetry.

504. Gille, Klaus F. "Heines 'Atta Troll'--'Das letzte freie Waldlied der Romantik'?" *Neophilologus* 62 (1978): 416-433.

Argues that *Atta Troll* is a continuation of Heine's argument with his hostile contemporaries; the urge to assert Heine's ideological superiority to all contemporaries misses unresolved ambivalences.

505. Gössmann, Wilhelm. "Deutsche Nationalität und Freiheit. Die Rezeption der Arminius-Gestalt in der Literatur von Tacitus bis Heine." *HJ 1977*, pp. 71-95.

Puts Heine's treatment of the Arminius theme in the *Wintermärchen* into its literary-historical context.

506. Grab, Walter. "Heinrich Heine als politischer Dichter." *Jahrbuch der Wittheit zu Bremen* 22 (1978): 69-92.

Well-meant but imprecise and indifferently informed praise of Heine as a political poet.

507. Grupe, Walther. "Heines 'schlesische Weber' auf einem Berliner Flugblatt." *DU* (East) 9 (1956): 426-428.

An altered version of the poem, confiscated from a Berlin worker in 1844.

508. ———. "Heines 'Wintermärchen' und die preußische Zensur. Nach Akten des Deutschen Zentralarchivs." *DU* (East) 16 (1963): 563-564.

A note on the speed with which the Prussian government proceeded to the confiscation of *Neue Gedichte* because of the *Wintermärchen*.

509. ⸺. "Der zensierte Heine." *NDL* 5, No. 8 (1957):
      169-171.

      On the proceedings of the Prussian government against
      the *Wintermärchen*.

510. Hahn, Karl-Heinz. "Die Wanderratten." Pp. 57-70 in
      Hahn, *Aus der Werkstatt deutscher Dichter: Goethe,
      Schiller, Heine*. Halle: Verlag Sprache und Literatur,
      1963. 371 pp. Reprinted Koopmann, ed., *Heinrich
      Heine*, pp. 117-132.

      Argues that Heine identifies with the proletariat;
      the image of them as rats satirizes the conventional
      bourgeois viewpoint.

511. Hammerich, Louis L. *Heinrich Heine som politisk digter:
      Tale ved mindehøjtideligheden på Københavns Universitet
      17. Februar 1956*. Tønder: Gads Forlag, 1957. 29 pp.
      Tr. as "Heinrich Heine als politischer Dichter." *OL*
      11 (1956): 125-137. Reprinted Koopmann, ed., *Heinrich
      Heine*, pp. 82-96.

      Praises Heine as a political poet, stressing the in-
      fluence of Marx, but also pointing out that the Nazaren-
      ism he scorned was in himself as well.

512. Hartwig, Helmut. "Ältere Erläuterungen zu Heines Gedicht
      'Deutschland.'" Pp. 229-249 in *Nationalismus in Germa-
      nistik und Dichtung: Dokumentation des Germanistentages
      in München vom 17.-22. Oktober 1966*, ed. Benno von
      Wiese and Rudolf Henss. Berlin: Erich Schmidt Verlag,
      1967. 363 pp.

      A socio-political interpretation of the poem "Deutsch-
      land" of 1840 in the context of a polemic against the
      way literature is taught in German schools.

513. Hasubek, Peter. "Heinrich Heines Zeitgedichte." *ZDP*
      91 (1972); Special Issue *Heine und seine Zeit*: 23-46.

      Seeks a characterization of the *Zeitgedichte* on the
      basis of their intentionality and their relationship
      to Heine's time.

514. Hermand, Jost. "Heines 'Wintermärchen'--Zum Topos der
      'deutschen Misere.'" *DD* 8 (1977): 234-249. Revised
      pp. 43-61 in Hermand, *Sieben Arten an Deutschland zu
      leiden*. Königstein: Athenäum, 1979. xii + 170 pp.

      Only the Left can appreciate the *Wintermärchen*, the

touchstone of the reader's political virtue. The poem
is unambiguous, and its negative satire implies a positive utopia.

515. Hinck, Walter. "Ironie im Zeitgedicht Heines. Zur
      Theorie der politischen Lyrik." Windfuhr, ed., *Heine-
      Kongreß*, pp. 81-104. Reprinted pp. 9-36 in Hinck,
      Von Heine zu Brecht: Lyrik im Geschichtsprozeß, suhr-
      kamp taschenbuch, 481. Frankfurt am Main: Suhrkamp,
      1978. 156 pp.

      Controversial suggestion that Heine's political verse
      is not above criticism but that his irony sometimes im-
      pedes the political effect.

516. Hinderer, Walter. "Die Suppe der Nützlichkeit oder Mit
      Speck fängt man Ratten." Pp. 118-127 in *Geschichte
      im Gedicht: Texte und Interpretationen, Protestlied,
      Bänkelsang, Ballade, Chronik*, ed. Walter Hinck. edi-
      tion suhrkamp, 721. Frankfurt am Main: Suhrkamp,
      1979. 308 pp.

      A careful analysis of Heine's ironic distance from
      both the proletariat, barbaric from hunger, and the
      threatened, pompous bourgeoisie in "Die Wanderratten."

517. Hooton, Richard Gary. *Heinrich Heine und der Vormärz.*
      Hochschulschriften Literaturwissenschaft, Vol. 30.
      Meisenheim am Glan: Hain, 1978. 146 pp.

      Thoughtful and useful observations on Heine's rela-
      tionship to contemporary political poets; helpful inso-
      far as it allows voices other than Heine's to be heard,
      but fails to confront all the problems owing to an
      insistence upon defending Heine's ideological superiority.

518. Kaufmann, Hans. "Deutschland--Ein Wintermärchen. Rede
      zur Heine-Ehrung der Humboldt-Universität in Berlin,
      18. Februar 1956." *WB* 2 (1956): 2-17.

      Explication and praise of the *Wintermärchen* in the
      light of the historical context and Heine's connection
      with Marx, though Heine could not quite reach a proletar-
      ian level of insight.

519. ————. "Gestaltungsprobleme in Heines 'Wintermärchen.'"
      WB 3 (1957): 244-266.

      Connects formal and ideological aspects of the *Winter-
      märchen*, sketching arguments developed in no. 521.

520.   ——————. "Heinrich Heine: 'Die schlesischen Weber.'"
       Junge Kunst 3, No. 7 (1959): 72-77. Reprinted pp.
       11-31 in Kaufmann, *Analysen, Argumente, Anregungen:*
       Aufsätze zur deutschen Literatur. Berlin: Akademie-
       Verlag, 1973. 216 pp; pp. 159-177 in *Methodische*
       Praxis der Literaturwissenschaft: Modelle der Inter-
       pretation, ed. Dieter Kimpel and Beate Pinkerneil.
       Kronberg: Scriptor Verlag, 1975. x + 323 pp.

       Examines the refunctioning and radical appropriation
       of older cultural and literary *topoi* in Heine's most
       famous political poem. The most recent publication
       adds remarks to the effect that only Marxist interpre-
       tation is adequate to such a poem.

521.   ——————. *Politisches Gedicht und klassische Dichtung:*
       Heine, Deutschland. Ein Wintermärchen. Berlin:
       Aufbau-Verlag, 1959. 220 pp.

       The most detailed orthodox Marxist examination of any
       work of Heine's makes worthwhile observations on style
       and other matters, but otherwise avoids problems in
       order to keep an ideologically untroubled view of the
       poem intact.

522.   Knipovič, Jewgenija F. "Deutschland. Ein Wintermärchen."
       Windfuhr, ed., *Heine-Kongreß*, pp. 190-201.

       An appreciation of the *Wintermärchen* from a Soviet
       perspective.

523.   Loeben, Maria-Beate von. "Deutschland. Ein Winter-
       märchen. Politischer Gehalt und poetische Leistung."
       GRM N.S. 20 (1970): 265-285.

       A judicious analysis of the relation of style and
       structure to the theme of reality versus illusion and
       the poem's complex, shifting structures.

524.   Maurer, Georg. "Der Leser wird zum Augenzeugen."
       Pp. 88-92 in Maurer, *Der Dichter und seine Zeit:*
       Essays und Kritiken. Berlin: Aufbau, 1956. 156 pp.

       Heine compared to Mayakovsky in the employment of
       poetic means to social and political purpose.

525.   Möller, Irmgard. "Historische Bezüge in Heines 'Zeit-
       gedichten.' Ein Beitrag zum Problem der Kommentie-
       rung." Pp. 232-259 in *Impulse: Aufsätze, Quellen,*
       Berichte zur deutschen Klassik und Romantik, ed.

Walter Dietze and Peter Goldammer. Folge 1. Berlin
and Weimar: Aufbau-Verlag, 1978. Pp. 414.

Examples of some of the problems of commentary on
Heine's political poems, doubtless in connection with
the editorial work on the East German edition.

526. Prawer, S.S. "Heine in His Workshop. The Evolution
of a Satiric Poem." *GR* 36 (1961): 82-93.

Examines the MS. variants of "Unsere Marine," showing a systematic parody of Freiligrath and very thoughtful composition.

527. ————. "Heines satirische Versdichtung." Pp. 179-195
in *Der Berliner Germanistentag 1968: Vorträge und Berichte*, ed. Karl Heinz Borck and Rudolf Henss. Heidelberg: Carl Winter, 1970. 221 pp.

Argues that some of the uneven quality of Heine's
satire may be owing to the loss of a tradition of wit
in Germany; interprets primarily *Lyrisches Intermezzo*
50, the *Wintermärchen*, *Atta Troll*, and "Jammertal."

528. Raddatz, Fritz J. "Heinrich Heines Wintermärchen."
Merkur 31 (1977): 545-555.

Assorted passages from Raddatz' forgettable book,
no. 126.

529. Reeves, Nigel. "Atta Troll and His Executioners: The
Political Significance of Heinrich Heine's Tragi-
comic Epic." *Euphorion* 73 (1979): 388-409.

An important and stimulating argument interpreting
the Gothic figures Laskaro and Uraka as symbols of the
Germanic paganism suppressed by Christianity and resus-
citated in modern times, destroying the opportunism of
literary liberals.

530. Reuter, Hans-Heinrich. "Heines politische Lyrik. Entwicklung, Haupttendenzen, Grundzüge." *DU* (East) 10
(1957): 309-326, 371-378.

Develops a typology of indirect political implications
in the early poetry, then follows the increasing ex-
plicitness of the political verse through its eventual
fading and last echo in "Enfant perdu."

531. Riemen, Alfred. "Gedichte und Publizistik. Zu Heinrich Heines lyrischem Stil." *HJ 1975*, pp. 50-69.

     Examines the stylistic strategies of Heine's political verse; concentrates on content rather than on the rhythm of thought and feeling.

532. Rose, Margaret A. "'Adam der Erste' und das Verlags-verbot vom 8. Dezember 1841." *HJ 1975*, pp. 70-76.

     A strained argument to play off Heine against Hoffmann von Fallersleben in connection with poems of each of similar theme and import.

533. ————. "Carnival and 'Tendenz': Satiric Modes in Heine's 'Atta Troll. Ein Sommernachtstraum.'" *AUMLA* 43 (May 1975): 33-49.

     Interesting observations on carnival elements from Shakespeare's *Midsummer Night's Dream* in *Atta Troll*, but oddly and not always intelligibly written with forced interpretations.

534. ————. "The Idea of the 'Sol Iustitiae' in Heine's 'Deutschland. Ein Wintermärchen.'" *DVLG* 52 (1978): 604-618.

     Identifies "astral" images drawn from myth, legend, Biblical and Messianic sources for satirical effect, symbolizing Heine's ambivalence in regard to revolution. Some of the argument is excessively ingenious.

535. Rüdiger, Horst. "Vitzliputzli im Exil." Pp. 307-324 in *Untersuchungen zur Literatur als Geschichte: Festschrift für Benno von Wiese*, ed. Vincent J. Günther, Helmut Koopmann, Peter Pütz, and Hans Joachim Schrimpf. Berlin: Erich Schmidt Verlag, 1973. 598 pp.

     An ingenious and erudite comparative examination, arguing that at the end of the poem Vitzliputzli threatens Europe with syphilis.

536. Sammons, Jeffrey L. "Hunting Bears and Trapping Wolves. 'Atta Troll' and 'Deutschland. Ein Wintermärchen.'" Kuttenkeuler, ed., *Heinrich Heine: Artistik und Engagement*, pp. 105-117.

     Interpretation of *Atta Troll* and the *Wintermärchen* in relation to one another. A chapter of no. 345.

537. ————. "'Der prosaisch bombastischen Tendenzpoesie
      hoffentlich den Todesstoß geben': Heine and the
      Political Poetry of the *Vormärz*." *GQ* 51 (1978): 150-
      159.

      A comparison with other political poets of the time
      shows that Heine never follows the waves of enthusiasm
      and disappointment as the others do, but remains through-
      out in a posture of negative, satirical rejection.

538. Schanze, Helmut. "Noch einmal: Romantique défroqué.
      Zu Heines 'Atta Troll,' dem letzten freien Waldlied
      der Romantik." *HJ 1970*, pp. 87-98. Reprinted Koop-
      mann, ed., *Heinrich Heine*, pp. 362-376.

      Despite Heine's ideological campaign against the
      Romantic School, he himself belongs to the Romantic
      movement while opposing the delusions of Romanticism
      and liberating its progressive potential.

539. Schmidt, Wolff A. von. "Zur Reflexion des Naturbereichs
      in der politischen Metaphorik Heinrich Heines." Pp.
      117-128 in *Kommunikative Metaphorik: Die Funktion des
      literarischen Bildes in der deutschen Literatur von
      ihren Anfängen bis zur Gegenwart*, ed. Holger A. Pausch.
      Studien zur Germanistik, Anglistik und Komparatistik,
      Vol. 20. Bonn: Bouvier, 1976. 199 pp.

      Some examples to show how Heine employs familiar nature
      images with surprising political effects.

540. Sengle, Friedrich. "'Atta Troll.' Heines schwierige
      Lage zwischen Revolution und Tradition." Windfuhr,
      ed., *Heine-Kongreß*, pp. 23-49.

      A controversial and polemical interpretation stresses
      the poem's dialectical relationship to the *Wintermärchen*,
      its traditional elements, and its critique of political
      partisanship.

541. Thomke, Hellmut. "Heine und Grandville." *HJ 1978*, pp.
      126-151.

      Although Heine never mentions Grandville, Thomke argues
      plausibly that his political animal caricatures must
      have been known to him and influenced *Atta Troll*.

542. Veit, Philipp F. "Heine's Imperfect Muses in *Atta Troll*.
      Biographical Romance or Literary Symbolism." *GR* 39
      (1964): 262-280.

One of the most worthwhile papers ever written on
Atta Troll interprets the three female figures of the
"Wild Hunt" as "imperfect Muses" of Heine's poetic
imagination.

543. Wadepuhl, Walter. "Atta Troll. Heines Sommernachts-
      traum." *DK* 25 (1973): 1-26.

      Treats the genesis of *Atta Troll* largely in connection
      with the *Börne* affair and Heine's duel with Salomon
      Strauss. Identical with the corresponding section in
      no. 161.

544. Woesler, Winfried. "Eine deutsche Verssatire in franzoe-
      sischer Uebersetzung. Sprachlich-stilistischer Ver-
      gleich der beiden Versionen von Heines 'Atta Troll.'"
      EG 33 (1978): 27-41.

      Specific lexical and stylistic categories show how
      the French prose translation necessarily reduced the
      force and charm of the German original.

545. ————. "Die Fabel vom Tanzbären." *Cahier Heine*,
      pp. 132-143.

      History of the dancing bear fable before *Atta Troll*.

546. ————. "Heines 'köstlichste' Trolliaden." *HJ 1976*,
      pp. 52-66.

      Demonstrates that some of the paralipomena to *Atta
      Troll* were composed after the completion of the poem,
      thus proving that the spirit of the *Wintermärchen* did
      not supersede it in Heine's attitudes.

547. ————. *Heines Tanzbär: Historisch-literarische Unter-
      suchungen zum "Atta Troll."* Heine-Studien, ed. Joseph
      A. Kruse. Hamburg: Hoffmann und Campe, Heinrich Heine
      Verlag, 1978. 474 pp.

      The most thorough study of *Atta Troll* and one of the
      most thorough of any work of Heine's in recent years
      covers genesis, reception, genre, setting, structure,
      metrics, style, and comparative connections; significant
      is an unusual readiness to analyze the poem as a work
      of art and to recognize that it is not friendly to
      revolution or proto-Marxist.

548. ————. "Das Liebesmotiv in Heines politischer Vers-
      dichtung." Windfuhr, ed., *Heine-Kongreß*, pp. 202-
      218.

Heine's employment of motifs of eros and marriage as political allegories.

549. Würffel, Stefan Bodo. "Heinrich Heines negative Dialektik. Zur Barbarossa-Episode des Wintermärchens." *Neophilologus* 61 (1977): 421-438.

A thoughtful and original critique of simplistic interpretations; a close reaaing of folkloric elements shows that the hope of revolution is douotful and elegaic.

550. Zagona, Helen Grace. "Heine's New Secular Approach: Salome's Emergence as a Heroine." Pp. 23-40 in Zagona, *The Legend of Salome and the Principle of Art for Art's Sake*. Geneva and Paris: Librairie E. Droz and Librairie Minard, 1960. 141 pp.

Places the figure of Herodias in *Atta Troll* at the head of a subsequent development in French symbolism. The treatment of *Atta Troll* itself is somewhat lacking in scholarly and critical precision.

4. Fiction

551. Altenhofer, Norbert. *Harzreise in die Zeit: Zum Funktionszusammenhang von Traum, Witz und Zensur in Heines früher Prosa*. Schriften der Heinrich Heine-Gesellschaft, 5. Düsseldorf: Heinrich Heine-Gesellschaft, 1972. 44 pp.

By extensive recourse to Freud, tries to distinguish the esoteric, hidden political significance of the text. Over-argued but stimulating.

552. Arendt, Dieter. "Parabolische Dichtung und politische Tendenz. Eine Episode aus den 'Bädern von Lucca.'" *HJ 1970*, pp. 41-57.

Stresses the political implications of the children's ball scene while doubting the presence of exact allegorical correspondences.

553. Brask, Peter. "Rebecca, er det mig som taler?" *Kritik* 36 (1975): 103-126.

Analyzes Hirsch's malapropisms in *Die Bäder von Lucca*,

rightly criticizing Freud's textually imprecise employment of the passage.

554. Cherubini, Bruno. "Heine und die Kirchen von Lucca."
      HJ 1971, pp. 16-19.

      Fact and imagination in Heine's description of sights
      in *Die Stadt Lucca*.

555. Elema, Hans. "Evelina und die Seelenwanderung: Zu
      Heines 'Ideen. Das Buch Le Grand.'" *HJ 1971*, pp.
      20-33.

      An effort to show that the dedicatee of *Buch Le Grand*
      is a composite image of all of Heine's loved and admired
      women.

556. Fancelli, Maria. "Heine Minore: Le *Florentinische
      Nächte*." *SG* N.S. 11 (1973): 51-70.

      Discusses autobiographical elements and self-censorship
      in Heine's effort to produce a harmless work, and sug-
      gests modern elements of decadence in the text.

557. Finke, Franz. "Zur Datierung des 'Rabbi von Bacherach.'"
      HJ 1965, pp. 26-32. Reprinted Koopmann, ed. *Heinrich
      Heine*, pp. 49-55.

      An important study of the MS. of the *Rabbi* showing
      that the third chapter and probably the second must
      have been written in 1840.

558. Freund, Lothar. *Zeitkritik in Heines Reisebildern.*
      Vaasan Kauppakorkeakoulun Julkaisuja. Tutkimuksia
      No. 2. Filologia. Vaasa: Vaasan Kauppakorkeakoulu,
      1970. 161 pp.

      Deals with Heine's elements of style, neologisms,
      and rhetorical devices in the *Reisebilder*. Derivative
      and largely paraphrase.

559. Grossklaus, Götz. "Heinrich Heine: Ideen. Das Buch Le
      Grand. Eine textsemantische Beschreibung." Pp. 169-
      196 in *Zur Grundlegung der Literaturwissenschaft*, ed.
      S.J. Schmidt. Munich: Bayerischer Schulbuch-Verlag,
      1972. 196 pp.

      Contains some of the results of no. 560 below.

560. —————. *Textstruktur und Textgeschichte: Die "Reise-
      bilder" Heinrich Heines: Eine textlinguistische und*

texthistorische Beschreibung des Prosatyps. Frankfurt
am Main: Athenäum, 1973. x + 175 pp.

A stunningly unreadable application of structural-
linguistic textual analysis charting recurrent elements
and binary oppositions in the *Reisebilder* text that
nevertheless achieves no results not easily accessible
to attentive literary criticism and some that are in-
exact and muddled.

561. Grözinger, Elvira. "Die 'doppelte Buchhaltung.' Einige
Bemerkungen zu Heines Verstellungsstrategie in den
'Florentinischen Nächten.'" *HJ 1979*, pp. 65-83.

A far-fetched, partly psychoanalytic allegorization
attempts to decode "esoteric" meaning in Heine's weak-
est major work.

562. Grubačić, Slobodan. *Heines Erzählprosa: Versuch einer
Analyse.* Studien zur Poetik und Geschichte der Lite-
ratur, Vol. 40. Stuttgart, Berlin, Cologne, and Mainz:
Kohlhammer, 1975. 166 pp.

Undertakes a rhetorical and stylistic microanalysis
of Heine's prose with a method in clear line of descent
from the Russian Formalists; weaves a dense fabric of
ingenious and acutely focused interpretations, arguing
that Heine's world view is anarchic, carnivalistic, and
disparate, but fails to get an evaluative focus on
texts.

563. Hamburger, Käte. "Zur Struktur der belletristischen
Prosa Heines." Pp. 286-306 in *Untersuchungen zur
Literatur als Geschichte: Festschrift für Benno von
Wiese*, ed. Vincent J. Günther, Helmut Koopmann, Peter
Pütz, and Hans Joachim Schrimpf. Berlin: Erich Schmidt
Verlag, 1973. 598 pp. Reprinted Kuttenkeuler, ed.,
Heinrich Heine: Artistik und Engagement, pp. 22-42.

An analysis of narrative structure in Heine's prose
fiction, correctly distinguishing the narrator from the
author's real self. But it is a question whether formal
narrative poetics are entirely appropriate to grasping
Heine's strategies.

564. Hermand, Jost. *Der frühe Heine: Ein Kommentar zu den
"Reisebildern."* Munich: Winkler, 1976. 226 pp.

Textual explications containing many useful observations without probing very deeply and mainly concerned

to demonstrate that Heine was in favor of progressive
ideas. Contains nos. 661, 565, 850, and 566.

565.   ———. "Heines 'Ideen' im 'Buch Le Grand.'" Windfuhr,
        ed., *Heine-Kongreß*, pp. 370-385.

An excellent article that explains some of the oddities
A rambunctious treatment of Heine's view of Goethe in
Buch Le Grand, leading to vigorous protests from the
East German representative at the conference. Included
in no. 564.

566.   ———. "Werthers Harzreise." Pp. 129-151 in Hermand,
        *Von Mainz nach Weimar (1793-1919): Studien zur deutschen
        Literatur.* Stuttgart: Metzler, 1969. 400 pp.

An exceedingly and perhaps excessively ingenious effort
to demonstrate that the *Harzreise* is informed by a thor-
oughgoing, hostile parody of Goethe. Included in no.
564.

567.   Hollosi, Clara. "The Image of Russia in Heine's Reise-
        bilder." *HJ 1976*, pp. 23-37.

An excellent article that explains some of the oddities
of Heine's expressed opinions on Russia.

568.   Hultberg, Helge. "Heines 'Die Harzreise.'" *HJ 1970*,
        pp. 58-69. Reprinted Koopmann, ed., *Heinrich Heine*,
        pp. 348-361.

A version of the *Harzreise* section in no. 95.

569.   Jacobs, Jürgen. "Zu Heines 'Ideen. Das Buch Le Grand.'"
        HJ 1968, pp. 3-11.

Discovers meaningful and ordered structure in Heine's
apparently aimless composition.

570.   Jahn, Maria-Eva. *Techniken der fiktiven Bildkomposition
        in Heinrich Heines "Reisebildern."* Stuttgarter Arbeiten
        zur Germanistik, 53. [ii] + 71 pp.

Examines fictionalized transformation of empirical
experience, illustrating the priority Heine gave to the
transforming, ideational imagination, charged with a
political message, over plain fact. Could have been
condensed into an article.

571.   Jennings, Lee B. "The Dance of Life and Death in Heine
        and Immermann." *GL&L* N.S. 18 (1964/65): 130-135.

The dance, "a graphic representation of vitality faced with extinction," is interpreted as the central motif of *Florentinische Nächte*.

572. Johnston, Otto W. "The Quest for Bonaparte in Heine's *Harzreise*." *RLV* 37 (1971): 176-180.

    It is not certain that the allusion to the Prometheus myth in *Die Harzreise* is a reference to Napoleon.

573. Kircher, Hartmut. "'Wie schlecht geschützt ist Israel...' Zur Szene am Frankfurter Ghetto-Tor in Heines 'Rabbi von Bacherach.'" *HJ 1972*, pp. 38-55.

    Offers a useful analysis of the Frankfurt scene in the *Rabbi*, but does not refute previous evaluations of the whole fragment, as the author supposes. A preliminary study to no. 680.

574. Kruse, Joseph A. "Die Qual dieser armen Schwäne: Zum Verhältnis von Realität und Fiktion in Heinrich Heines Hamburg-Darstellung." *AION* 20, No. 1 (1977): 131-154.

    Reviews the fictional aspect of Heine's relationship to Hamburg treated in greater detail in no. 100.

575. Mayer, Hans. "Die Platen-Heine-Konfrontation." *Akzente* 20 (1973): 273-286. Reprinted pp. 207-223 in Mayer, *Aussenseiter*. Frankfurt am Main: Suhrkamp, 1975. 511 pp.

    For the first time within memory a decent balance of judgment is brought to bear on Heine's intemperate attack on Platen. Mayer suggests that both Heine and Platen were pariahs of a repressive society.

576. Möhrmann, Renate. "Der naive und der sentimentalische Reisende. Ein Vergleich von Eichendorffs 'Taugenichts' und Heines 'Harzreise.'" *HJ 1971*, pp. 5-15.

    Shows Heine's dependence on Romantic tradition as well as the way in which he points to new developments.

577. Müller, Joachim. "Heines Napoleondichtung." *Wissenschaftliche Zeitschrift der Universität Jena. Gesellschafts- und Sprachwissenschaftliche Reihe* 21 (1972): 235-243.

    Comments on Heine's symbolization of Napoleon as a mythic hero and questions whether he went too far in ignoring Napoleon's defects.

578. ———. *Heines Prosakunst*. Abhandlungen der sächsischen
      Akademie der Wissenschaften zu Leipzig. Philologisch-
      historische Klasse, Vol. 65, Fascicle 2. Berlin:
      Akademie-Verlag, 1975. 179 pp. 2nd edition, 1977.

      Treats Heine's prose fiction as narrative art with de-
      tailed close reading, stressing the fictive narrator,
      epic integration, sentence rhythm, and associative tex-
      ture. The focus is welcome, but Müller tends to catalogue
      and describe rather than get texts into focus, and the
      study is very much out of touch with contemporary scholar-
      ship.

579. Owen, Claude R. "Charruas und Tacuabé. Interpretation
      zu einem dunklen Passus in Heinrich Heines 'Tableaux
      de Voyage.'" *HJ 1965*, pp. 38–41.

      A passage in a French preface to the *Reisebilder* is
      explained as a reference to the exhibit of the last
      living members of a Uruguayan tribe in Paris.

580. Pabel, Klaus. *Heines "Reisebilder": Ästhetisches Be-
      dürfnis und politisches Interesse am Ende der Kunst-
      periode*. Munich: Fink, 1977. 304 pp.

      The purpose is to show that for Heine the aesthetic
      is not a category of unreal harmonization but a vehicle
      of the promise of sensuality and gratification that can
      only be realized in revolutionary emancipation. The
      point is by now conventional, though Pabel endeavors
      to give it a stronger textual foundation through detailed
      explication.

581. Riesel, Elise. "Sprache und Stil von Heines 'Harzreise.'"
      DU (East) 9 (1956): 11–18, 79–95.

      An explication of the *Harzreise* originally intended
      for foreign-language students in the Soviet Union.

582. Rose, Margaret A. "Über die strukturelle Einheit von
      Heines Fragment 'Der Rabbi von Bacherach.'" *HJ 1976*,
      pp. 38–51.

      Unconvincingly argues the unity of the *Rabbi* on the
      basis of an archetypal narrative scheme.

583. Rosenthal, Ludwig. "Einige Glossen zu dem Notizblatt
      Heines für den 'Rabbi von Bacherach' mit der Über-
      schrift 'Vita Abarbanelis' im Heine-Archiv in Düssel-
      dorf." *HJ 1971*, pp. 20–25.

      Identifies a source for the *Rabbi*.

584. Sammons, Jeffrey L. "Ein Meisterwerk. 'Ideen: Das Buch Le Grand." Koopmann, ed., *Heinrich Heine*, pp. 307-347.

     Analysis of the meaningful composition and structure of *Buch Le Grand*. Tr. of a chapter of no. 345.

585. ————. "Heine's Composition: Die Harzreise." *HJ 1967*, pp. 40-47.

     Seeks a structural pattern correlating with the meaning of the text. Included in revised form in no. 345.

586. ————. "Heine's *Rabbi von Bacherach*: The Unresolved Tensions." *GQ* 37 (1964): 26-38.

     Offers internal reasons why Heine could not complete the *Rabbi*. Included in revised form in no. 345.

587. Sandor, Andras. "Auf der Suche nach der vergehenden Zeit. Heines 'Florentinische Nächte' und die Probleme der Avantgarde." *HJ 1980*, pp. 101-139.

     Endeavors to rescue *Florentinische Nächte* from the customary view of it as a regressive and weak work by interpreting it as a metaphorical treatment of the relation of art and life, pointing part way to modernism and the absurd. Ingenious, challenging, and hermetically difficult.

588. Sauerland, Karol. "Heinrich Heines Reisebilder—ein besonderes literarisches Genre?" *Streitbarer Humanist*, pp. 145-158.

     Argues that Heine created a new poetic genre with the *Reisebilder*. Much shadow-boxing with "bourgeois" criticism.

589. Scher, Steven Paul. "Heine's Paganini Portrait: Translation of Music into 'Theater.'" Pp. 79-105 in Scher, *Verbal Music in German Literature*. Yale Germanic Studies, 2. New Haven and London: Yale University Press, 1968. xii + 181 pp.

     An exceptionally sensitive interpretation of the Paganini passage of *Florentinische Nächte* in the context of a study of the reproduction of musical experience in literature.

590. Schillemeit, Jost. "Das Grauenhafte im lachenden Spiegel des Witzes. Zum historischen Kontext einer

ästhetischen Idee in Heines 'Buch Le Grand.'" *Jahrbuch
des Freien Deutschen Hochstifts* (1975): 324-345.

An important contribution that derives from Solger and
Jean Paul Heine's aesthetic considerations on the short
space from the sublime to the ridiculous.

591. Schneider, Ronald. "Die Muse 'Satyra.' Das Wechsel-
      spiel von politischem Engagement und poetischer Re-
      flexion in Heines 'Reisebildern.'" *HJ 1977*, pp. 9-19.

      A major critical article analyzes the interplay and
      shifting distribution of moral satire and artistic humor
      in the *Reisebilder*.

592. ————. "'Themis und Pan': Zu literarischer Struktur und
      politischem Gehalt der 'Reisebilder' Heinrich Heines."
      AION 18, No. 3 (1975): 7-42.

      An important article, if arguable in details, analyzes
      the duality of political engagement and aesthetic play
      in the *Reisebilder*.

593. Schuller, Marianne. "Überlegungen zur Textkonstitution
      der Heineschen 'Reisebilder.'" *LiLi* 3, No. 12 (Decem-
      ber 1973): 81-98.

      Semiotic methods are employed to describe the distinc-
      tion between Heine's text type and that of the Romantic
      "system"; a case of fashionable methodology leading to
      conventional results.

594. Thanner, Josef. "Tektonische und weltanschauliche
      Strukturen der Raumdarstellung in Heinrich Heines
      'Die Harzreise.'" *University of Dayton Review* 10,
      No. 2 (Fall 1973): 57-64.

      Heine treats the setting of the Harz journey not by
      empirical description but with subjective associations
      derived from radical social experience. Out of touch
      with scholarship on the subject.

595. Thomas, Barry G. "The van der Pissen Scene in Heinrich
      Heine's *Schnabelewopski*: A Suggestion." *GQ* 51 (1978):
      39-46.

      Convincingly explicates one of the most puzzling scenes
      in Heine's prose.

596. Veit, Philip F. "Heine's Polemics in *Die Bäder von
      Lucca*." *GR* 55 (1980): 109-117.

Efforts to identify the fictional characters with
Eduard Gans, David Friedländer, Rahel Varnhagen, Friederike Robert, and Friedrich de la Motte Fouqué range
from the ingenious to the implausible.

597. Wadepuhl, Walter. "Eine ungedruckte Vorrede zu Heines
Reisebildern." Wadepuhl, *Heine-Studien*, pp. 91-96.

Prints and comments upon the previously unpublished
preface to the fourth *Reisebilder* volume.

598. ————. "Eine unveröffentlichte Episode aus Heines
'Florentinischen Nächten.'" Wadepuhl, *Heine-Studien*,
pp. 109-113.

A suppressed passage critical of Prussia.

599. Werner, Michael. "Heines 'Reise von München nach Genua'
im Lichte ihrer Quellen." *HJ 1975*, pp. 24-46.

Heine's confrontation with and deviation from tradi-
tional accounts of Italian journeys.

600. Windfuhr, Manfred. "Heines Fragment eines Schelmenromans
*'Aus den Memoiren des Herren von Schnabelewopski.'"
HJ 1967, pp. 21-39. Reprinted Koopmann, ed., *Heinrich
Heine*, pp. 232-256.

Places *Schnabelewopski* in the picaresque tradition.

601. Zlotkowski, Edward A. "Die Bedeutung Napoleons in
Heines Reisebilder II." *EG* 35 (1980): 145-162.

Napoleon, upon whom Heine projects his values, is a
link between the unity of the past and the unity of the
future across the present of disunity, and a symbol for
the possibility of a new aesthetic. A version of a section of no. 602 below.

602. ————. *Heinrich Heines Reisebilder: The Tendency of
the Text and the Identity of the Age*. Abhandlungen
zur Kunst-, Musik- und Literaturwissenschaft, Vol.
307. Bonn: Bouvier, 1980. 221 pp.

This ideological study of the first two *Reisebilder*
volumes remains closely attentive to the internal relations and rhythms of Heine's texts without polemic or
the heavy load of extraneous philosophical apparatus
common to discussions of the subject, and offers one of
the finest interpretations of the *Harzreise* so far attempted. The comparison with Shelley is both apt and
long overdue, and deserves further consideration.

5. Dramas and Ballets

603. Henning, Hans. "Heine und Faust oder Klassik und Roman-
      tik in Heines Faust-Poem." *Streitbarer Humanist*, pp.
      379–384.

      Argues that Heine's Faust ballet exhibits allegiance
      to German classicism and to Goethe, and that the con-
      clusion symbolizes the doom of the bourgeoisie. Imper-
      ceptive and weak.

604. ———. "Heines Tanzpoem 'Der Doktor Faust.'" *Faust-
      Blätter*, No. 29 (1975): 1011–1024.

      Takes up the topic of the preceding item in somewhat
      more substantial fashion, thoughtfully discussing the
      antithesis of Nazarenism and Hellenism, the relationship
      to Goethe, and the premonition of Heine's religious
      return, but fails to grasp the demonic aspect of eros
      and dance.

605. Lea, Charlene A. ["ALMANSOR by HEINRICH HEINE."] Pp.
      27–33 in Lea, *Emancipation, Assimilation and Stereo-
      type: The Image of the Jew in German and Austrian
      Drama (1800–1850)*. Modern German Studies, ed. Peter
      Heller, George Iggers, Volker Neuhaus, and Hans H.
      Schulte, Vol. 2. Bonn: Bouvier, 1978. viii + 171 pp.

      Quite properly examines Heine's Moorish drama in a
      section entitled "The Camouflaged Jew."

606. Niehaus, Max. *Himmel, Hölle und Trikot: Heinrich Heine
      und das Ballett*. Munich: Nymphenburger Verlag, 1959.
      95 pp.

      A useful and informative account of the circumstances
      of Heine's ballet scenarios as well as his inspiration
      for the ballet *Giselle*.

607. Stiefel, Robert E. "Heine's Ballet Scenarios, An Inter-
      pretation." *GR* 44 (1969): 186–198.

      A sensitive interpretation of the dynamics of the
      ballet texts.

608. Turóczi-Trostler, József. "Heine und Faust." Pp. 203–
      207 in Turóczi-Trostler, "Faust-Studien." *Acta Lit-
      teraria Academiae Scientiarum Hungaricae* 6 (1964):
      203–219.

      A brief account of the background and circumstances of
      Heine's *Faust*, calling attention to the great enthusiasm
      for Goethe and his *Faust* in France at that time.

609. Weiss, Gerhard. "Die Entstehung von Heines 'Doktor
     Faust.' Ein Beispiel deutsch-englisch-französischer
     Freundschaft." *HJ 1966*, pp. 41-57.

     A thorough discussion of the genesis of Heine's *Faust*.

610. Wiese, Benno von. "Mephistophela und Faust. Zur Inter-
     pretation von Heines Tanzpoem 'Der Doktor Faust.'"
     Pp. 225-240 in *Herkommen und Erneuerung: Essays für
     Oskar Seidlin*, ed. Gerald Gillespie and Edgar Lohner.
     Tübingen: Niemeyer, 1976. xiv + 434 pp.

     A number of accurate observations on sensualism and
     spiritualism in the ballets, although Heine is made too
     much of the sensualist Devil's party. Included in no.
     371.

6. Literature, Art, Music, Religion, Philosophy, Politics, Journalism

611. Badia, Gilbert. "Heine journaliste." *Europe*, Nos.
     125/126 (May-June 1956): 78-91.

     A modestly well-informed account of Heine's journal-
     istic career.

612. Barnard, Frederick. "Nationality, Humanity and the
     Hebraic Spirit: Heine and Herder." Immerwahr and
     Spencer, eds., *Heinrich Heine*, pp. 56-67.

     An unusual comparison of Heine with Herder, more
     learned about Herder than about Heine.

613. Basso, Lelio. "Heine e Marx." *Belfagor* 11 (1956):
     121-136.

     Reviews the relationship of Heine with Marx and its
     connection to the *Wintermärchen*, including the whole
     correspondence in Italian translation. Basso argues
     that Heine yielded to Marx's influence, but rejects
     Heine's criticisms of Communism.

614. Baumgarten, Michael, and Wilfried Schulz. "Topoi
     Hegelscher Philosophie der Kunst in Heines 'Roman-
     tischer Schule.'" *HJ 1978*, pp. 55-94.

     An effort, under the aegis of Ernst Bloch, to draw
     Heine into the context of Hegel's aesthetics, which the
     authors admit he cannot have known.

112

Criticism

615. Bech, Françoise. "Literatur und Wissenschaft. 'Streit-
      objekt Heine.'" *Sprache im technischen Zeitalter* No.
      68 (October–December 1978): 290–301.

      Treats Heine's pantheism as a progressive variant of
      Hegel's identity of nature and spirit; ingenious, but
      makes Heine too unproblematical.

616. Becker, Karl Wolfgang. "Klassik und Romantik im Denken
      Heinrich Heines." *Streitbarer Humanist*, pp. 255–276.

      An argument that Heine repudiated Romanticism as re-
      actionary and developed via Goethean Classicism to
      activist political engagement.

617. Benda, Gisela. "Heines 'Testament' in deutscher Denk-
      tradition." *PLL* 11 (1975): 46–53.

      Heine's wish, expressed in his will of 1846, that the
      Germans might acquire a lighter spirit and more cheer-
      fulness, is set in a tradition of similar sentiments
      from Goethe to Nietzsche and the Brothers Mann.

618. Bock, Helmut. "Die ökonomisch-politischen Auffassungen
      Heinrich Heines in den Briefen an die Augsburger
      Allgemeine Zeitung von 1840–1843." *Zeitschrift für
      Geschichtswissenschaft* 5 (1957): 826–835.

      Argues a development carrying Heine beyond the limita-
      tions of Saint-Simonianism and close to "the political-
      social goals of the proletarian revolution."

619. ———. "Zur Entwicklung des historischen Denkens bei
      Heinrich Heine. Des Dichters Weg zum revolutionären
      Demokratismus (1797–1831)." *Streitbarer Humanist*,
      pp. 109–131.

      An uncritical encomium with little relation to reality.

620. Bodi, Leslie. "Heine und die Revolution." Pp. 169–177
      in *Dichtung, Sprache, Gesellschaft: Akten des IV. Inter-
      nationalen Germanisten-Kongresses in Princeton*, ed.
      Victor Lange and Hans-Gert Roloff. Frankfurt am Main:
      Athenäum, 1971. 635 pp.

      Examines the "Promethean imagery" of revolution as
      erotic passion and bacchanal, and acknowledges Heine's
      fear of revolution.

621. ———. "Kopflos—ein Leitmotiv in Heines Werk." Wind-
      fuhr, ed., *Heine-Kongreß*, pp. 227–244.

On the political implications of Heine's motif of
decapitation.

622. Bollacher, Martin. "Aufgeklärter Pantheismus.' Die
      Deutung der Geschichte in Heines Schrift *Zur Geschichte
      der Religion und Philosophie in Deutschland*." *DVLG*
      49 (1975): 265-314. Reprinted Kuttenkeuler, ed., *Hein-
      rich Heine: Artistik und Engagement*, pp. 144-186.

      Attempts to account for Heine's repudiation of the
      essay later in life and the ambivalence of his perora-
      tion, separating the argument from Marxist interpreta-
      tions and arguing correctly that Heine associated panthe-
      ism with the liberating sensuality of art against idealism
      and materialism.

623. Booss, Rutger. *Ansichten der Revolution: Paris-Berichte
      deutscher Schriftsteller nach der Juli-Revolution 1830.
      Heine, Börne u.a.* Cologne: Pahl-Rugenstein, 1977.
      272 pp.

      An observant and instructive comparison of Heine's
      and Börne's reportage on the aftermath of the July
      Revolution with that of other contemporaries, although
      Heine is conventionally praised at Börne's expense and
      the grasp of French history of the period is drawn
      exclusively from Marxism.

624. ————. "Empirie und Fiktion. Die Juli-Revolution und
      die Anfänge von Heines Pariser Berichterstattung."
      Kuttenkeuler, ed., *Heinrich Heine: Artistik und Engage-
      ment*, pp. 66-85.

      A compressed version of some of the results of the
      study above, with a rather eccentric defense of the
      fictions and inventions in Heine's reportage.

625. Braun, Jürgen. "Zwischen Kunst und Leben. Zu Heines
      Geschichts- und Kunstauffassung." *TK* 18/19 (1968):
      36-39.

      Heine could no longer believe in the Romantic aesthetic
      interpretation of historical eschatology, but his own
      effort to amalgamate the aesthetic with progressive
      activity ended in failure and resignation.

626. Broicher, Ursula. "Studien zu Heines Solidarität."
      HJ 1974, pp. 10-33.

      Criticizes the canonization of Heine as a modern
      political revolutionary, pointing out that his "solidar-
      ity" with the people maintained an aesthetic distance.

627. Brünn, Max F. "Heine og jødedommen." *Samtiden* 66 (1957): 109-116.

Heine's complicated allegiances in a time when the relationship of Jewry to its environment was undergoing great change.

628. Cadot, Marie-Thérèse. "Trois Allemands de bonne foi en quête de la vraie Pologne." *RdA* 3 (1971): 524-547.

Heine compared as a sympathetic observer of Poland with Alfred Döblin and the contemporary journalist Hansjakob Stehle.

629. Calvié, Lucien. "Heine und die Junghegelianer." Windfuhr, ed., *Heine-Kongreß*, pp. 307-317.

An unusually precise and learned set of distinctions between Heine and the Young Hegelians and socialists of his time with careful attention to nuance and chronology.

630. Cantimori, Delio. "Eine literarische Parallele zwischen Kant und Robespierre." Pp. 519-527 in *Maximilien Robespierre 1758-1794: Beiträge zu seinem 200. Geburtstag*, ed. Walter Markov and Georges Lefebre. Berlin: Rütten & Loening, 1958. 628 pp. Reprinted pp. 469-477 in *Maximilien Robespierre 1758-1794*, ed. Walter Markov. Berlin: Rütten & Loening, 1961. 606 pp. Reprinted as "Un parallelo letterario fra Kant e Robespierre." Pp. 655-664 in Cantimori, *Studi di storia*. Turin: Einaudi, 1959. xx + 867 pp.

Heine's parallel in *Zur Geschichte der Religion und Philosophie in Deutschland* of Kant and Robespierre as revolutionary terrorists in the realms of theory and action respectively is found elsewhere in literary and political sources about the French Revolution.

631. Chawtassi, Grigorij. "Weltergänzung durch Poesie: Zu ästhetischen Ansichten Heinrich Heines." *WB* 18, No. 2 (1972): 145-161.

An orthodox Marxist insistence on Heine's consistent materialism, focused primarily on *Shakespeares Mädchen und Frauen*.

632. Chiarini, Paolo. "Heine contra Börne ovvero critica dell'impazienza rivoluzionaria." *SG* N.S. 10 (1972): 355-392.

An introduction to an Italian translation of *Börne*

defends Heine's strategies of working on the consciousness of the public by aesthetic means in order to modify
its authoritarian and spiritualist predilections as superior to Börne's radical political impatience.

633. ⸻. "Heine e le radici storiche della 'miseria'
tedesca." *Rivista di letterature moderne e comparate*
11 (1958): 231-244. Reprinted pp. 33-50 in Chiarini,
Romanticismo e realismo nella letteratura tedesca.
Padua: Liviana Editrice, 1961. viii + 293 pp.

Finds Heine's view of the positive and negative German
qualities summarized in his portrait of Luther.

634. ⸻. "Heinrich Heine fra decadentismo e marxismo."
Società 16 (1960): 383-404. Reprinted pp. 81-103 in
Chiarini, *Romanticismo e realismo nella letterature
tedesca.* Padua: Liviana Editrice, 1961. viii + 293
pp.

A study of *Lutezia* attempts to refine Heine's location
between "Marxism," i.e., democratic allegiances, and
emerging French decadence.

635. ⸻. "Heinrich Heine; il letterato e il politico.
Note in margine ai 'Französische Zustände.'" *SG*
N.S. 10 (1972): 561-589.

Some random observations on Heine's views on the differences of national character in Germany and France
that require different models of revolution.

636. Clasen, Herbert. *Heinrich Heines Romantikkritik: Tradi-
tion--Produktion--Rezeption.* Heine-Studien, ed.
Joseph A. Kruse. Hamburg: Hoffmann und Campe, Heinrich Heine Verlag, 1979. 405 pp.

Primarily focused on *Die Romantische Schule*, the
Wintermärchen, and (very briefly) *Faust*, the study endeavors to show that Heine retained productive and progressive aspects of early Romanticism, which is said
to be an anti-feudal, anti-bourgeois, anti-capitalist
movement which, however, was falsified into a reactionary tendency in the bourgeoisie's resistance to the
revolutionary proletariat. Some good local observations,
but the execution is weakened by the rigidity of the
political assumptions and an uncritical naïveté.

637. De Leeuwe, Hans. "Was Heine über Holland nicht gesagt
hat." *DK* 28 (1976): 97-102.

        Guesses at the origin of an aphorism falsely attributed to Heine about Holland's backwardness.

638.   Demetz, Peter. "Persönliche Kontakte: Marx, Engels und Heine." Pp. 106-114 in Demetz, *Marx, Engels und die Dichter: Zur Grundlagenforschung des Marxismus.* Stuttgart: Deutsche Verlags-Anstalt, 1959. 350 pp. Reprinted pp. 78-85 in *Marx, Engels und die Dichter: Ein Kapitel deutscher Literaturgeschichte.* Ullstein Buch No. 4021/4022. Frankfurt am Main: Ullstein, 1969. 271 pp. Tr. as "Personal Contacts: Marx, Engels, and Heine." Pp. 74-82 in *Marx, Engels, and the Poets: Origins of Marxist Literary Criticism.* Chicago and London: University of Chicago Press, 1967. x + 278 pp.

        A skeptical view of the relationship with Marx, stressing Heine's late repudiations of Communism. Though regularly attacked in the Marxist camp, the argument bears consideration.

639.   Doerksen, Victor G. "June Bugs and Hornets: A Contextual Consideration of Heine's 'Schwabenspiegel.'" Immerwahr and Spencer, eds., *Heinrich Heine*, pp. 34-45.

        An original and unusual look at the other side of Heine's quarrel with the Swabian School, suggesting that there might be something to be said for Heine's opponents.

640.   Dresch, Joseph. "Heine et Victor Cousin." *EG* 11 (1956): 122-132.

        Examines Heine's contempt for Cousin's distortions of German philosophy, deriving it from Heine's allegiance to Hegel.

641.   Eisner, F.H. "Ein Aufsatz Heines in 'Le Globe,' Februar 1832?" *WB* 5 (1959): 421-425.

        An essay by an anonymous "Prussian" confessing devoted allegiance to Saint-Simonianism is ascribed to Heine. Possible but questionable.

642.   Emmerich, Karl. "Heinrich Heines politisches Testament in deutscher Sprache." *WB* 4 (1958): 202-214.

        First publication of a German draft of the famous preface to the French edition of *Lutezia*.

643. Fairley, Barker. "Heine, Goethe, and the *Divan*." *GL&L*
      N.S. 9 (1955/56): 166-170.

      Very skeptical about Heine's grasp of Goethe's *West-
      östlicher Divan*.

644. Fest, Joachim. "Über eine Metapher von Heinrich Heine."
      Pp. 21-32 in *Deutsche Akademie für Sprache und Dichtung
      --Jahrbuch 1978*, No. 2. Heidelberg: Lambert Schneider,
      1979. 147 pp.

      The metaphor in question is Heine's comment on German
      philosophy that the thought precedes the deed as light-
      ning precedes the thunder. Fest is more willing than
      most contemporary observers to relate it to German ten-
      dencies to force an unmediated, sometimes terroristic
      juncture between ideas and action.

645. Fleischmann, Jakob. "Heine und die Hegelsche Philosophie."
      Deutsche Universitätszeitung 14 (1959): 418-426.

      Argues that Heine intuitively grasped the enormous
      significance of reason in history according to Hegel.
      Assertions virtually without demonstration.

646. Francke, Renate. "Zum Aspekt der Volkstümlichkeit in
      Heines 'Romantischer Schule.'" *Streitbarer Humanist*,
      pp. 375-378.

      Heine's literary criticism shows that he was devoted
      to the people.

647. Frank, Manfred. "Heine und Schelling." Windfuhr, ed.,
      Heine-Kongreß, pp. 281-306.

      A remarkable, thought-provoking, and perhaps debatable
      contribution suggests that Heine was closer to Schelling
      philosophically than his explicit dismissals would sug-
      gest.

648. Fridlender, Georgi Michailowitsch. "Heinrich Heine und
      die Ästhetik Hegels." *Streitbarer Humanist*, pp. 159-
      171. Reprinted *WB* 19, No. 4 (1973): 35-48.

      Hegel's reading of history affected Heine's view of
      the end of the "epoch of art," but Heine was unwilling
      to steer a course of creative renewal in social aware-
      ness between Hegel and Romantic art-religion.

649. Frühwald, Wolfgang. "Heinrich Heine und die Spätromantik:
      Thesen zu einem gebrochenen Verhältnis." Immerwahr

and Spencer, eds., *Heinrich Heine*, pp. 46-55.

Shows a subtle debate between Heine and the late
Romantics; the reactionary Görres and the radical Börne
agreed on the utilitarian employment of literature, while
Heine and Brentano appeared to agree on the issue of
autonomy.

650.   Fuhrmann, Alfred. *Recht und Staat bei Heinrich Heine.*
       Schriften zur Rechtslehre und Politik, ed. Ernst v.
       Hippel, Vol. 33. Bonn: Bouvier, 1961. xviii + 210 pp.

       A compendium of Heine's various views on religious,
political, and legal institutions. Useful for reference.

651.   Galley, Eberhard. "Politische Aspekte in Heines italie-
       nischen Reisebildern." Windfuhr, ed., *Heine-Kongreß*,
       pp. 386-398.

       Endeavors to work out the chronology of Heine's politi-
cal attitudes in the period of the *Reisebilder*.

652.   Geisler, Ulrich. "Die sozialen Anschauungen des revolu-
       tionären Demokraten Heinrich Heine." *Wissenschaftliche
       Zeitschrift der Karl-Marx-Universität Leipzig. Gesell-
       schafts- und Sprachwissenschaftliche Reihe* 14 (1965):
       7-15.

       An orthodox East German Party view of Heine's political
standpoint.

653.   Girndt, Eberhardt. "Heines Kunstbegriff in 'Französische
       Maler' von 1831." *HJ 1970*, pp. 70-86.

       A disappointingly opaque and abstruse attempt to offer
a differentiated explication of Heine's aesthetics ade-
quate to his formal and social instincts.

654.   Grappin, Pierre. "Heiné [sic] in Frankreich: Vorkämpfer
       der Aussöhnung." *Europäische Gemeinschaft* (1972, No.
       12): 24-26.

       Heine's efforts to mediate between French and German
cultures.

655.   Hahn, Karl-Heinz. "Zwischen Tradition und Moderne. Zu
       Heinrich Heines Essay 'Die Romantische Schule.'" Wind-
       fuhr, ed., *Heine-Kongreß*, pp. 416-446.

       Argues that Heine takes a Goethean position against

Romanticism, leading to a new concept of revolution
embracing all areas of life and coming close to Marxist
positions, though hindered by remnants of idealism.

656. Harich, Wolfgang. "Heinrich Heine und das Schulgeheimnis
der deutschen Philosophie." *SuF* 8, No. 1 (1956): 27–
59. Expanded pp. 7–52 in Heine, *Zur Geschichte der
Religion und Philosophie in Deutschland*, ed. Harich.
sammlung insel, 17. Frankfurt am Main: Insel, 1965.
245 pp.

The East German semi-dissident takes a very orthodox
line, arguing that "bourgeois" critics misunderstand the
text and that German philosophy can only be understood
as culminating in Marxism, a process into which Heine's
text can be placed.

657. Heise, Wolfgang. "Zum Verhältnis von Hegel und Heine."
Streitbarer Humanist, pp. 225–254. Reprinted as
"Heine und Hegel: Zum philosophisch-äesthetischen
Standpunkt Heines." *WB* 19, No. 5 (May 1973): 5–36.

Heine accepted Hegel's historicism, but radicalized
it with a stronger sense of the human need of material
happiness; he was inferior to Marx in that he could not
see the revolutionary potential of the working class.
Well written but undistinguished.

658. Hengst, Heinz. *Idee und Ideologieverdacht: Revolutionäre
Implikationen des deutschen Idealismus im Kontext der
zeitkritischen Prosa Heinrich Heines*. Munich: Fink,
1973. 170 pp.

Stresses Heine's non-utopian, practical concentration
on human emancipation and his defense of the artistic
domain and of the individual. The most informative
part is a chapter comparing Heine with the Right Hegelians.

659. Henning, Hans. "Heines Buch über Shakespeares Mädchen
und Frauen." *Shakespeare Jahrbuch* 113 (1977): 103–
117.

A basically informational lecture, undifferentiated
and nearly uncritical. A list of treatments of Heine
and Shakespeare ignores the best of them, no. 734.

660. Hermand, Jost. "Auf andere Art so große Hoffnung.
Heine und die USA." Pp. 81–92 in *Amerika in der
deutschen Literatur: Neue Welt--Nordamerika--USA*,
ed. Sigrid Bauschinger, Horst Denkler, and Wilfried

Malsch. Stuttgart: Reclam, 1975. 416 pp.

Heine's changing opinions on America from republican
admiration to quite negative criticism of boorish egali-
tarianism and slavery are put in the historical context
of his views.

661. ———. "Heines 'Briefe aus Berlin.' Politische
      Tendenz und feuilletonistische Form." Pp. 284-305
      in *Gestaltungsgeschichte und Gesellschaftsgeschichte:
      Literatur-, kunst- und musikwissenschaftliche Studien*,
      ed. Helmut Kreuzer with Käte Hamburger. Stuttgart:
      Metzler, 1969. xii + 624 pp.

      In their stress on the social and political function
      of art the *Briefe aus Berlin* are one of Heine's earliest
      statements of fundamental principle. Included in no.
      564.

662. Hinderer, Walter. "Nazarener oder Hellene: Die politisch-
      ästhetische Fehde zwischen Börne und Heine." *Monats-
      hefte* 66 (1974): 355-365.

      Takes the rather uncommon position of respecting
      Börne's views on Heine's elitist and quasi-aristocratic
      posture.

663. Hoffmann, Gerd. "Über Heines Beziehungen zur Musik
      und zu Musikern." *Aufbau* 12 (1956): 127-132.

      An uncritical review of Heine's music criticism, with
      some remarks on settings of his poems.

664. Hohendahl, Peter Uwe. "Geschichte und Modernität: Heines
      Kritik an der Romantik." *JDSG* 17 (1973): 318-361.
      Reprinted pp. 50-101 in Hohendahl, *Literaturkritik
      und Öffentlichkeit*. Munich: Piper, 1974. 234 pp.

      A well-written and instructive essay argues that Heine
      extracted the modern component of early Romanticism and
      opposed it to the conservative apologetics of late Romanti-
      cism.

665. ———. "Kunsturteil und Tagesbericht. Zur ästhetischen
      Theorie des späten Heine." Kuttenkeuler, ed., *Heinrich
      Heine: Artistik und Engagement*, pp. 207-241.

      A detailed and differentiated Neo-Marxist analysis of
      Heine's art and literary criticism against the back-
      ground of bourgeois society in France.

666. ————. "Talent oder Charakter: Die Börne-Heine-Fehde
      und ihre Nachgeschichte." *MLN* 95 (1980): 609-626.

      Proposes to clarify correctly the meaning of the
      Börne-Heine feud by concentrating on its reception,
      but the result is the wholly conventional Neo-Marxist
      view defending Heine's deeper and more revolutionary
      insight. The complexities of the *Börne* text are evaded,
      and the analysis of reception yields no detectable ad-
      vance in understanding.

667. Höltgen, Karl Joseph. "Über 'Shakespeares Mädchen und
      Frauen.' Heine, Shakespeare und England." Windfuhr,
      ed., *Heine-Kongreß*, pp. 464-488.

      Endeavors to estimate Heine's knowledge of Shakespeare
      and analyze the strengths of the book without overesti-
      mating them. Unusually urbane and sensible.

668. Holub, Robert C. "Spiritual Opium and Consolatory
      Medicine. A Note on the Origin of 'Opium des Volks.'"
      HJ 1980, pp. 222-227.

      Finds in Heine's characterization of religion as
      "spiritual opium," taken over by Marx, a parody of a
      passage in Börne's review of *De l'Allemagne* on the con-
      soling medicine of religion in the Roman world.

668a. Hultberg, Helge. "Heines Bewertung der Kunst." *HJ 1967*,
      pp. 81-89.

      Quotes Heine's ambivalent statements on the value of
      art, concluding that they are ambivalent and lead to
      no new aesthetics.

669. Iggers, Georg G. "Heine and the Saint-Simonians: A Re-
      examination." *CL* 10 (1958): 289-308.

      An important paper by a major modern student of the
      Saint-Simonian movement offers a fresh interpretation
      of Heine's relationship to it.

670. Jacobi, Ruth [L.]. "Heines 'Romantische Schule.'
      Eine Antwort auf Madame de Staëls 'De l'Allemagne.'"
      HJ 1980, pp. 140-168.

      Reviews the different responses to Staël through
      French history, giving a fair account of her and her
      book, but reproduces unanalytically Heine's familiar
      assertions and does not grasp the manifest contradic-
      tions in his opposition to Staël.

671.   ————. *Heinrich Heines jüdisches Erbe*. Abhandlungen
        zur Kunst-, Musik- und Literaturwissenschaft, 243.
        Bonn: Bouvier, 1978. 184 pp.

        A dissertation on Heine's Jewish inheritance, highly
        derivative of previous scholarship, sometimes without
        acknowledgment, inaccurate, and unanalytic.

672.   Jacobs, Jürgen. "Nach dem Ende der 'Kunstperiode.'
        Heines Aporien und ihre Aktualität." Kuttenkeuler,
        ed., *Heinrich Heine: Artistik und Engagement*, pp.
        242-255.

        Discusses the survival of Heine's dilemma between art
        and activism in modern literature.

673.   Johnston, Otto W. "Signatura Temporis in Heine's *Lutezia*."
        GQ 47 (1974): 215-232.

        Describes Heine's change from destroying myths to
        literary myth-making with materials in his own time in
        search of the recognizable "signature" of his age.

674.   Käfer, Karl-Heinz. *Versöhnt ohne Opfer: Zum geschichts-*
        theologischen Rahmen der Schriften Heinrich Heines
        1824-1844. Meisenheim am Glan: Hain, 1978. xii + 260
        pp.

        Develops an influence of Schelling on Heine, first
        suggested by M. Frank (no. 647) alongside that of Hegel,
        Marx, and Feuerbach. Exhibits accurate insights into
        the persistently religious or para-religious character
        of Heine's utopian thinking, but consistently overesti-
        mates Heine's philosophical competence by elaborate and
        abstruse extrapolation. Extremely difficult reading.

675.   Karst, Roman. "Heine und Polen." *NDL* 4, No. 8 (August
        1956): 79-89.

        Reviews Heine's essay *Über Polen* and his later reaction
        to the Polish revolution.

676.   Kaufmann, Hans. "Die Denkschrift 'Ludwig Börne' und
        ihre Stellung in Heines Werk." Windfuhr, ed., *Heine-*
        Kongreß, pp. 178-189. Reprinted pp. 65-77 in *Heinrich*
        Heine und die Zeitgenossen.

        An orthodox East German view of *Börne* ascribing to
        Heine higher intuitions and intimations of Marxism.

677.   ————. "Heines Schönheitsbegriff und die Revolution
        von 1848." *WB* 6 (1960): 266-277.

Heine sees no more possibility for beauty on earth after the failure of the 1848 Revolution.

678. ———. "Zur Entwicklung der Weltanschauung Heinrich Heines in den Jahren 1840-1844." *Wissenschaftliche Zeitschrift der Humboldt-Universität zu Berlin. Gesellschafts- und Sprachwissenschaftliche Reihe* 6 (1956/57): 59-69.

Prepublication of part of Kaufmann's book on the *Wintermärchen* (no. 521).

679. Kiba, Hiroshi. "Das Problem des Judentums bei Heinrich Heine. Zu dessen Grundlegung." *Doitsubungaku-Ronkô* 9 (1969): 1-18.

Reviews Heine's shifting relationship to Judaism, arguing that it is neglected in German scholarship. (Japanese with German abstract.)

680. Kircher, Hartmut. *Heinrich Heine und das Judentum.* Literatur und Wirklichkeit, ed. Karl Otto Conrady, Vol. 11. Bonn: Bouvier, 1973. 306 pp.

The first section is devoted to an account of the history and condition of the German Jews in Heine's time, a middle section reviews the Jewish aspects of Heine's biography, and the third part analyzes texts, the centerpiece being Kircher's previously published study of the *Rabbi* (no. 573). Thoroughly researched and pleasantly written, though it contains little that is new and some dubious assumptions uncritically accepted.

681. Klenner, Hermann. "Zur Stellung Heinrich Heines in der Geschichte der Staats- und Rechtstheorie." *Staat und Recht* 5 (1956): 696-710.

Examines Heine's opposition to the repressive legal theories of his day and endeavors to make him a direct forerunner of Marx and Engels.

682. Knüfermann, Volker V. "Heinrich Heine--Intellektualität als gedankliches und ästhetisches Problem--zur Krise des Kunstbewußtseins im neunzehnten Jahrhundert." *Seminar* 8 (1972): 181-197.

Heine's sensitivity to the potential for decadence in the modern intellect is a nontranscendental version of F. Schlegel's ideas pointing ahead to Nietzsche and Thomas Mann.

683. Koch, Franz. "Börne und Heine." Pp. 23-60 in Koch,
     *Idee und Wirklichkeit: Deutsche Dichtung zwischen
     Romantik und Naturalismus*, Vol. I. Düsseldorf: Louis
     Ehlermann, 1956. 327 pp.

     An account intended for a general reader reviews the
     careers of Heine and Börne and endeavors to weigh their
     conflict even-handedly.

684. Koch, Hans-Gerhard. "Heinrich Heine und die Religion.
     Eine Auseinandersetzung mit dem marxistischen Heine-
     Bild." *Zeitwende: Die neue Furche* 32 (1961): 742-753.

     Dates the East German enthusiasm for Heine from the
     intervention of a Soviet cultural officer in 1947. Other-
     wise mostly quotations without a penetrating confrontation
     with the Marxist view.

685. Kofta, Maria. "Heinrich Heine und die polnische Frage."
     WB 6 (1960): 506-531.

     Defends Heine's attitude toward Poland as Hegelian
     and historically justified.

686. Koopmann, Helmut. "Heine in Weimar: Zur Problematik
     seiner Beziehungen zur Kunstperiode." *ZDP* 91 (1972),
     Special Issue *Heine und seine Zeit*: 46-66.

     In Heine's shifting and self-contradictory attitude
     toward Goethe is reflected the younger generation's
     inability to solve the problem of a non-autonomous art.

687. ———. "Heines Geschichtsauffassung." *JDSG* 16 (1972):
     453-476.

     Heine's view of history is both dualistic and static;
     art is a vehicle for the resolution of dualities. Koop-
     mann relates Heine's pattern to contemporary ideas and
     traces it to the eighteenth century.

688. ———. "Heines politische Metaphorik." Immerwahr and
     Spencer, eds., *Heinrich Heine*, pp. 68-83.

     A study of Heine's metaphors for revolution comes to
     the unexpected conclusion that Book II of *Börne* was in
     fact largely written in 1830, as Heine claimed, rather
     than 1840. Debatable but significant argument.

689. ———. "Heinrich Heine und die Politisierung des
     Mythos." Pp. 141-158 in *Mythos und Mythologie in der
     Literatur des 19. Jahrhunderts*, ed. Koopmann. Studien

zur Philosophie und Literatur des neunzehnten Jahr-
hunderts, Vol. 36. Frankfurt am Main: Vittorio Kloster-
mann, 1979. 385 pp.

Heine not only politicized the materials he drew freely
from Classical and Germanic mythology; he mythologized
politics. Consequently his vision of the revolutionary
future became apocalyptic and ran the risk of becoming
located in a realm beyond reality.

690. Krämer, Helmut. *Heinrich Heines Auseinandersetzung mit
zeitgenössicher Philosophie: Eine Studie an ausgewählten
Beispielen.* Europäische Hochschulschriften, Series I,
Vol. 335. Frankfurt am Main, Bern, and Cirencester:
Peter D. Lang, 1980. 108 pp.

An unscholarly, popularizing, often erroneous, meager,
and superfluous ramble reviewing aspects of Heine's
commentary on philosophy.

691. Kreutzer, Leo. *Heine und der Kommunismus.* Kleine Vanden-
hoeck-Reihe, 322. Göttingen: Vandenhoeck & Ruprecht,
1970. 38 pp.

Despite its brevity, the most important study of this
subject, arguing that Heine opposed Communism not in the
modern sense, but in the form of the iconoclastic and
reductively egalitarian doctrines of Babeuf. Widely
accepted in subsequent scholarship.

692. Krüger, Edward. *Heine und Hegel: Dichtung, Philosophie
und Politik bei Heinrich Heine.* Monographien Literaturwissenschaft, 33. Kronberg: Scriptor, 1977. 312
pp.

Hews eruditely to the orthodox Marxist line of Heine
as a follower of Hegel, postulating an influence of
Hegel's *Aesthetics* on Heine years before it was published.
Selective quotation, forced evidence, and vast inflation
of Heine's philosophical competence.

693. Kruse, Joseph A. "'Die Romantische Schule.'" Windfuhr,
ed., *Heine-Kongreß*, pp. 447-463.

Analyzes Heine's attachment to Romanticism in this
anti-Romantic work.

694. Kuttenkeuler, Wolfgang. *Heinrich Heine: Theorie und
Kritik der Literatur.* Sprache und Literatur, 72.
Stuttgart: Kohlhammer, 1972. 160 pp.

The development of Heine's literary theory and criticism
from 1820 to 1835 is investigated in order to demonstrate
that he attempted to rebut Hegel's thesis of the end of
art. Many useful and perceptive results; the difficult
monograph will repay the stressful reading it requires.

695. Lefebvre, Jean-Pierre. "Marx und Heine." *Streitbarer
Humanist*, pp. 41-61.

An initially promising effort to see the relationship
of Heine and Marx in the context of the history of the
two men eventuates in absurd claims of harmony and identification with the proletariat on Heine's part.

696. Leschnitzer, Franz. "Heine contra Börne." *Die Weltbühne*
11 (1956): 212-217, 241-245.

An orthodox defense of Heine against Börne, drawing
on the opinions of Marx and Engels but going beyond them
to denounce Börne as a reactionary.

697. Lindner, Burkhardt. "Literarische Öffentlichkeit und
politische Subjektivität. Literatursoziologische
Thesen, konkretisiert an Heines auktorialer Prosa."
Pp. 153-190 in *Germanistik und Deutschunterricht:
Zur Einheit von Fachwissenschaft und Fachdidaktik*,
ed. Rudolf Schäfer. Munich: Fink, 1979. 331 pp.

Combines text-oriented Neo-Marxist literary sociology
with a version of speech-act theory to argue that Heine's
subjective manner is congruent with his revolutionary
purpose and his destruction of the "epoch of art"; his
narcissism displays his complicated role as a spokesman
for a people that does not yet exist.

698. Lukács, Georg. "Heine und die ideologische Vorbereitung
der achtundvierziger Revolution." *Aufbau* 12, No. 2
(1956): 103-118. Reprinted pp. 24-44 in *Geist und
Zeit* 1, No. 5 (1956): 24-44, and *TK* 18/19 (1968):
25-34. As "Heine et la révolution de 1848." *Europe*,
No. 125/126 (1956): 47-66. As "Heine e la preparazione
ideologica della rivoluzione del Quarantotto." *Società*
12 (1956): 225-245.

The fame of this essay, originally published in the
Soviet Union in 1941, owes more to the prestige of its
author than to its intrinsic merit. Focussed primarily
on the *Wintermärchen*, it argues in orthodox fashion
Heine's superiority to "petty-bourgeois radicals," his
Romantic aspect as an anti-capitalist affect, and his

failure to reach a position of Marxist insight as
historically conditioned.

699. Magnani, Luigi. "Heine e la musica romantica." *Paragone*,
      No. 84 (December 1956): 3-19. Reprinted pp. 95-115
      in Magnani, *Le frontiere della musica: Da Monteverdi
      a Schoenberg*. Milan and Naples: Ricciardi, 1957.
      328 pp.

      Finds in Heine's music criticism an intuitive affinity
      for enduring and progressive musical values.

700. Maier, Willfried. *Leben, Tat und Reflexion. Unter-
      suchungen zu Heinrich Heines Ästhetik*. Literatur und
      Wirklichkeit, ed. Karl Otto Conrady, Vol. 5. Bonn:
      Bouvier, 1969. 247 pp.

      An analysis of Heine's utterances on aesthetics
      contributes to our understanding but imposes more philo-
      sophical order on his views than is actually there.

701. Malsch, Sara Ann. "Die Bedeutung von Goethes Pantheismus
      und seiner satirischen Brechung für Heines Demokratiebe-
      griff." *HJ 1978*, pp. 35-54.

      A thoughtful and valuable essay argues that Heine
      satirically transmits Goethe's pantheism to the prac-
      tical present, though it makes Heine more singleminded
      and democratic than he was.

702. Malter, Rudolf. "Heine und Kant." *HJ 1979*, pp. 35-64.

      Another effort to argue Heine's philosophical compe-
      tence; very learned, but translates his attitude into
      a more philosophical idiom and claims its correctness.

703. Mann, Michael. "Französische Quellen für Heinrich Heines
      Berichte über 'Die musikalische Saison.'" *GRM* N.S. 12
      (1962): 253-267.

      Source studies of Heine's musical reportage. A pre-
      study to no. 705 below.

704. ————. "Heinrich Heine und G.W.F. Hegel zur Musik."
      Monatshefte 54 (1962): 343-353.

      A prestudy to no. 705 below.

705. ————. *Heinrich Heines Musikkritiken*. Heine-Studien,
      ed. Manfred Windfuhr. Hamburg: Hoffmann und Campe,
      Heinrich Heine Verlag, 1971. 167 pp.

An unedited dissertation on Heine's music criticism absolving him from charges of corruption but showing that he knew little about music and that he wavered between a popular, democratic standard and an elitist, aesthetic one. Provides the philological basis for Mann's edition (no. 8).

706. Mayr, Josef. "Heinrich Heines Cholerabericht. Eine Stellungnahme des Künstlers zu seiner Zeit." *Quaderni di lingue e litterature* 1 (1976): 151-160.

A largely paraphrasing explication of Heine's account of the cholera epidemic in *Französische Zustände* as an exposé of the betrayal of the people by the ruling classes; not without accurate observation but marked by a rather naive view of Heine's political engagement and factual accuracy.

707. Meinhold, Peter. "Heinrich Heine als Kritiker seiner Zeit." *Zeitschrift für Religions- und Geistesgeschichte* 8 (1956): 319-345.

Heine's analysis of his times is a tragic effort to expose and promote, in the midst of his critical opposition to them, their progressive possibilities. Praises Heine's acuteness and seriousness, and correctly remarks that he underestimated his own "spiritualism."

708. ———. "'Opium des Volkes'? Zur Religionskritik von Heinrich Heine und Karl Marx." *Monatsschrift für Pastoraltheologie* 49 (1960): 161-176.

Shows that Heine's critique of religion was fully conceived before his acquaintance with Marx, that it owed nothing to Marx except a temporary radicality of expression, and the subsequent development of the two men was totally divergent.

709. Mende, Fritz. "Bekenntnis 1837. Heinrich Heines 'Einleitung zum Don Quixote.'" *HJ 1967*, pp. 48-66.

Detects in the Cervantes essay a revolutionary social viewpoint distinguishing Heine from Ludwig Börne.

710. ———. "Heinrich Heine an einen Goetheaner." *SG* N.S. 10 (1972): 343-354.

Gives reasons for Heine's sudden outbreak of criticism of Goethe in the fall of 1827 as a consequence of feeling himself ignored and disrespected by Goethe.

711.   ———. "Heinrich Heine: Kommunist?" *Philologia Pra-*
        gensia 14 (1971): 177-189.

        A close analysis of Heine's relationship to the Com-
        munist movement, with copious quotations.

712.   ———. "Heinrich Heine und die Deutschen." *EG* 17
        (1962): 251-258.

        Argues against overstressing Heine's Jewish or Rhenish
        origins or his cosmopolitanism and in favor of seeing
        him in the context of the democratic, national literary
        movement in Germany. The argument is shaped by the of-
        ficial position on patriotism and nationalism in the
        Soviet Union and East Germany.

713.   ———. "Heinrich Heine und die Folgen der Julirevolu-
        tion." Pp. 182-207 in *Goethe-Almanach auf das Jahr*
        1968, ed. Helmut Holtzhauer and Hans Henning. Berlin:
        Aufbau-Verlag, 1967. 339 pp.

        Analyzes Heine's developing understanding of the
        bourgeois capitalist character of the July Monarchy
        and attempts to deal with his opposition to republican-
        ism and claims of monarchism, concluding that he remained
        a bourgeois writer with progressive instincts.

714.   ———. "'Indifferentismus.' Bemerkungen zu Heines
        ästhetischer Terminologie." *HJ 1976*, pp. 11-22.

        Traces the concept of "indifferentism" from a religious
        to a social and aesthetic usage.

715.   ———. "Zu Heinrich Heines Goethe-Bild." *EG* 23 (1968):
        212-231.

        Reviews Heine's shifting and ambivalent view of Goethe,
        accounting for it exclusively in social-political terms.

716.   ———. "Zur Bedeutung des Wortes 'Freiheit' bei Hein-
        rich Heine." *Streitbarer Humanist*, pp. 368-374. Ex-
        panded as "Zu Heinrich Heines politischer Terminologie."
        EG 29 (1974): 319-330.

        Traces Heine's usage of "freedom," "democracy," "rea-
        son," and "cosmopolitanism"; but more than a catalogue
        of passages is needed to get at his meaning.

717.   Milska, Anna. "Heine über Polen." *SuF* 8 (1956): 66-
        77.

        A view of Heine's opinions on Poland as perceptive,

sympathetic, and revolutionary is achieved by selective
quotation. Also reviews the history of Heine's reputation
in Poland.

718. Mittenzwei, Johannes. "Musikalische Inspiration in
      Heines Erzählung 'Florentinische Nächte' (I) und die
      Auffassung des Dichters über das 'Zeitalter der Musik.'"
      Pp. 231-251 in Mittenzwei, *Das Musikalische in der
      Literatur: Ein Überblick von Gottfried von Straßburg
      bis Brecht*. Halle: VEB Verlag Sprache und Literatur,
      1962. 576 pp.

      Claims a musical quality to Heine's poetry, sketches
      Schumann's relationship to Heine, endeavors to show with
      the Paganini episode of *Florentinische Nächte* and other
      passages how Heine's imagination could be inspired by
      music, and summarizes Heine's criticism of musical events
      and personalities. The study is not well focused and
      overestimates Heine's musical receptivity.

719. Motekat, Helmut. "Hegel und Heine." Pp. 65-79 in *A
      Hegel Symposium*, ed. D.C. Travis. Austin: Department
      of Germanic Languages, University of Texas, 1962. 137
      pp.

      Looks at the question largely from the vantage point
      of Heine's late repudiation of Hegel, and argues that
      Hegel sharpened Heine's discernment of the issues of
      the modern world.

720. Musgrave, Miriam. "Heinrich Heine's Anti-Slavery Thought."
      Negro American Literature Forum 6 (1972): 91-93, 84.

      Reviews Heine's views on slavery and on America.

721. Netter, Lucienne. "La Genèse des articles XL et XXV de
      'Lutezia' ou les anachronismes de Heine." *EG* 29
      (1974): 83-88.

      Establishes that Article XXV was written earlier in
      1842 than believed and then predated 1840.

722. ———. *Heine et la peinture de la civilisation parisi-
      enne 1840-1848*. Publications Universitaires Européens,
      Series I, Vol. 336. Frankfurt am Main, Bern, and
      Cirencester: Peter D. Lang, 1980. 424 pp.

      Lucienne Netter's extensive and fruitful studies in
      Heine's reportage for the Augsburg *Allgemeine Zeitung*,
      revised in *Lutezia*, and the contemporary French journalism

with which they are intimately connected, have eventuated
in the first detailed study of Heine's journalism of the
1840s. The learned and thoroughly documented study,
though it is too much inclined to defend and affirm Heine
as incomparably perceptive and prophetic, will be a funda-
mental resource for future scholarship.

723.   ————. "Heine, l'affair des juifs de Damas et la presse
       parisienne." *HJ 1972*, pp. 56-65.

       Shows that the resuscitation of the *Rabbi* occurred on
       the day after Heine learned of the pogrom against the
       Damascus Jews.

724.   ————. "Heine als Journalist in den vierziger Jahren."
       Streitbarer Humanist, pp. 350-354.

       A brief extract from the results of Netter's researches
       into Heine's journalism, stressing the growing dissonance
       with the increasingly conservative policies of the Augs-
       burg *Allgemeine Zeitung*.

725.   Obermann, Karl. "Heinrich Heine und seine Rolle in der
       deutschen Geschichte der dreißiger und vierziger Jahre
       des 19. Jahrhunderts." *Heinrich Heine und die Zeitge-
       nossen*, pp. 7-36.

       A recapitulation of Heine's radicalization in the
       1830s and 1840s attempts to show that he had a signifi-
       cant impact on the pre-revolutionary situation. But
       the citations from a few liberal contemporaries, censors,
       and spies, along with the reiteration of the episode
       with Marx, do not make the case.

726.   Oehler, Dolf. "Heines Genauigkeit. Und zwei komplemen-
       täre Stereotypen über das Wesen der proletarischen
       Massen." *DD* 8 (1977): 250-271.

       Endeavors to demonstrate, with bizarre distortion of
       the meaning of texts, that Heine was an unambiguous
       partisan of Communism.

727.   ————. *Pariser Bilder I (1830-1848): Antibourgeoise
       Ästhetik bei Baudelaire, Daumier und Heine*. edition
       suhrkamp, 725. Frankfurt am Main: Suhrkamp, 1979.
       301 pp.

       Primarily a book about Baudelaire; Heine and Daumier
       are employed comparatively. Employs the same distortive
       hermeneutic to discover a pro-Communist secret message
       in Heine's texts as in no. 726.

728. Oellers, Norbert. "Die zerstrittenen Dioskuren: Aspekte
      der Auseinandersetzung Heines mit Börne." *ZDP* 91 (1972),
      Special Issue *Heine und seine Zeit*: 66-90.

      Illuminates the quarrel with Börne through contemporary
      commentary and a speculative reconstruction of motives,
      though not close enough to the peculiarities of Heine's
      text to satisfy in every respect.

729. Oesterle, Günter. *Integration und Konflikt: Die Prosa
      Heinrich Heines im Kontext oppositioneller Literatur
      der Restaurationsepoche.* Stuttgart: Metzler, 1972.
      195 pp.

      A strictly Marxist effort to make precise Heine's
      transitional position between affirmative and emancipa-
      tory literature, with serious insensitivities, especially
      on the quarrel with Platen, but much learning and valuable
      isolated observations.

730. Oesterle, Ingrid, and Günter Oesterle. "Der literarische
      Bürgerkrieg. Gutzkow, Heine, Börne wider Menzel.
      Polemik nach der Kunstperiode und in der Restauration."
      Pp. 151-185 in *Demokratisch-revolutionäre Literatur in
      Deutschland: Vormärz*, ed. Gert Mattenklott and Klaus
      R. Scherpe. Literatur im historischen Prozess, 3/2.
      Kronberg: Scriptor, 1975. 263 pp.

      Good on analysis of Menzel's and Gutzkow's weaknesses,
      but primarily apologetic in its treatment of Heine.

731. Oosawa, K. "Heine als Literaturhistoriker." *DB* 57
      (Fall 1976): 21-29.

      An uncritical paraphrase of *Die Romantische Schule*,
      suggesting implications pointing to Nietzsche. (Japa-
      nese with German abstract.)

732. Peters, Eckehard, and Eberhard Kirsch. *Religionskritik
      bei Heinrich Heine.* Erfurter Theologische Schriften,
      13. Leipzig: St. Benno-Verlag, 1977. 140 pp.

      A most unusual publication by two members of a Catholic
      theological faculty in East Germany. Both show the
      strain of this situation. Peters' is an anemic reproduc-
      tion of familiar aspects of Heine's religious argument,
      while Kirsch argues on a higher plane, his main concern
      a reconciliation of Marxist humanism with emancipatory
      Christianity, for which Heine is used, not uncritically,
      as an occasion.

733. Pfeiffer, Hans. "Heinrich Heine und das Theater."
     Theater der Zeit 11, No. 3 (1956): 17-21.

     All of Heine's commentary on the theater derives from
     his revolutionary democratic position, which was as
     correct as it could be for a pre-Marxist.

734. Prawer, Siegbert. *Heine's Shakespeare: A Study in
     Contexts. An Inaugural Lecture Delivered Before the
     University of Oxford on 5 May 1970.* Oxford: Clarendon
     Press, 1970. 40 pp.

     A graceful presentation of the allusive, critical, and
     self-revealing uses Heine makes of Shakespeare and his
     works. Best essay yet written on this subject.

735. Preisendanz, Wolfgang. "Der Sinn der Schreibart in
     Heines Berichten aus Paris 1840-1843 'Lutezia.'"
     Pp. 115-139 in *Deutsche Weltliteratur von Goethe bis
     Ingeborg Bachmann: Festgabe für J. Alan Pfeffer*, ed.
     Klaus W. Jonas. Tübingen: Niemeyer, 1972. xii +
     304 pp. Reprinted in no. 341.

     Heine's reportorial style shows the transitoriness of
     public events and an awareness of the opacity of their
     surface and the contradictory truth of immediate situ-
     ations. Highly regarded in subsequent scholarship.

736. Rasch, Wolfdietrich. "Die Pariser Kunstkritik Heinrich
     Heines." Pp. 230-244 in *Beiträge zum Problem des Stil-
     pluralismus*, ed. Werner Hager and Norbert Knopp. Studien
     zur Kunst des neunzehnten Jahrhunderts, Vol. 38. Munich:
     Prestel-Verlag, 1977. 255 pp.

     Rasch shows the limitations of Heine's competence as
     an art critic and argues that he derived from Romantic
     theory a conviction that every age brings forth its own
     characteristic style, and that he was therefore put off
     and bewildered by the modern pluralism of styles in the
     Paris exhibitions.

737. Reissner, H.G. "Heinrich Heine's Tale of the 'Captive
     Messiah.'" Pp. 327-340 in *Der Friede: Ideen und Ver-
     wirklichung. The Search for Peace: Festgabe für Adolf
     Leschnitzer*, ed. Erich Fromm and Hans Herzfeld. Heidel-
     berg: Lambert Schneider, 1961. 435 pp.

     Seeks a Rabbinical Messianic source for a passage in
     Börne, Book IV.

738. Rippmann, Inge. "Heines Denkschrift über Börne: Ein Doppelporträt." *HJ 1973*, pp. 41-70.

A substantial analysis of the interaction of the personalities of Börne and Heine by a major Börne expert.

739. Rose, Ernst. "The Beauty from Pao: Heine--Bierbaum--Hesse." *GR* 32 (1957): 5-18.

Discovers the source of a Chinese anecdote in *Die Romantische Schule* in an English translation of Chinese poetry, and traces its subsequent course through literature.

740. Rose, Margaret A. "Heines 'junghegelianisches' Bild von Delacroix." *HJ 1979*, pp. 27-34.

A confusing and unconvincing effort to ascribe an esoteric Young Hegelian meaning to Heine's description of Delacroix's freedom painting in *Französische Maler*.

741. Rose, William. *Heinrich Heine: Two Studies of his Thought and Feeling*. Oxford: Clarendon Press, 1956. xii + 163 pp.

In one of the major early contributions to the modern phase of Heine studies, Rose examines his political and social attitude with sympathy while insisting that his consciousness was that of a poet, and judiciously reviews his complex Jewish feeling.

742. Rosenberg, Rainer. "Heinrich Heine--das Programm einer politischen Literatur." *WB* 18, No. 4 (1972): 104-132.

A superficial, paraphrasing review of the writings of Heine's middle period.

743. Rosenthal, Ludwig. *Heinrich Heine als Jude*. Frankfurt am Main and Berlin: Ullstein, 1973. 388 pp.

A conscientious effort to give a comprehensive account of Heine as a Jew, with vast knowledge of Jewish culture and much original research, though very elementary, repetitious, and in places tedious to read.

744. Sammons, Jeffrey L. "Heine and William Cobbett." *HJ 1980*, pp. 69-77.

Identifies the sources for the passages from Cobbett in the *Englische Fragmente*, explains why the repressive and reactionary aspects of Cobbett could not be congenial to Heine, and estimates Heine's command of English.

745. Saueracker-Ritter, Ruth. *Heinrich Heines Verhältnis zur Philosophie.* Munich: Dissertationsdruck-Schön, 1974. 178 pp.

This little-known publication contains, amidst much conventional criticism of Heine's philosophical competence, a most interesting and probably important discovery: that Heine's basic sources for his philosophical understanding appear to be his boyhood schoolbooks.

746. Schmidt, Johann Michael. "Thron und Altar. Zum kirchengeschichtlichen Hintergrund von Heines Kritik des preußischen Protestantismus." *HJ 1977*, pp. 96-128.

A learned essay on the development of reactionary Protestantism at the Prussian court in Heine's time.

747. Schmitz, Gerhard. *Über die ökonomischen Anschauungen in Heinrich Heines Werken.* Weimar: Arion-Verlag, 1960. 143 pp.

Presentation of Heine's social criticism as "economic views" comparable to those of Marx and Engels and employable as a weapon against West Germany.

748. Schöll, Norbert. "'Ich bin der Krankste von Euch Allen.' Zum Stil in Heines Berichten über das Zeitgeschehen." *HJ 1980*, pp. 49-68.

Denies a conflict of art and commitment in Heine, accepting Heine's claims uncritically and defending his position against Börne as one of realistic integrity.

749. Seeba, Hinrich C. "Die Kinder des Pygmalion: Die Bildlichkeit des Kunstbegriffs bei Heine. Beobachtungen zur Tendenzwende der Ästhetik." *DVLG* 50 (1976): 158-202.

Shows how Heine used and altered the Pygmalion image in order to differentiate the new activist and sensual concept of art; very erudite and worthwhile, but does not quite deal with Heine's deep ambivalence about sensualism and the erotic.

750. Simon, Ernst. "Heine und die Romantik." Pp. 135-156 in Simon, *Brücken: Gesammelte Aufsätze.* Heidelberg: Lambert Schneider, 1965. 531 pp.

Describes the early development of Heine's use of the
concept of Romanticism and his estrangement from it.

751. ————. "Heines Stellung zum Judentum, Spätzeit (Résumé)."
Windfuhr, ed., *Heine-Kongreß*, pp. 318–319.

An abstract, with a promise of full publication elsewhere, of an indifferently informed ramble on the subject of Heine's Jewishness that was very popular with
the audience at the Düsseldorf conference.

752. Söhn, Gerhart. "In der Tradition der literarischen
Kunstbetrachtung: Heinrich Heines 'Französische Maler.'"
HJ 1978, pp. 9–34.

Describes Heine's art criticism, supplying several
plates of the (today rather forgotten) paintings he dis-
cussed.

753. Sourian, Eve. *Madame de Staël et Henri Heine: Les deux
Allemagnes*. Essais et Critiques, 18. Paris: Didier,
1974. 198 pp.

A welcome rehabilitation of Madame de Staël against
Heine's dismissive view of her, but a little thin in
Heine scholarship and limited by the employment of the
French versions of Heine's texts only.

754. Spencer, Hanna. "Heine: Between Hegel and Jehovah."
Immerwahr and Spencer, eds., *Heinrich Heine*, pp. 23–
33.

Discounts some of the significance of Heine's religious
return by attempting to show that it was not a sharp
break with his customary views, which Spencer assimilates
to Hegel.

755. ————. "Heine und Nietzsche." *HJ 1972*, pp. 126–161.

Collects familiar comparisons and observations on
Heine's prefigurations of Nietzsche. Reprinted in no.
353.

756. ————. "Heines 'Briefe aus Helgoland'--synchronische
Chronik?" *WW* 22 (1972): 404–411.

A detailed analysis of the contrapuntal coherence and
thematic composition of Book II of *Börne* leads to the
conclusion that it must be a largely fictional product.
Reprinted as "Gipfel oder Tiefpunkt? Die Denkschrift
für Ludwig Börne" in no. 353.

757. ———. "Heines Spiel mit Goethes Erbmantel." *Seminar*
9 (1973): 109-126.

Shows parallels and comparisons between *Buch Le Grand*
and Goethe's autobiography, the Italian pieces and Goethe's
Italienische Reise, along with other parodistic echoes.
Reprinted in no. 353.

758. Starke, Fritz. "Zeitkritik in Heinrich Heines 'Englischen
Fragmenten.' Unterrichtsentwurf zu einem fast verges-
senen Feuilleton." *DD* 9 (1978): 100-112.

The *Englische Fragmente* are recommended as a school
text to show Heine's dialectical understanding of England;
the article contains much potted Marxist history, and the
author is unacquainted with the first fundamentals of
Heine's view of England.

759. Sternberger, Dolf. "Heine—ein politischer Denker? Ein
Referat, das nicht gehalten wurde." Pp. 169-178 in
Der Berliner Germanistentag 1968: Vorträge und Berichte,
ed. Karl Heinz Borck and Rudolf Henss. Heidelberg:
Carl Winter, 1970. 221 pp.

In a paper so controversial that its delivery was pre-
vented by student demonstrations, Sternberger argues
that Heine was not a political thinker in the strict
sense at all.

760. ———. "Heinrich Heines Götter." Pp. 167-194 in *Das
Altertum und jedes neue Gute: Für Wolfgang Schadewalt
zum 15. März 1970*, ed. Konrad Gaiser. Stuttgart, Berlin, Cologne, and Mainz: Kohlhammer, 1970. 560 pp.

Argues that with the gods of the past Heine symbolizes
men themselves who will have overcome sin in a future
utopia. Related to no. 356.

761. Stöcker, Jakob. "Heinrich Heine im Jahre 1844. Begegnungen mit Karl Marx—Deutschland, ein Wintermärchen."
Geist und Zeit 4 (1959): 103-113.

A popular and in places imprecise account of the year
1844, with the *Wintermärchen* and the association with
Marx as the creative high point of Heine's life.

762. Streller, Siegfried. "Das Verhältnis von Nationalem
und Internationalem in Heines Auffassung des Patrio-
tismus." *Steitbarer Humanist*, pp. 360-367.

Heine's idea of humanity, realized in the proletariat,
dialectically relating patriotism and internationalism,
which is an effective weapon against West German imperialism.

763. Strich, Fritz. "Heinrich Heine und die Überwindung der
      Romantik." Pp. 118–138 in Strich, *Kunst und Leben:*
      Vorträge und Abhandlungen zur deutschen Literatur.
      Bern and Munich: Francke, 1960. 241 pp.

      Shows that Heine controlled his Romantic proclivities
      with a sharp intellect and a strong sense of mundane
      reality, and that his irony is not Romantic but directed
      at Romanticism.

764. Tonelli, Giorgio. *Heine e la Germania: Saggio intro-*
      duttivo e interpretativo su "Atta Troll" e "Deutsch-
      land ein Wintermärchen." Quaderni di critica storica
      e letteraria, 3. Palermo: Istituto di storia dell'
      Università, 1963. 233 pp. Tr. as *Heinrich Heines*
      politische Philosophie (1830-1845). Studien und
      Materialien zur Geschichte der Philosophie, Vol. 9.
      Hildesheim and New York: Olms, 1975. 216 pp.

      In drastic divergence from the main line of contempor-
      ary criticism, Tonelli presents Heine as a tactically
      opportunist but stable supporter of constitutional
      monarchy in the direction of Caesarism. Stimulating
      and valuable if debatable, and marred by implausible
      allegorizations.

765. Tramer, Friedrich. "Heine und Fichte." *Zeitschrift*
      für die Geschichte der Juden 3 (1966): 31-36.

      An orthodox Marxist view of Heine's "socialist" and
      "democratic" views of Fichte, seen here as a proto-Nazi.

766. Trilse, Christoph. "Das Goethe-Bild Heinrich Heines."
      Goethe. Neue Folge des Jahrbuchs der Goethe-Gesell-
      schaft 30 (1968): 154-191.

      A detailed if occasionally selective review of Heine's
      relationship to Goethe aruges that he matured to a
      critical but admiring view after outgrowing Börne's
      bad influence. The essay has some correct perceptions,
      but it overestimates Heine's insight into Goethe and
      is trimmed to the official East German appropriation
      of the Classical tradition.

767. ———. "Heinrich Heine als Literatur- und Theater-
      kritiker. Betrachtungen über eine exemplarische
      Methode." *Streitbarer Humanist*, pp. 341-349.

      Heine knew everything about literature and his criti-
      cism is a model for modern Marxist procedure.

768. Turóczi-Trostler, József. "Heine, die Weltliteratur
     und die ungarische Dichtung (I)." *Acta Litteraria
     Academicae Scientiarum Hungaricae* 1 (1957): 99-178.

     A detailed discussion of Heine's relationship to
     contemporary and traditional literature. Hungarian
     literature is not mentioned here; a continuation did
     not appear.

769. Vermeil, Edmond. "Heine als Politiker." *SuF* 8 (1956)
     407-424.

     A general account of Heine's political views, admit-
     ting that he was an intellectual aristocrat and feared
     Communism.

770. ————. "Henri Heine." *Europe*, Nos. 125/126 (May-
     June 1956): 12-32.

     Similar to the item above, but more specifically aimed
     at a French audience.

771. Voisine, Jacques. "Heines als Porträtist in der 'Lu-
     tezia.'" Windfuhr, ed., *Heine-Kongreß*, pp. 219-226.

     Analyzes Heine's art of characterization in *Lutezia*.

772. Wadepuhl, Walter. "Heines Nachruf für Ludwig Markus."
     Wadepuhl, *Heine-Studien*, pp. 135-151.

     An attempt to establish a philologically reliable
     text for Heine's memoir of Markus. The result has been
     severely criticized by Michael Werner in no. 779.

773. ————. "Heines Verhältnis zu Goethe." *Goethe: Neue
     Folge des Jahrbuchs der Goethe-Gesellschaft* 18 (1956):
     121-131.

     A forced interpretation finds hidden vengeance against
     Goethe in *Schnabelewopski*.

774. ————. "Heines 'Vorrede zu den Französischen Zuständen.'
     Ein Beitrag zur Geschichte der preußischen Zensur."
     Wadepuhl, *Heine-Studien*, pp. 97-108.

     Researches the circumstances of the suppression and
     separate publication of the preface.

775. ————. "'Shakespeares Mädchen und Frauen.' Heine
     und Shakespeare." Wadepuhl, *Heine-Studien*, pp. 114-
     134.

Describes the stages of Heine's experience with Shakespeare and the circumstances of the book's publication,
arguing that it was derivative and more about Heine than
about Shakespeare.

776. Weiss, Gerhard. "Heines Amerikabild." *HJ 1969*, pp.
      21–44. Reprinted pp. 295–318 in *Deutschlands litera-
      risches Amerikabild: Neuere Forschungen zur Amerika-
      rezeption in der deutschen Literatur*, ed. Alexander
      Ritter. Hildesheim and New York: Olms, 1977. 615 pp.

      Detailed and scholarly study with many interesting
      sidelights on a somewhat unprofitable topic.

777. ————. "Heinrich Heines 'Französische Maler' (1831)––
      Sprachkunstwerk und Referat. Eine rezeptions- und
      einflußgeschichtliche Studie über Literatur und Malerei."
      HJ 1980, pp. 78–100.

      An observant evaluation, including specifics of Heine's
      direct borrowings from French criticism, showing that
      many of his most dubious judgments arise from it, and
      tracing the echoes of Heine's reportage in subsequent
      art historiography.

778. Werner, Hans–Georg. *Heine: Seine weltanschauliche Ent-
      wicklung und sein Deutschlandbild*. Bucharest: Espla
      Staatsverlag für Kunst und Literatur, 1958. 124 pp.

      A very general, sometimes paraphrasing account of
      Heine's ideological development from a partly Romantic,
      partly humanistic position to a critique of capitalism
      close to materialism. It is admitted that he did not
      reach a proletarian standpoint in the Marxist sense,
      and he is quite severely criticized for this failing.

779. Werner, Michael. "Das 'Augsburgische Prokrustesbett.'
      Heines Berichte aus Paris 1840–1847 (*Lutezia*) und die
      Zensur." *Cahier Heine*, pp. 42–65.

      A detailed, intelligent, and significant analysis of
      the censorship situation as it affects the text of *Lu-
      tezia*.

780. Wieland, Wolfgang. "Heinrich Heine und die Philosophie."
      DVLG 37 (1963): 232–248. Reprinted Koopmann, ed.,
      Heinrich Heine, pp. 133–155.

      Without overestimating Heine's technical philosophical
      command, Wieland thoughtfully examines Heine's response to

philosophical concerns and argues that he applied more effort to them than previously assumed. One of the most judicious assessments of the relationship to Hegel.

781. Wilczek, Stanislaw. "Heinrich Heine und Polen." *Begegnung mit Polen* 5 (1968): 347-352.

A brief review of Heine's observations and opinions on Poland.

782. Wilhelm, Kurt. "Heine: 'Verein für Kultur und Wissenschaft der Juden.'" *Judisk Tidskrift* 29 (1956): 54-58.

A brief general account of Heine's relations with the Jewish *Verein*, with a fairly severe judgment on the organization.

783. Windfuhr, Manfred. "Heine und Hegel. Rezeption und Produktion." Windfuhr, ed., *Heine-Kongreß*, pp. 261-280.

A level-headed assessment of the contentious question of Heine's relationship to Hegel.

784. ———. "Heinrich Heine zwischen den progressiven Gruppen seiner Zeit. Von den Altliberalen zu den Kommunisten. Ein Arbeitspapier." *ZDP* 91 (1972), Special Issue *Heine und seine Zeit*: 1-23.

A descriptive and general account of Heine's placement among the various political and philosophical movements of his time.

785. Winterberg, Inge. "Heines Bemerkungen zur italienischen Literatur." *HJ 1978*, pp. 211-217.

Discusses Heine's very sparing references to Italian literature.

786. Wolffheim, Hans. "Heine und das deutsch-französische Verhältnis. Ein politisches Panorama aus seinen Schriften." *TK* 18/19 (1968): 15-24.

A commented sequence of quotations, taking the conventional position that Heine was a mediator between the two nations of modern relevance.

787. Zepf, Irmgard. *Heinrich Heines Gemäldebericht zum Salon 1831: Denkbilder. Eine Untersuchung der Schrift "Französische Maler."* Munich: Fink, 1980. 264 pp.

The first full monographic study of Heine's report on
the 1831 Salon insists upon the importance of its literary aspect and the employment of the artistic imagination
to mediate revolutionary and emancipatory views. Methodo-
logically elaborate and occasionally over-argued, but
stimulating. Black-and-white plates of twenty of the
paintings Heine discusses.

788. Zisserman, N. "Heinrich Heine and Russia: Random Notes
     on Heine and Pushkin." *New Zealand Slavonic Journal*
     9 (Winter 1972): 73-100.

   Finds a plausible source for Heine's claimed admiration of Czar Nicholas I, though distressingly inaccurate
in regard to Heine.

VIII

RECEPTION, REPUTATION, INFLUENCE,
AND COMPARATIVE STUDIES

789. Altenhofer, Norbert. "Die verlorene Augensprache.
Marginalien zum Problem der 'Wirkung' Heinescher
Texte." *DD* 8 (1977): 304-317.

Takes Heine at his word that he had a "secret" he was
unable to express except esoterically. Much of the interesting argument is focused on *Buch Le Grand* and the
long failure to perceive its importance.

790. Angelet, Christian. "Gide, Heine et le Roman Parodique."
Les Lettres Romanes 31 (1977): 220-242.

In numerous echoes Gide indicates his perception of
a decadent Heine.

791. Anstett, J.-J. "Le Congrès Henri Heine à Weimar (8-13
Octobre 1956)." *EG* 11 (1956): 351.

A report on the East German anniversary conference,
stressing the announcement of a critical edition.

792. Arendt, Dieter. "Die Heine-Rezeption im Werk Wilhelm
Raabes." *HJ 1980*, pp. 188-221.

A sensitive and thoughtful consideration of Raabe's
response to Heine and the transformation of Heine's
aggression into Raabe's more tolerant but still critical
humor. A long-needed gesture of fairness to Raabe on
this matter.

793. Arnold, Armin. *Heine in England and America: A Bibliographical Check-List*. London: Linden Press, 1959.
80 pp. Reprinted New York: International Publications
Service, 1959.

A first resource for Heine in English. Some inaccur-
acies.

794. Arnsberg, Paul. "Heinrich Heine als linksintellektuelles
     'Anti'-Symbol. Ein Bildersturm im vorigen Jahrhundert."
     Tribüne 2 (1963): 643-657.

     A somewhat rambling essay presenting Heine as an ex-
     emplary case of a leftist scorned for his wit and criti-
     cism. Includes a history of the conflict over efforts
     to erect a monument to Heine.

795. Babler, Otto F. "Ein Heine-Gedicht als georgisches
     Volkslied." *HJ 1965*, pp. 64-67.

     A Georgian folk version of "Du schönes Fischermädchen."

796. Baldauf, Helmut. "Deutsche Heine-Rezeption." *NDL* 13,
     No. 11 (1965): 146-150.

     Praise of Kaufmann's edition (no. 2) at the expense
     of its West German reprint and other Western scholarship.

797. Bark, Joachim. "Literaturgeschichtsschreibung über
     Heine. Zur Wirkungsgeschichte im 19. Jahrhundert."
     Kuttenkeuler, *Heinrich Heine: Artistik und Engagement*,
     pp. 284-304.

     A useful beginning toward a more accurate account of
     Heine criticism in the nineteenth century, disposing of
     the misapprehension that he was universally vilified or
     regularly rejected on anti-Semitic grounds.

798. Benda, Gisela. "Angst vor dem kommenden Chaos: Heine
     und Büchner als Vorgänger Nietzsches." *GN* 8 (1979):
     4-8.

     In a series of comparative quotations a line of nine-
     teenth-century pessimism is traced from Heine and Büch-
     ner to Nietzsche. Much too brief for this disputed con-
     tention, and postulates an influence from Schopenhauer,
     though there is no evidence that Heine or Büchner had
     ever heard of him.

799. Benn, Maurice. "Büchner and Heine." *Seminar* 13 (1977):
     215-226.

     Suggests parallels between the early *Reisebilder* and
     Leonce und Lena, and supplies evidence that Büchner read
     Die Romantische Schule and *Zur Geschichte der Religion
     und Philosophie in Deutschland*.

800. Berendsohn, Walter A. "Heine im Norden." Windfuhr, ed.,
     Heine-Kongreß, pp. 413-415.

A sketch of Heine's reputation in Scandinavia.

801. Beyer, Harald. "Striden omkring Heinrich Heine." *Sam-tiden* 65 (1956): 531-537.

    A brief but sensible review of Heine's past and present reputation, ending with some remarks on his importance for Norwegian literature.

802. Bianquis, Geneviève. "L'Année Heine en Allemagne et en France." *EG* 11 (1956): 349-350.

    A brief account of anniversary activities in Germany and France.

803. Block, Haskell M. "Heine and the French Symbolists." Pp. 25-39 in *Creative Encounter: Festschrift for Herman Salinger*, ed. Leland R. Phelps with A. Tilo Alt. North Carolina Studies in the Germanic Languages and Literatures, 91. Chapel Hill: University of North Carolina Press, 1978. xxii + 182 pp.

    The much-discussed subject of Heine's influence on French symbolist poetry is treated with succinct good judgment and restraint. Discusses Nerval, Gautier, Banville, Baudelaire, Mallarmé, and Jules Laforgue.

804. Boeck, Oliver. "Beobachtungen zum Thema 'Heine und Brecht.'" *HJ 1973*, pp. 208-228.

    Thematic parallels between Heine and Brecht; more iconography than literary study.

805. ————. *Heines Nachwirkung und Heine-Parallelen in der französischen Dichtung*. Göppinger Arbeiten zur Germanistik, No. 52. Göppingen: Verlag Kümmerle, 1972. 245 pp.

    Heine's influence on Nerval, Gautier, Banville, the Parnasse and Verlaine, Baudelaire, Symbolism, and Mallarmé; Boeck disapproves of all this French literature on ideological grounds, arguing that the poets failed to grasp Heine's progressive commitment. Devoid of literary sensibility.

806. Bopp, Marianne O. de. "Heinrich Heine: Bibliografía en México." *Anuario de Letras* 1 (1961): 181-190.

    A chronological list of Mexican Heine translations.

807. Borries, Mechthild. *Ein Angriff auf Heinrich Heine:*
     Kritische Betrachtungen zu Karl Kraus. Studien zur
     Poetik und Geschichte der Literatur, Vol. XIII. Stutt-
     gart, Berlin, Cologne, and Mainz; Kohlhammer, 1971.
     108 pp.

     For the first time, Kraus's unjust attack on Heine is
     criticized, showing Kraus's irrational neo-idealism and
     stubbornly conservative canon of literature and language.
     A welcome deflation.

808. Bouchard, Edmond. "Henri Heine et sa Statue. Mit einem
     Nachwort von Fritz H. Eisner, London." *HJ 1970*, pp.
     134-139.

     A discovered memorandum by the son-in-law of Campe's
     son, concerning the fate of the statue once owned by
     Empress Elizabeth of Austria.

809. Bunke, Horst. "Die illustrierten deutschen Heine-
     Ausgaben 1910-1971. Eine Bibliographie." *Marginalien*
     48 (1972): 33-47.

810. ———, and Gert Klitze. *Illustrationen zu Heinrich*
     Heine. Leipzig: Deutsche Bücherei, 1972. 57 pp.

     Examples of illustrations of Heine's works from his
     own time to the present, with a historical commentary.

811. Butler, Elsie M. "Heine in England and Matthew Arnold."
     GL&L N.S. 9 (1955/56): 157-165.

     A fairly severe criticism of Arnold's essay as in-
     sensitive to literary values.

812. Cwojdrak, Günther. "Heine und die Literaturhistoriker."
     NDL 4, No. 2 (February 1956): 11-22.

     On the class character and distortions of treatments
     of Heine in "late bourgeois" scholarship.

813. De Graaf, Daniel A. "Quelques rencontres avec Henri
     Heine dans la littérature française." *Les Langues*
     Modernes 59 (1956): 140-144.

     Echoes of Heine in Mérimée, Baudelaire, Nerval, Sainte-
     Beuve, Rimbaud, and Laforgue.

814. Delille, Maria Manuela. "Heine em Portugal. Heine na
     literatura portuguesa dos séculos XIX e XX." *Biblos*
     54 (1978): 1-66.

Translations (mostly lyrical), influence and reception
of Heine in Portugal.

815. Demetz, Peter. "Ezra Pound's German Studies." *GR* 31
(1956): 279-262.

Contains comments on Pound's Heine translations and
his difficulties with them.

816. Deutsch, Alexander. "Heine in der UdSSR." Windfuhr,
ed., *Heine-Kongreß*, pp. 405-412.

Discusses the history of Heine in Russia and the
Soviet Union, with much Soviet self-praise and little
analysis.

817. Dresch, Joseph. "Heine et la critique en France depuis
sa mort." *Allemagne d'aujourd'hui* (March-April 1956):
79-83.

Extracts from the final chapter of no. 67.

818. ————. "Heine--Musset--Baudelaire zum Gedenken."
Antares: Kunst, Literatur, Wissenschaft aus Frankreich
5, No. 5 (August 1957): 18-22.

Discusses the Paris Heine exhibit of 1956 and the con-
nections with Musset and Baudelaire brought to mind by
exhibits of those poets.

819. Dubruck, Alfred. "*Poésies Allemandes* and the Heine
Translations." Pp. 99-125 in Dubruck, *Gérard de Nerval
and the German Heritage*. Studies in French Literature,
IV. The Hague: Mouton, 1965. 136 pp.

Examines Nerval's Heine translations in the context
of his relation to and knowledge of German literature,
arguing that Nerval turned inward to a "private code"
that opened a gap from Heine.

820. Dymschitz, Alexander. "Heinrich Heine in Russland und
in der Sowjetunion." *WB* 4 (1958): 535-544.

History and influence of Heine in Russia and the
Soviet Union.

821. Englekirk, John E. "Heine and Spanish-American Modernism." Pp. 488-500 in *Comparative Literature: Pro-
ceedings of the Second Congress of the International
Comparative Literature Association*, ed. Werner P.
Friedrich. Vol. II. UNC Studies in Comparative

Literature, No. 24. Chapel Hill: University of North
Carolina Press, 1959.

An introductory study of the impact of the "Bécquer-
Heine school" on Spanish-American modernism.

822. Feise, Ernst. "Some Notes on Translating Heine." *GL&L*
N.S. 9 (1955/56): 189-191.

Thoughtful considerations by one of the most accomplished translators of Heine's poetry into English.

823. Feiwel, M. "Bécquer, Heine y la tradición poética."
RLC 51 (1977): 395-416.

A critical examination of Heine's influence on
Gustavo Adolfo Bécquer.

824. Feuerlicht, Ignace. "Heine and his 'Atta Troll' in
Spain." *Monatshefte* 49 (1957): 83-86.

A note on the farcical dramatization of *Atta Troll*
by Alejandro Casona.

825. Fischer, Heinz. "Heinrich Heine und Georg Büchner.
Zu Büchners Heine-Rezeption." *HJ 1971*, pp. 43-51.
Reprinted pp. 9-17 in Fischer, *Georg Büchner: Untersuchungen und Marginalien*. Bonn: Bouvier, 1972. 104
pp.

An attempt to establish an influence of Heine on Büchner by verbal parallels, none of which are compelling.

826. Freadman, Anne. "Le Portrait de Heine par Suarès."
La Revue des Lettres Modernes, Nos. 484-490 (1976):
77-95.

Analysis of a 1945 essay in which André Saurès con-
flated an inaccurate perception of Heine with his own
experience of exile, anti-Semitism, and the deceptions
of love and liberty.

827. Friesen, Gerhard. "Heine II." Immerwahr and Spencer,
eds., *Heinrich Heine*, pp. 96-113.

Identifies the author of a fierce imitation of the
Wintermärchen, directed against the Germany of 1872
and published in the United States, as the Baden radical
Otto Hörth.

828. Fueger, Wilhelm. "Harry Heine." *Wake Newslitter* N.S.
13 (1976): 114-115.

Suggests allusion to Heine's name and "Du bist wie
eine Blume" in Joyce's *Finnegans Wake*.

829. Galinsky, Hans. "Echowirkungen von Coleridges 'Kubla
Khan' und 'Dejection: An Ode' in Longfellows erstem
Heine-Essay." Pp. 117-140 in Galinsky, *Sprache und
Sprachkunstwerk in Amerika: Studien und Interpreta-
tionen*. Heidelberg: Quelle & Meyer, 1961. 208 pp.

Finds and accounts for linguistic echoes of Coleridge
in Longfellow's Heine essay.

830. Galley, Eberhard. "Dichtung als Provokation: Heine und
seine Kritiker (1821-1856)." *HJ 1979*, pp. 118-138.

A balanced review of Heine's reputation during his
lifetime, pointing out that the critical objections to
him were moralistic, not political, but also stressing
that there was always much praise of Heine.

831. ———. "Heine und sein Werk in Deutschland nach 1945.
Eine kritische Übersicht." *Düsseldorfer Jahrbuch* 50
(1960): 151-162.

A critical examination of the developing split between
East and West in Heine interpretation.

832. ———. *Heinrich Heine im Widerstreit der Meinungen
1825-1965*. Schriften der Heinrich Heine-Gesellschaft
Düsseldorf, 3. Düsseldorf: Heinrich Heine-Gesellschaft,
1967. 23 pp. Reprinted in part as "Heine in Deutschland. Zwischen allen Stühlen." *Europäische Gemeinschaft* (1972, No. 12): 26-31.

A brief essay on the long history of dispute over
Heine's reputation, concluding that we are still only
on the threshold of a just understanding.

833. ———. "Die Illustration Heinescher Werke: Ein Kapitel
aus der Rezeptionsgeschichte deutscher Literatur."
Pp. 85-93 in *Bibliothek und Buch in Geschichte und
Gegenwart: Festgabe für Friedrich Adolf Schmidt-
Künsemüller zum 65. Geburtstag am 30. Dez. 1975*,
ed. Otfried Weber. Munich: Verlag Dokumentation, 1976.
317 pp.

Traces the shifts in illustration from Campe's lack
of interest through the luxury editions beginning in

the 1880s, the avant-garde illustrations in the early
twentieth century, and the more recent decline.

834. Geldrich, Hanna. *Heine und der spanisch-amerikanische
     Modernismo*. German Studies in America, ed. Heinrich
     Meyer, No. 7. Bern and Frankfurt am Main: Herbert
     Lang, 1971. 298 pp.

     Describes Heine's thematic and stylistic influence on
     the renovation of both poetry and prose by the Latin
     American *modernistas* at the end of the nineteenth cen-
     tury, a major chapter in the history of Heine's inter-
     national influence.

835. Gilman, Sander. "Parody and Parallel: Heine, Nietzsche,
     and the Classical World." Pp. 199-213 in *Studies in
     Nietzsche and the Classical Tradition*, ed. James C.
     O'Flaherty, Timothy F. Sellner, and Robert M. Helm.
     University of North Carolina Studies in the Germanic
     Languages and Literatures, No. 85. Chapel Hill: Uni-
     versity of North Carolina Press, 1976. xviii + 278
     pp. Revised as "Nietzsche and Heine," pp. 57-76 in
     Gilman, *Nietzschean Parody: An Introduction to Reading
     Nietzsche*. Studien zur Germanistik, Anglistik und
     Komparatistik, Vol. 38. Bonn: Bouvier, 1976. 135 pp.

     Follows Nietzsche's changing views of Heine as a pat-
     tern of Nietzsche's internal biography.

836. Gohdes, Clarence. "Heine in America: A Cursory Survey."
     Georgia Review 11 (1957): 44-49.

     A brief account of the rise of Heine's reputation in
     the United States and his influence, especially on W.D.
     Howells.

837. Goldammer, Peter. "Das Werk Heinrich Heines in den Ver-
     lagen der DDR." *Streitbarer Humanist*, pp. 455-460.

     Unanalyzed statistics on Heine publications in East
     Germany, with misleading commentary.

838. Gössmann, Wilhelm, with Hans Peter Keller and Hedwig
     Walwei-Wiegelmann, eds. *Geständnisse: Heine im Be-
     wußtsein heutiger Autoren*. Düsseldorf: Droste Verlag,
     1972. 275 pp.

     Responses of ninety German authors to an inquiry on
     Heine's importance to them; a mixed bag of amiable if
     often melancholy reminiscences, pious clichés, obscure

meditations, imaginative appropriations, rebel yells,
and an occasional thoughtful illumination.

839. Gössmann, Wilhelm. "Das Heine-Denkmal von Bert Gerres-
      heim." *HJ 1980*, pp. 252-253.

      A comment on a new modern sculpture of Heine.

840. ————. "Konservativ oder liberal? Heine und die
      Droste." *HJ 1976*, pp. 115-139.

      Discusses the contemporaneity of Heine and Annette
      von Droste-Hülshoff, concluding that even a conserva-
      tive might have some humane views.

841. Gotsche-Meister, Helga. "Heine-Haus im Herzen der Alt-
      stadt." *Düsseldorf* (1972, No. 3): 16-18.

      Interview with Eberhard Galley about the new head-
      quarters of the Heine Institute.

842. Gottgetreu, Erich. "Der Gymnasiast Thomas Mann und Heine."
      NDH 20, No. 140 (1973): 92-99.

      On Thomas Mann's spirited schoolboy defense of Heine's
      greatness against sentimentalizing attempts to render
      him harmless.

843. Grandjonc, Jacques, and Michael Werner. *Wolfgang Strähls
      "Briefe eines Schweizers aus Paris" 1835: Zur Geschichte
      des Bundes der Geächteten in der Schweiz und zur Rezep-
      tion Heines unter deutschen Handwerkern in Paris.*
      Schriften aus dem Karl-Marx-Haus, No. 21. Trier:
      Karl-Marx-Haus, 1978. 85 pp.

      This instructive study reprints and comments on a
      lengthy critique of Heine's prophecy of the birth of
      German revolution out of the spirit of German philosophy
      at the end of *Zur Geschichte der Religion und Philosophie
      in Deutschland*, found in a MS. of a Swiss revolutionary
      artisan. His position is close to Börne and Lamennais
      and is marked by moralistic religiosity, anti-intellec-
      tualism, utopian nationalism, and a deep suspicion of
      Heine's upper-class immoralism, but also by a genuine
      commitment to democracy. The erratically educated,
      barely literate artisan could not comprehend Heine's
      complexity; it is easy to see why Heine was repelled by
      such people, and vice-versa.

844. Grzimek, Waldemar. "Gedanken zu meinem Heine-Denkmal."
      Bildende Kunst 4 (1956): 310-314.

      The sculptor describes his controversial monument to
      Heine erected near East Berlin.

845. Hansen, Volkmar. *Thomas Manns Heine-Rezeption.* Heine-
      Studien, ed. Manfred Windfuhr. Hamburg: Hoffmann
      und Campe, Heinrich Heine Verlag, 1975. 331 pp.

      An industrious dissertation searches Mann's published
      and unpublished writings, yielding a surprising quantity
      of reference and allusion to Heine, and arguing that much
      in Mann that appears to be in the Nietzsche tradition
      may actually go back to Heine.

846. ————. "Thomas Manns Erzählung 'Das Gesetz' und Heines
      Moses-Bild." *HJ 1974,* pp. 132-149.

      A segment of no. 845.

847. Hasubek, Peter. "Ausbürgerung--Einbürgerung? Heinrich
      Heine als Schullektüre. Ein Beitrag zur Rezeptions-
      geschichte." Kuttenkeuler, ed., *Heinrich Heine:
      Artistik und Engagement,* pp. 305-332.

      A discussion of Heine's place in schoolbooks in the
      Wilhelminian period and in modern East and West Germany
      offers details but no unfamiliar results.

848. Hellendall, F. "Heinrich Heine and Düsseldorf--A City
      Afraid of its Great Son." *Monatshefte* 63 (1971): 56-
      59.

      An account of the dispute over the naming of the Uni-
      versity of Düsseldorf after Heine, without documentation
      or penetration.

849. Hemmerdinger, Bertrand. "Le Thème de Cartouche banquier
      chez Eugène Pottier et Heine (1831)." *Belfagor* 23
      (1968): 484.

      Implausible suggestion that Heine may have referred
      to a motif of Pottier, the author of the *Internationale,*
      when Pottier was fifteen years old.

850. Hermand, Jost. "Heines frühe Kritiker." Pp. 113-133
      in *Der Dichter und seine Zeit: Politik im Spiegel
      der Literatur. Drittes Amherster Kolloquium zur
      modernen deutschen Literatur 1969,* ed. Wolfgang
      Paulsen. Literatur und Geschichte: Eine Schriftenreihe,

Vol. 1. Heidelberg: Lothar Stiehm, 1970. 227 pp.

Examples of accusation of egotistical subjectivity,
irreverence, sacrilege, obscenity, lack of patriotism,
and rootless Jewishness in the reviews of the *Reisebilder* from 1828 to 1835. Generally leaves out the
positive reception of Heine at the time. Included in
no. 564.

851. Hessmann, Pierre. "Heinrich Heine und Gérard de Nerval."
      Studia Germanica Gandensia 5 (1963): 185-206.

A brief but worthwhile discussion stressing not only
Nerval's discipleship to Heine, but also the significant
differences between them.

852. Höck, Wilhelm. "Deutsche Dichter im Wandel des Urteils.
      Eine Aufsatzreihe (VI). Heinrich Heine." *Der junge
      Buchhandel* 17, No. 12 (Enclosure to Supplement No. 97,
      December 4, 1964): 186-192.

Points out that Heine's name rarely appeared in West
German university course catalogues between 1959 and
1964.

853. Hörling, Hans. *Heinrich Heine im Spiegel der politischen
      Presse Frankreichs von 1831-1841: Ansatz zu einem
      Modell der qualitativen und quantitativen Rezeptions-
      forschung.* Europäische Hochschulschriften, Series I,
      Vol. 172. Frankfurt am Main, Bern, and Las Vegas:
      Peter Lang, 1977. 350 pp.

An elaborate statistical examination of discussions of
Heine in Parisian newspapers from 1831 to 1841, giving
a detailed account of the history, financing, and partisan coloration of each paper. A most scholarly, informative, and important study with many new insights.

854. Hofman, Alois. "Heine bei den Tschechen." *Streitbarer
      Humanist*, pp. 434-442.

History and importance of Heine in Czechoslovakia.

855. Hohendahl, Peter Uwe. "Erzwungene Harmonie. Bürger-
      liche Heine-Feiern." Pp. 123-142, 179-183 in *Deutsche
      Feiern*, ed. Reinhold Grimm and Jost Hermand. Wies-
      baden: Athenaion, 1977. 187 pp.

Discusses public celebrations of Heine in 1897, 1906,
and 1972, in order to show that all were marked by conservative and reactionary views of Heine. Hohendahl

bends the evidence considerably to make the point.

856. Hollosi, Clara. "Views on Heine in Russia in the Begin-
      ning of the 20th Century." *HJ 1978*, pp. 175-185.

      Stresses Heine's importance for anti-realistic, "ex-
      istentialist" Russian writers at the turn of the century.

857. Horch, Hans Otto. "'Das Schlechte ... mit demselben
      Vergnügen wie das Gute.' Über Theodor Fontanes Be-
      ziehungen zu Heinrich Heine." *HJ 1979*, pp. 139-176.

      Describes Fontane's life-long Heine echoes, especially
      the exceptional integration of Heine allusions in *Effi
      Briest*.

858. Hotz, Karl. *Heinrich Heine: Wirkungsgeschichte als
      Wirkungsästhetik. Materialien zur Rezeptions- und
      Wirkungsgeschichte Heines*. Stuttgart: Klett, 1975.
      176 pp.

      A resource text for schoolteaching based on criticisms
      of Heine from "bourgeois" criticism of the poetry to
      contemporary reactions, badly written and full of con-
      ventional bias about Heine and his reputation.

859. Huppert, Hugo. "Heine im Pantheon der Sowjetkultur."
      NDL 4, No. 2 (February 1956): 3-40.

      Heine's importance in the early Soviet Union and in
      nineteenth-century Russia.

860. ———. "Eine Vorwegnahme modernen Menschtums: Zur
      Heine-Rezeption in Rußland." *SuF* 24 (1972): 1138-
      1152.

      Illustrates the different responses before and after
      the Bolshevik Revolution to Heine, who replaced Schiller
      among the younger, progressive writers as a model.

861. Inoue, Shozo. *Der Dichter Heine im fernen Osten*.
      (Special Printing on the Occasion of the Tenth Anni-
      versary of the City University of Tokyo.) Tokyo:
      [City University of Tokyo], 1960. 27 pp.

      The major contemporary Japanese translator and expli-
      cator of Heine describes his history and importance in
      Japan.

862. Jonzeck, Marianne. "Westdeutsche Traditionspflege:
      Ein Beitrag zum Heine-Jubiläumsfeier 1972." *Der*

Bibliothekar 26 (1972): 765-771.

An East German propaganda piece, charging neglect and distortion of Heine in West Germany.

863. Kabaktschiewa, Maria. "Heinrich Heine in Bulgarien." *Streitbarer Humanist*, pp. 443-447.

History and importance of Heine in Bulgaria.

864. Kaltwasser, Gerda. "Der Heinrich-Heine-Preis der Landeshauptstadt Düsseldorf. Ein Diskussionsbeitrag." *HJ 1980*, pp. 247-251.

A comment on the questionable and contentious award of the Düsseldorf Heine Prize to Sebastian Haffner in 1979, moderate in tone but saying nothing about the meretricious international campaign mounted against it by supposed friends of Heine.

865. Kämmerling, Bernd. "Die wahre Richtung des Angriffs. Über Karl Kraus' Heine und die Folgen." *HJ 1972*, pp. 162-169.

An effort to be fair to Kraus, apparently directed against no. 807, but obliged to some of the same insights.

866. Kesten, Hermann. "Deutschland, Ein Wintermärchen." Pp. 62-78 in Kesten, *Der Geist der Unruhe: Literarische Streifzüge*. Cologne and Berlin: Kiepenheuer & Witsch, 1959. 346 pp.

Originally the preface to an English edition of the *Wintermärchen* published in New York in 1944, the moving and biting essay describes how Kesten rallied his fellow prisoners in a French concentration camp by reading Heine's satirical poem.

867. ———. "Heinrich Heine und Joseph Roth." Pp. 259-273 in *Publications of the Leo Baeck Institute Year Book XX*. London: Secker & Warburg, 1975. xxxii + 379 pp.

Similarities and dissimilarities of Heine and Roth, impelled by Kesten's personal affection for Roth; the encomium on Heine is eloquent though imprecise.

868. Kleinknecht, Karl Theodor, ed. *Heine in Deutschland: Dokumente seiner Rezeption 1834-1956*. Deutsche Texte, ed. Gotthart Wunberg, 36. Tübingen and Munich: Deutscher Taschenbuch Verlag and Niemeyer, 1976. xxxii + 176 pp.

A selection of critical documents concentrating on
Heine's Paris years and the Wilhelminian period, in-
telligently edited but skimping on the great phase of
Heine scholarship in the Empire and the Republic.

869. Knüfermann, Volker. "Jean Paul, Heine und Büchner:
     Ein Beitrag zur Rezeptionsgeschichte." *HJ 1973*, pp.
     200-207.

     Endeavors to find a line of influence from Jean Paul's
     Rede des toten Christus via Heine to Büchner.

870. ————. "Zweimal deutsche Kulturgeschichtsschreibung.
     Heinrich Heine und Hugo Ball." *HJ 1976*, pp. 140-165.

     Shows how the cultural criticism of the Dadaist Hugo
     Ball derived from and criticized Heine's.

871. Kolbe, Jürgen. *Ich weiss nicht was soll es bedeuten:
     Heinrich Heines Loreley. Bilder und Gedichte.*
     Munich: Hanser, 1976. 48 pp.

     A short essay, with examples, on the Loreley tradition
     in poetry, including incredibly hideous nineteenth-
     century illustrations of the motif. Doubtless one of
     the most amusing items on Heine published in our time.

872. Koopmann, Helmut. "Heines 'Millenium' und Eichendorffs
     'alte schöne Zeit.' Zur Utopie im frühen 19. Jahr-
     hundert." *Aurora: Jahrbuch der Eichendorff-Gesell-
     schaft* 37 (1977): 33-50.

     Eichendorff found a correlative of the lost paradise
     in his own personal history, blaming the fallen world
     on Protestantism and modernity; Heine turned the motif
     around, projecting paradise into the future.

873. ————. "Heinrich Heine in Deutschland. Aspekte seiner
     Wirkung im 19. Jahrhundert." Pp. 312-333 in *Nationa-
     lismus in Germanistik und Dichtung: Dokumentation des
     Germanistentages in München vom 17.-22. Oktober 1966*,
     ed. Benno von Wiese and Rudolf Henss. Berlin: 1967.
     363 pp. Reprinted Koopmann, ed., *Heinrich Heine*, pp.
     257-287.

     One of the first detailed examinations of the history
     of Heine's reputation in the modern phase of scholarship.

874. Krahé, Peter. "Heine und Ruskin. Shakespeare-Bild und
     nationales Vorurteil." *HJ 1980*, pp. 169-187.

A comparison of the completely different and unrelated views of Heine and Ruskin on Shakespeare.

875. Kramer, Aaron. "The Link Between Heine and Emma Lazarus." *Publication of the American Jewish Historical Society* 45 (1955/56): 248-257.

A critical view of Emma Lazarus' translations, arguing that Heine contributed to her development into a strong, prophetic writer.

876. Kruse, Joseph A. "Ablehnung, Zustimmung, und konsolidiertes Interesse. Heine-Chronik 1973/74." *HJ 1975*, pp. 171-182.

A review of the commentary on Heine in the wake of the anniversary of 1972.

877. ————. "Historische und kulturpolitische Aspekte der Heine-Ausstellungen." *HJ 1980*, pp. 242-246.

Discusses the background and international exhibition activities of the Heinrich Heine-Gesellschaft.

878. Kubacki, W. "Heinrich Heine und Polen." *HJ 1966*, pp. 90-106.

History, importance, and translations of Heine in Poland.

878a. Lambert, José. "Heine, Nerval et un vers d'*El Desdichado*." *Les Lettres Romanes* 29 (1975): 43-51.

Urges a reexamination of the relationship between Nerval and Heine.

879. Landsberg, Abraham. "Last Traces of Heinrich Heine in Hamburg." *Year Book of the Leo Baeck Institute* 1 (1956): 360-369.

Describes the few memorials to Heine still remaining in Hamburg.

880. Lauer, Reinhard. *Heine in Serbien: Die Bedeutung Heinrich Heines für die Entwicklung der serbischen Literatur 1847-1918.* Osteuropastudien der Hochschulen des Landes Hessen, Series 3, Vol. 4. Meisenheim am Glan: Hain, 1961. 268 pp.

History and importance of Heine in Serbia.

881. Lehnert, Herbert. "Heine, Schiller, Nietzsche und der
     junge Thomas Mann." *Neophilologus* 48 (1961): 51-56.

     Criticizes and revises no. 918.

882. Lehrmann, Lucienne. "Du nouveau sur Heine." *Europe*,
     No. 124 (April 1956): 169-171.

     A prepublication review of an edition by Georges
     Cogniot, remarking that only the revolutionary proletar-
     iat (and Lenin and Stalin) appreciated Heine.

883. Lewik, Wilhelm. "Heine und die russische Poesie."
     Streitbarer Humanist, pp. 414-424.

     Observations on Heine's impact on Russian poetry and
     the problems of translating him. Rather more interest-
     ing than the usual national influence study of this
     kind.

884. Löschburg, Winfried. "Alfred Meißners Erinnerungen an
     Heine." *NDL* 4, No. 8 (August 1956): 162-163.

     Sketches Meissner's career, correctly arguing that
     his memoirs of Heine are among the most valuable we
     have.

885. Machado da Rosa, Alberto. "Heine in Spain (1856-67)--
     Relations with Rosalía de Castro." *Monatshefte* 49
     (1957): 65-82.

     Corrects previous opinions on Heine's influence on
     Rosalía de Castro, putting it in the context of Heine's
     reputation in Spain.

886. Malieniemi, Irja. "Heinrich Heine in der Literatur
     Finnlands bis etwa 1920." *Nerthus: Nordisch-deutsche
     Beiträge* 1 (1964): 9-105.

     History and reputation of Heine in Finland, with a
     bibliography of Finnish translations to 1938.

887. Marcuse, Ludwig. "Heines Parodien, Heine-Parodien."
     TK 18/19 (1968): 43-44.

     On Heine's parodies of other poems, and the parodies
     of others of his.

888. Mayser, Erich. *H. Heines "Buch der Lieder" im 19.
     Jahrhundert.* Stuttgarter Arbeiten zur Germanistik,
     No. 58. Stuttgart: Akademischer Verlag Hans-Dieter

Heinz, 1978. [viii] + 230 + xx pp.

A detailed and thoughtful analysis of the reaction to Heine's poetry among critics and other writers through 1828; the discussion of the situation after 1830 is less thorough and analytic.

889. Meier-Lenz, D.P. *Heinrich Heine--Wolf Biermann: Deutschland. ZWEI Wintermärchen--ein Werkvergleich.* Abhandlungen zur Kunst-, Musik- und Literaturwissenschaft, Vol. 246. Bonn: Bouvier, 1977. 158 pp.

A comparison of Heine's *Wintermärchen* with the East German dissident Wolf Biermann's modern version is not badly informed in regard to Biermann, as the author was himself an East German writer, but imprecise and full of errors of judgment in regard to Heine, and overall very simplistic.

890. Mende, Fritz. "Heine und Ruge. Ein Kapitel Heine-Rezeption in der Zeit des Vormärz." *WB* 14 (1968): 797-827.

A detailed discussion of Ruge's shifting views of Heine as an example of the deficiencies of petty-bourgeois criticism persisting into the present.

891. ———. "Heines *Französische Zustände* im Urteil der Zeit. (Eine wirkungsgeschichtliche Studie zur Heine-Rezeption in Deutschland und Frankreich)." *Philologica Pragensia* 11 (1968): 77-85, 152-164.

Summarizes the German and French commentary on *Französische Zustände*, carefully differentiating points of view and estimating Heine's own part in instigating the French reception.

892. Merkelbach, Valentin. "Heinrich Heine in lesebüchern der Bundesrepublik." *DD* 8 (1977): 317-332.

Some improvement in the once sorry status of Heine in school anthologies is found, but the situation continues to be unsatisfactory except for one schoolbook organized to sharpen pupils' class-consciousness.

893. Mitsuno, Masyuki. "Umriß einer Geschichte der Heine-Rezeption in Japan." *HJ 1979*, pp. 218-232.

The history of Heine's reception in Japan reviewed from a Marxist standpoint.

894. Müller, Beatrix. *Die französische Heine-Forschung 1945-
      1975.* Hochschulschriften Literaturwissenschaft, 28.
      Meisenheim am Glan: Hain, 1977. 471 pp.

      One of the most thorough studies of Heine scholarship
      in a foreign country reviews editions, biographical
      study, criticism, and thematology. A most valuable
      effort despite certain insecurities of judgment and
      accent.

895. Murdoch, Brian. "Poetry, Satire and Slave-Ships: Some
      Parallels to Heine's 'Sklavenschiff.'" *Forum for
      Modern Language Studies* 15 (1979): 323-335.

      Compares similar poems on the slave trade by William
      Cowper, Béranger, and Chamisso, showing that the Béranger
      poem regularly given as Heine's source is quite differ-
      ent in implication.

896. Nabrotzky, Ronald H.D. "Die DDR: Heinrich Heines ver-
      wirklichter Lebenstraum." *MLN* 92 (1977): 535-548.

      A welcome beginning to an inspection of the assertions
      of East German Heine scholarship measures the claims
      made for Heine as a prophet of the East German state
      against his actual views, but lacks a systematic, in-
      clusive, and historical analysis of the problem.

897. ————. "Heines Prophezeiung vom Sieg des Kommunismus:
      Zur Rezeption der französischen *Lutezia*-Vorrede in
      der DDR." *MLN* 93 (1978): 482-492.

      Challenges the pro-Communist interpretation that has
      sometimes been put on the French *Lutezia* preface; has
      similar virtues and weaknesses as the preceding item,
      and suffers from somewhat insufficient scholarship.

898. Nicolaus, Norbert. "Das Heine-Jahr 1972. Eine Chronolo-
      gie der Ereignisse." *HJ 1974*, pp. 159-167.

      A chronicle of public events during the anniversary
      year of 1972.

899. ————. "Rezeption und Vermittlung. Das Heine-Jahr
      1972 im Medium der Presse." *HJ 1974*, pp. 150-158.

      A review of the press accounts of the anniversary
      year of 1972.

900. Owen, Claude R. "Darío and Heine." *Susquehanna Uni-
      versity Studies* 8 (1970): 329-349.

Ruben Darío probably never read a line of Heine in the original, but alludes to him frequently, sometimes appositely, sometimes not.

901. ————. "Ezequiel Martínez Estrada and Heine." *HJ 1971*, pp. 52–75.

Contains an energetic but confusing unpublished essay on Heine by the Argentine poet written for the anniversary year of 1956.

902. ————. *Heine im spanischen Sprachgebiet: Eine kritische Bibliographie.* Spanische Forschungen der Görresgesellschaft, Series 2, XII. Münster: Aschendorff, 1968. xii + 336 pp.

Very professional and thorough critical bibliography of Heine's works, imitations, critical studies, and other written treatments in the Spanish-speaking world.

903. ————. "Heinrich Heine im spanischen Sprachgebiet. Eine kritische Bibliographie. Nachträge." *Spanische Forschungen der Görresgesellschaft* 27 (1973): 1–172.

Supplement to no. 902.

904. ————. "Ramiro de Maeztu über Heinrich Heine." *HJ 1967*, pp. 90–98.

Admiration of Heine by a Spanish conservative.

905. Pageard, Robert, and G.W. Ribbans. "Heine and Byron in the *Semanario popular* (1862–1865)." *Bulletin of Hispanic Studies* 33 (1956): 78–86.

Lists the numerous Heine translations in a mid-nineteenth-century Spanish weekly.

906. Pepperle, Ingrid. "Das Verhältnis der junghegelianischen Kritik zu Heine." *Streitbarer Humanist*, pp. 355–359. Expanded as "Die junghegelianische Kritik und Heine." Pp. 127–141 in *Heinrich Heine und die Zeitgenossen*.

A learned and detailed account of the criticism of Heine by the Left Hegelians, dealing primarily with Arnold Ruge.

907. Perez, Hertha. "Das Heine-Bild in Rumänien." *Arcadia* 10 (1975): 72–76.

History and importance of Heine in Rumania.

162   *Reception, Reputation, Etc.*

908. Peschken, Bernd. *Versuch einer germanistischen Ideo-
      logiekritik; Goethe, Lessing, Novalis, Tieck, Hölderlin,
      Heine in Wilhelm Diltheys und Julian Schmidts Vorstel-
      lungen.* Texte Metzler, 23. Stuttgart: Metzler, 1972.
      195 pp.

      Demonstrates how an official canon of German literature
      arose in the Wilhelminian period and on what grounds
      Heine was excluded from it.

909. Politi, Francesco. "Carducci zwischen Platen und Heine."
      Pp. 124-140 in *Studien zur deutsch-italienischen
      Geistesgeschichte,* ed. Istituto Italiano di Cultura
      and Petrarca-Institute of the University of Cologne.
      Studi Italiani, Vol. 3. Cologne and Graz: Böhlau
      Verlag, 1959. 182 pp. Reprinted pp. 525-546 in
      Carducci: Discorsi nel cinquentenario della morte.
      Bologna: Zanichelli, 1959. viii + 546 pp.

      Although Carducci admired Platen, he was far superior
      to him as a poet and more closely related to Heine, with
      whom he shared anti-Christian and political themes,
      though with less irony and complexity.

910. ————. "Heine und Carducci." Pp. 189-200 in Politi,
      Studi di letteratura tedesca e marginalia. Bari:
      Adriatica Editrice, 1963. 267 pp.

      On Carducci's great enthusiasm for Heine and the
      similarities and differences between them.

911. Poschmann, Henri. "Heine und Büchner. Zwei Strategien
      revolutionär-demokratischer Literatur im 1835." *Hein-
      rich Heine und die Zeitgenossen,* pp. 203-228.

      Exhibits Büchner's borrowings from Heine, shows how
      both employed the figure of Camille Desmoulins to reflect
      upon their own situation as revolutionaries, and argues
      that Büchner rejects Heine's poetic subjectivity in
      favor of an uncompromising realism.

912. Prang, Helmut. "Heine im Schatten Hölderlins." *NDH*
      2 (1955/56): 472-475.

      Shows how the modernist aesthetic has been increasing-
      ly preoccupied with Hölderlin at the expense of Heine,
      who is more suited to the French and Anglo-American
      than the German mentality.

913. Preisendanz, Wolfgang. "Die umgebuchte Schreibart.
      Heines literarischer Humor in Spannungsfeld von

Begriffs-, Form- und Rezeptiongeschichte." Kuttenkeuler, ed., *Heinrich Heine: Artistik und Engagement*,
pp. 1-21.

Examines with admirable precision the characterization
of Heine by himself and his contemporaries as a humorist
rather than a satirist and shows how Heine shifted the
concept of humor from an idealistic to a modern-realistic
and critical position.

914. Prox, Lothar. "Wagner und Heine." *DVLG* 46 (1972):
684-698.

Describes and explains Wagner's later denial of his
debt to Heine, and points out that Heine, too, subse-
quently edited his recollections of Wagner in an un-
complimentary direction.

915. Radford, F.L. "Heinrich Heine, the Virgin, and the
Hummingbird: *Fifth Business*--A Novel and its Sub-
conscious." *English Studies in Canada* 4 (1978):
95-110.

Employment of motifs from Heine's *Faust* and "Vitzliputzli" in a novel by Robertson Davies.

916. Raphael, J. "Heinrich Heine--Eine hebräische Bibliographie." *HJ 1968*, pp. 39-57.

Bibliography of Heine in Hebrew translation.

917. ———. "Heinrich Heine in der jiddisch-literarischen
Welt." *HJ 1970*, pp. 140-147.

A brief history of Heine's influence on Yiddish culture and a selective bibliography of translations.

918. Reed, T.J. "Thomas Mann, Heine, Schiller: The Mechanics
of Self-Interpretation." *Neophilologus* 47 (1963):
41-50.

Connects Heine to Mann's aristocratic, unegalitarian
view of the artist, though Mann publicly credited Schiller instead. See also no. 881.

919. Reese, Walter. *Zur Geschichte der sozialistischen Heine-
Rezeption in Deutschland.* Europäische Hochschulschrif-
ten, Series I, Vol. 313. Frankfurt am Main, Bern, and
Circencester: Peter D. Lang, 1979. 457 pp.

The first and long-needed detailed, historically

accurate examination of the treatment of Heine in the
German Democratic Republic traces the development to
mid-nineteenth-century and Wilhelminian Socialist reception. Reese criticizes the East German development,
sometimes severely, from the point of view of utopian
Neo-Marxism; but his informational detail, based on
much primary research, will be of value to readers of
less stringent beliefs. The book is burdened by a
hundred pages of reception theory of the most extreme
presentism, which the reader interested in Reese's
subject might well skip.

920. Reimann, Paul. "Heine und die tschechische Literatur.
      Zum 100. Todestag des Dichters." Pp. 28-33 in Reimann,
      *Von Herder bis Kisch: Studien zur Geschichte der
      deutsch-österreichisch-tschechischen Literaturbezie-
      hungen.* Berlin: Dietz, 1961. 292 pp.

      Heine's importance to the national movement of the
      Czechoslovakian peoples and to the working class.

921. Richter, Karl. "Heinrich Heine in Richard Wagners
      autobiographischen Schriften und in den Tagebüchern
      von Cosima Wagner." *HJ 1979*, pp. 209-217.

      Material from Cosima Wagner's diary showing how Wag-
      ner's hysterical anti-Semitism led to his repression
      of Heine's importance to him.

922. ————. "Zum Verhältnis Richard Wagners zu Heinrich
      Heine. 'Der fliegende Holländer'—ein Test." *Emuna*
      4 (1969): 221-225.

      A compact account of all the details concerning Wag-
      ner's relationship to Heine and the *Flying Dutchman*
      material, brief but of unusual solidity.

923. Rinsler, Norma. "Gérard de Nerval and Heinrich Heine."
      RLC 33 (1959): 94-102.

      Suggests specifics of the influence of Heine's memoirs
      and poems on Nerval's images and imagination.

924. Rogge, Helmuth. "Heinrich Heine und die 'Briefe der
      frommen Männer des 19. Jahrhunderts.'" *HJ 1969*,
      pp. 45-68.

      Discovery of a fairly witless satire on Heine of 1831
      from Pietistic circles.

925. Rømhild, Lars Peter. "En tekstsammenligning: to digte af Heine og Chr. Winther." Pp. 214-231 in Rømhild, *Laesere: Artikler og foredrag.* Munksgaardserien 42. Copenhagen: Munksgaard, 1971. 294 pp.

A demonstration of a comparative interpretation of Heine's *Lyrisches Intermezzo* 58 and a poem of a Danish contemporary with a similar disillusioning ending.

926. Rose, Margaret. "Kenneth Slessor's 'Heine in Paris.'" *Quadrant* No. 129 (April 1978): 56-59. Tr. in excerpt as "Kenneth Slessors 'Heine in Paris'--Anmerkungen zu Heine in Australien." *HJ 1980*, pp. 234-241.

Discusses the importance of Heine's works for Slessor's poem on Heine's dying hours.

927. Rose, William. "Heine Conference at Weimar." *GL&L* N.S. 10 (1956/57): 162-163.

A brief report on the East German anniversary conference of 1956.

928. Rosenberg, Rainer. "Die Wiederentdeckung des Lesers: Heine und Prutz." *Heinrich Heine und die Zeitgenossen*, pp. 178-202.

Primarily concerned with a worthwhile discussion of Robert Prutz's very advanced analysis of the literary situation of his time in its political and social context, which, though Rosenberg shies away from the point, is more penetrating and realistic than Heine's.

929. Rukser, Udo. "Heine in der hispanischen Welt." *DVLG.* 30 (1956): 474-510.

Heine's influence is shown to be important for a revival of Spanish and Spanish-American literature from a low point in the early nineteenth century, an influence that continues to the present.

930. Salinger, Herman. "Heinrich Heine's Stature After a Century." *Monatshefte* 48 (1956): 309-316.

Heine's place in world literature, such as it may be, is based upon his wit.

931. Schaub, Uta. "Liliencron und Heine im Urteil von Karl Kraus. Ein Beitrag zum Problem der literarischen Wertung." *HJ 1979*, pp. 191-201.

Shows how Kraus's condemnation of Heine and admiration

for Liliencron exhibits the problem of the persistence
of restrictive canonical norms in German criticism--
paradoxical in this case, since Liliencron was an ob-
vious pupil of Heine.

932. Scheffener, D. "Heine in Nederland." *Levende Talen*
      No. 185 (1956): 318-325.

      Dutch intellectual opinion on Heine from his death to
      the 1930s.

933. Schiller, Dieter. "Heine heute. Bericht über die wis-
      senschaftliche Konferenz vom 6. bis 9. 12. 1972 in
      Weimar." *WB* 19, No. 4 (1973): 184-192.

      An ideologically watchful account of the 1972 Weimar
      conference.

934. Schmidt, Egon. "Zur Rezeption von Heines Dichtung
      'Deutschland. Ein Wintermärchen' in der sozialdemo-
      kratischen Parteiliteratur der siebziger Jahre."
      Streitbarer Humanist, pp. 396-403.

      Social-democratic imitations of Heine's *Wintermärchen*.

935. Schoenermark, Erna. "Gedanken zur Heine-Ehrung 1972."
      DU (East) 25 (1972): 712-715.

      Description of a tenth-grade discussion of Heine,
      with revolutionary music in the background and the
      conclusion that he is an ally in the fight against the
      enemies of mankind.

936. Schönfeldt, Otto, ed. "Und alle lieben Heinrich Heine
      ...." Cologne: Pahl-Rugenstein, 1972. 195 pp.

      A documentation of the international "citizen's
      initiative" to have the University of Düsseldorf named
      after Heine. Exhibits the widespread interest and
      concern in this matter, as well as the shrill, arrogant,
      and simplistic argumentation of some of the proposal's
      supporters, which did not contribute to its success.

937. Schumacher, Ernest. "Heinrich Heine und die Chinesen."
      Pp. 494-501 in Schumacher, *Lotosblüten und Turbinen:
      China zwischen gestern und morgen*. Düsseldorf: Pro-
      gress-Verlag Johann Fladung, [1958]. 514 pp.

      A report on a centenary celebration in Peking, which
      is compared to the indifference to Heine in West Germany.

938. Schweikert, Alexander. *Heinrich Heines Einflüsse auf die deutsche Lyrik 1830-1900.* Abhandlungen zur Kunst-, Musik- und Literaturwissenschaft, Vol. 57. Bonn: Bouvier, 1969. 259 pp.

Examines Heine's influence on five generations of subsequent German poets and writers, primarily Gutzkow, Herwegh, Weerth, Storm, Keller, Scheffel, F.T. Vischer, Wilhelm Busch, and Christian Morgenstern. The results are, on the whole, aesthetically depressing, nor does Schweickert exhibit any refined discrimination or critical sensibility. An informative beginning on an important enterprise.

939. ————. "Notizen zu den Einflüssen Heinrich Heines auf die Lyrik von Kerr, Klabund, Tucholsky und Erich Kästner." *HJ 1969*, pp. 69-107.

Carries the above inquiry into the twentieth century.

940. Secci, Lia. "Die Götter im Exil—Heine und der europäische Symbolismus." *HJ 1976*, pp. 96-114.

Takes up again the question of Heine and European symbolism, correcting some of the misjudgments of no. 804.

941. ————. "Heine in Italien: Croce und die Folgen." *Europäische Gemeinschaft* (1972, No. 12): 32-33.

The contemporary recovery of Heine's reputation in Italian scholarship from Croce's influential devaluation.

942. Seifert, Siegfried. "Der unbewältigte Heine." *NDL* 13, No. 1 (1965): 172-179.

Praise of East German treatment of Heine in contrast to West Germany.

943. Sengle, Friedrich. "Zum Problem der Heinewertung. Ein Vortrag." Pp. 376-391 in *Geist und Zeichen: Festschrift für Arthur Henkel zu seinem 60. Geburtstag*, ed. Herbert Anton, Bernhard Gajek, and Peter Pfaff. Heidelberg: Winter, 1977. 482 pp.

Enlightening, forceful, and arguable effort to defuse the evaluative contentiousness about Heine by looking at his reputation in the historical light of his times.

944. Senn, Alfred. "Heines *Nordsee* in litauischer Übersetzung und Bemerkungen zu Balŷs Srŭogas Dichtersprache."

Die Welt der Slaven 8 (1963): 18-33.

A largely philological examination of a modern Lithuanian translation.

945. Snamenskaja, Galina. "Die Traditionen von Heinrich Heine im Schaffen Heinrich Manns." *Streitbarer Humanist*, pp. 62-77.

Heinrich Mann as a continuator of Heine as a politically progressive writer.

946. Söhn, Gerhart. *Heinrich Heine in seiner Vaterstadt Düsseldorf.* Düsseldorf: Triltsch, 1966. 69 pp.

A historical retrospect on Heine's home town by a dedicated amateur. Numerous illustrations; can be used as a guidebook.

947. Sprinchorn, Evert. "Heine, Hummel, and the Hyacinth Girl." *Meddelanden från Strindbergssälskapet* No. 56 (May 1976): 16-17.

Argues that Hummel in Strindberg's *Ghost Sonata* is modelled on Hyacinth Hirsch in Heine's *Bäder von Lucca*, a figure drastically misunderstood as a "rascally Jewish speculator."

948. Stanescu, Heinz. "Heine-Literatur in Rumänien." *NDL* 4, No. 7 (July 1956): 157-158.

Brief account of Heine's texts and discussion in Rumania.

949. Stauffacher, Werner. "'Ein Stern in der Jauche.' Bemerkungen zu Carl Spittelers Heine-Lektüre." *HJ 1979*, pp. 177-190.

Explores the ambivalent and evidently quite peripheral relationship of Spitteler to Heine.

950. Steinhauer, Harry. "Heinrich Heine." *Antioch Review* 16 (1956/57): 445-458.

Observations on the oddities of Heine's reputation.

951. Stekelenburg, Dick van. "Heinrich Heine als Beziehungsfigur. Zum Internationalen Heine-Kongress 15-19 X 1972, Düsseldorf." *DK* 25 (1973): 27-40.

A skeptical but on the whole reasonable report on the events and occasional uproar of the Düsseldorf conference.

952. Stern, Martin. "'Poetische Willkür.' Heine im Urteil Gottfried Kellers." *HJ 1977*, pp. 49-70.

    A readable and sensible discussion of Gottfried Keller's relation to Heine.

953. Suzuki, Kazuko. "Heine in Japan." *Streitbarer Humanist*, pp. 448-454.

    Examines the interest in Heine in Japan up to 1911 and the involvement of Heine enthusiasts in opposition to reactionary government.

954. Tesdorpf, Ilse-Maria. *Die Auseinandersetzung Matthew Arnolds mit Heinrich Heine, des Kritikers mit dem Kritiker: Ein besonderer Fall von konstruktivem Mißverstehen und eigenwilliger Entlehnung.* Neue Beiträge zur Anglistik und Amerikanistik, Vol. 6. Frankfurt am Main: Athenäum, 1971. 184 pp.

    The most precise account of Heine's influence on Matthew Arnold, showing Arnold's sources and severely criticizing Arnold's alterations of Heine's concepts.

955. Tiedemann, Rüdiger von. "Der Tod des großen Pan-- Bemerkungen zu einem Thema bei Heinrich Heine und Gérard de Nerval." *Arcadia* (1978): Special Issue *Horst Rüdiger zum siebzigsten Geburtstag*: 41-55.

    An interesting study of the similarities and differences in Heine's more polemical and Nerval's more elegaic and syncretistic Neopaganism.

956. Tieder, Irène. "Heine et Michelet." *EG* 29 (1974): 487-494.

    Discusses Heine's interest in Michelet and particularly his influence on Michelet's account of Luther in his later historical work.

957. Töteberg, Michael. "Die Rezeption Heines in der neuschottischen Literatur." *HJ 1975*, pp. 167-170.

    The importance of Heine translation for the birth of the "New Scottish Renaissance" in the 1920s, with bibliography.

958. Tronskaja, Maria. "Heine in der russischen revolutionär-demokratischen Kritik." *Streitbarer Humanist*, pp. 404-413.

    A review of the reception of Heine among nineteenth-century Russian dissidents, especially Belinsky, Pissarev, Dobrolyubov, and Chernyshevsky.

959. Ude, Karl. "Heinrich Heine und der 'Schneider Wibbel.'" *WuW* 27 (1972): 347–350.

A loose connection with an element of *Buch Le Grand* and the early twentieth-century playwright Hans Müller-Schösser.

960. Vajda, György M. "Heine und Petöfi." *Streitbarer Humanist*, pp. 425–433.

Affinities and mutual interest of Heine and the Hungarian revolutionary poet Sándor Petöfi.

961. Vontin, Walther. "La recherche de la paternité. Heine, Wagner und der 'Fliegende Holländer.'" Pp. 78–82 in *Richard Wagner und das neue Bayreuth*, ed. Wieland Wagner. List-Bücher, 237. Munich: List, 1962. 236 pp.

Wagner's youthful discipleship to Heine, with remarks on *The Flying Dutchman* and Wagner's setting of a French version of "Die Grenadiere."

962. Wadepuhl, Walter. "Das Bronze-Medaillon Heinrich Heines." Wadepuhl, *Heine-Studien*, pp. 86–90.

History and circumstances of a bronze medal of Heine struck in 1834.

963. ———. "Zur amerikanischen Gesamtausgabe von Heines Werken." Wadepuhl, *Heine-Studien*, pp. 174–180.

Circumstances of the pirated Philadelphia edition of 1855.

964. Walwei-Wiegelmann, Hedwig. "Wolf Biermanns Versepos 'Deutschland. Ein Wintermärchen'--in der Nachfolge Heinrich Heines?" *HJ 1975*, pp. 150–166.

Respectful but skeptical and critical analysis of Biermann's modern Heine imitation.

965. Weidl, Erhard. "Die zeitgenössische Rezeption des 'Buchs der Lieder.'" *HJ 1975*, pp. 3–23.

A study of the very extensive public criticism of Heine's poems as they appeared before their compilation in *Buch der Lieder*.

966. Welzig, Werner. "Heine in deutschen Balladenanthologien." *GRM* N.S. 27 (1977): 315-328.

Shows how little change there has been in the Heine ballads chosen for anthologies from the beginning to the present. One of the most concise and instructive contemporary reception studies.

967. Werner, Alfred. "A Century after Heine's Death." *South Atlantic Quarterly* 55 (1956): 171-178.

Some comments on American translations and on Heine's "hedonism."

968. ———. "Heine in America." *American-German Review* 22, No. 6 (August-September 1956): 4-7.

Summarizes Heine's comments on America and cites some older American comment on him.

969. ———. "Heinrich Heine: Anniversary Notes." *Chicago Jewish Forum* 16 (1957/58): 102-106.

A not always accurate review of English-language publications on Heine in the centenary year.

970. Werner, Hans-Georg. "Zur Wirkung von Heines literarischem Werk." *Streitbarer Humanist*, pp. 190-224. Reprinted *WB* 19, No. 9 (September 1973): 35-73.

A highly biased sketch of the history of Heine's reception in Germany, arguing that only in East Germany and the Soviet Union has he been rightly appreciated.

971. Wiesenberger, Fritz. "Düsseldorf und Heinrich Heine." *Düsseldorf* (1972, No. 3): 26-29.

Düsseldorf's difficulties in preserving Heine's reputation. Includes a comment on the quarrel over naming the university after Heine.

972. Windfuhr, Manfred. "Heinrich Heines deutsches Publikum (1820-1860): Vom Lieblingsautor des Adels zum Anreger der bürgerlichen Intelligenz." Pp. 260-283 in *Literatur in der sozialen Bewegung: Aufsätze und Forschungsberichte zum 19. Jahrhundert*, ed. Alberto Martino, Günter Häntzschel, and Georg Jäger. Tübingen: Niemeyer, 1977. 542 pp.

Argues that up to 1835 Heine's public had been noble and upper class, but his turn to political and public themes earned him a new, larger, bourgeois public. Interesting but doubtful upon close examination.

973. ———. "Eine Zeitungsfamilie und ein umstrittener Autor: Heinrich Heine in der früheren Düsseldorfer Presse." *Düsseldorf* (1972, No. 3): 10-15.

Of two Düsseldorf newspaper-publishing brothers in the 1840s, one showed a continuing interest in Heine, while the other printed only ill-willed gossip.

974. Wright, Charles P. "Matthew Arnold on Heine as 'Continuator' of Goethe." *Studies in Philology* 65 (1968): 693-701.

Finds Arnold's view of Heine as Goethe's continuator incorrect and misleading.

975. Zagari, Luciano. "Heine in der italienischen Kritik." *HJ 1965*, pp. 51-63. Tr. as "Heine nella critica italiana." Pp. 221-232 in Zagari, *Studi di letteratura tedesca dell' Ottocento*. Rome: Ateneo, 1965. 239 pp.

Phases of Heine's reputation in Italian criticism.

976. ———. "Ritorno di Heine." *Nuova Antologia* 489 (September-December 1963): 513-530.

A research report on contemporary Heine studies and translations in Italy.

977. Zamudio, José. *Heinrich Heine en la literatura chilena: Influencia y traducciones*. [Santiago]: Bello, 1958. 195 pp.

History and importance of Heine in Chile, with an anthology of translations.

INDEX OF AUTHORS AND EDITORS

Abels, Kurt 272
Abraham, Pierre 246
Abusch, Alexander 247
Adorno, Theodor W. 378
Alker, Ernst 274
Altenhofer, Norbert 6, 275, 551, 789
Angelet, Christian 790
Anglade, René 3, 379
Anstett, J.-J. 791
Arbogast, Hubert 380, 381
Arendt, Dieter 382, 552, 792
Arnold, Arnim 793
Arnsberg, Paul 794
Atkins, Stuart 7, 170, 225-228, 383-385
Atkinson, Ross 498
Ayrault, Roger 386

Babler, Otto F. 795
Badia, Gilbert 611
Baldauf, Helmut 796
Bandet, Nicole 3
Bark, Joachim 499, 797
Barnard, Frederick 612
Bartelt, Frauke 49
Basso, Lelio 613
Baum, Wilhelm 170a
Baumgarten, Michael 614
Bayerdörfer, Hans-Peter 387, 388, 500, 501
Bech, Françoise 615
Becker, Eva D. 12, 13
Becker, Heinz 50
Becker, Karl Wolfgang 3, 276, 616

Behal, Michael 277
Bein, Alex 248
Beissner, Friedrich 171
Benda, Gisela 51, 617, 798
Benn, Maurice 799
Berendsohn, Walter A. 14, 389, 390, 800
Bergenthal, Hugo 15
Bernhard, Hans Joachim 249
Betz, Albrecht 278, 487
Beyer, Harald 801
Bianquis, Geneviève 52, 802
Biermann-Ratjen, Hans Harder 250
Bloch, Ernst 391
Block, Haskell M. 803
Bock, Helmut 618, 619
Bockelkamp, Marianne 172
Bodi, Leslie 620, 621
Boeck, Oliver 7, 804, 805
Böhm, Hans 3
Boie, Bernhild 392
Bollacher, Martin 277, 622
Booss, Rutger 173, 623, 624
Bopp, Marianne O. de 806
Borries, Mechthild 807
Bouchard, Edmond 808
Boucher, Maurice 251
Brand, Jean-Jacques 53
Brandt, Helmut 276, 393
Brask, Peter 553
Brate, Gertrud 394

Braun, Jürgen 625
Briegleb, Klaus 1, 54, 55
Brinitzer, Carl 56, 57
Brod, Leo 58
Brod, Max 59
Brody, Elaine 488
Broicher-Stöcker, Ursula
   279, 626
Brokerhoff, Karl Heinz 280
Brünn, Max F. 627
Brummack, Jürgen 277, 281,
   395
Buchheit, Gert 396
Bühler, Hans-Eugen 60, 61
Bürger, Peter 282
Bunke, Horst 809, 810
Butler, E.M. 62, 63, 811

Cadot, Marie-Thérèse 628
Calvié, Lucien 629
Cantimori, Delio 630
Carlssohn, Erich 174
Chawtassi, Grigorij 631
Cherubini, Bruno 554
Cheval, René 64
Chiarini, Paolo 283, 284,
   632-635
Christmann, Helmut 397
Clasen, Herbert 636
Colleville, Maurice 252
Cuby, Louis 65
Cwojdrak, Günther 16, 812

David, Claude 3
Deblüe, Vera 285
De Graaf, Daniel A. 813
De Leeuwe, Hans 637
Delille, Maria Manuela 814
Demetz, Peter 638, 815
Derré, Jean-René 3
Destro, Alberto 398
Deutsch, Alexander 816
Dirrigl, Michael 66
Djordjević, Miloš 286
Dmitrejew, Alexander
   Sergejewitsch 399
Doerksen, Victor G. 639
Dresch, Joseph 17, 67, 640,
   817, 818

Dubruck, Alfred 819
Dück, Hans-Udo 400
Dyck, Joachim 175
Dymschitz, Alexander 820

Eckhoff, Annemarie 489
Ederer, Hannelore 287
Eggert, Jens 253
Ehrmann, Bruce L. 210
Eisner, Fritz H. 3, 68,
   176-180, 229-231, 641,
   808
Elema, Hans 232, 555
Emmerich, Karl 642
Englekirk, John E. 821
Erler, Gotthard 2
Estermann, Alfred 233
Ezergailis, Inta 401

Fairley, Barker 288, 289,
   643
Fancelli, Maria 556
Feise, Ernst 402, 822
Feiwel, M. 823
Fendri, Mounir 403
Fest, Joachim 644
Feudel, Werner 18
Feuerlicht, Ignace 404,
   405, 824
Fingerhut, Karl-Heinz 290,
   406
Finke, Franz 19, 69, 181,
   407, 557
Fischer, Heinz 825
Flake, Otto 254
Fleischmann, Jakob 645
Fowkes, Robert A. 488
Fränkel, Jonas 70, 291
Francke, Renate 3, 182,
   646
François-Poncet, André
   255
Frank, Manfred 647
Freadman, Anne 826
Freund, Lothar 558
Freund, Winfried 502,
   503
Fridlender, Georgi Michae-
   lowitsch 648
Friesen, Gerhard 827

Frühwald, Wolfgang 649
Fueger, Wilhelm 828
Fuerst, Norbert 292
Fuhrmann, Alfred 650

Galinsky, Hans 829
Galley, Eberhard 10, 48, 71-
  79, 167, 183-187, 651, 830-
  833
Gebhard, Hella 408
Gebhardt, Christoph 409
Geiger, Barbara 190
Geis, Robert 256
Geisler, Ulrich 652
Geldrich, Hanna 834
Germann, Dietrich 188
Giese, Gerhard 20
Giesen, Christiane 5
Gille, Klaus F. 504
Gilman, Sander 835
Girndt, Eberhard 653
Gishdeu, Sergej Pawlowitsch
  410
Görsch, Eva 21
Gössmann, Wilhelm 80, 505,
  838-840
Gohdes, Clarence 836
Goldammer, Peter 837
Goranow, Kristo 293
Gotsche-Meister, Helga 841
Gottgetreu, Erich 842
Grab, Walter 506
Grabowska, Maria 81
Grandjonc, Jacques 82, 843
Grappin, Pierre 3, 5, 189,
  411, 654
Grésillon, Almuth 190
Grözinger, Elvira 561
Grossklaus, Götz 559, 560
Grubačić, Slobodan 562
Grupe, Walter 83-85, 507-
  509
Grzimek, Waldemar 844
Guichard, Léon 86, 234

Häntzschel, Günter 1
Hagström, Tore 22
Hahn, Karl-Heinz 3, 190,
  510, 655

Hamburger, Käte 563
Hamburger, Michael 294
Hamelau, Karin 23
Hammerich, Louis L. 412,
  511
Hansen, Volkmar 5, 192,
  845, 846
Harich, Wolfgang 656
Hart-Nibbrig, Christiaan L.
  413
Hartwig, Helmut 512
Hasubek, Peter 513, 847
Hatfield, Henry 295
Hay, Louis 24, 193
Hecht, Wolfgang 296
Heim, Harro 87
Heinegg, Peter 88
Heinemann, Gerd 89, 90,
  194, 195, 224
Heinemann, Gustav 257
Heise, Wolfgang 657
Heissenbüttel, Helmut 414
Hellendall, F. 848
Hemmerdinger, Bertrand 849
Hengst, Heinz 658
Henning, Hans 603, 604,
  659
Hermand, Jost 5, 25, 415,
  514, 564-566, 660, 661,
  850
Hermlin, Stephan 258
Hermstrüver, Inge 196, 197
Hess, John A. 91, 297
Hessmann, Pierre 851
Heymann, Fritz 92
Hilscher, Eberhard 93
Hinck, Walter 416-418, 515
Hinderer, Walter 516, 662
Hirsch, Helmut 94
Höck, Wilhelm 852
Höllerer, Walter 298, 419
Höltgen, Karl Joseph 198,
  667
Hörling, Hans 857
Hövelmann, Gregor 61
Hoffmann, Gerd 663
Hofman, Alois 854
Hofrichter, Laura 299, 300

Hohendahl, Peter Uwe 664–
  666, 855
Hollosi, Clara 567, 856
Holtzhauer, Helmut 199
Holub, Robert C. 668
Hooton, Richard Gary 517
Horch, Hans Otto 857
Hotz, Karl 858
Huder, Walter 259
Hueppe, Frederick E. 301
Hultberg, Helge 95, 586,
  668a
Huppert, Hugo 859, 860

Iggers, Georg G. 669
Immerwahr, Raymond 26, 302
Inoue, Shozo 861

Jacobi, Ruth L. 670, 671
Jacobs, Jürgen 420, 569,
  672
Jahn, Maria-Eva 570
Jaspersen, Ursula 421–423
Jennings, Lee B. 303, 304,
  571
Johnston, Otto W. 96, 572,
  673
Jonzeck, Marianne 862

Kabaktschiewa, Maria 863
Kadt, J.d. 305
Käfer, Karl-Heinz 674
Kämmerling, Bernd 865
Kahn, Robert L. 27
Kaltwasser, Gerda 864
Kanowsky, Walter 97, 98
Karger, Irmingard 306
Karst, Roman 260, 675
Kaufmann, Eva 2
Kaufmann, Hans 2, 307, 308,
  424, 518–521, 676–678
Keller, Hans Peter 838
Kesten, Hermann 261, 866,
  867
Kiba, Hiroshi 679
Killy, Walther 425, 426
Kircher, Hartmut 573, 680
Kirsch, Eberhard 732

Klaar, Walter 1
Kleinknecht, Karl Theodor
  868
Klenner, Hermann 681
Klitze, Gert 810
Klusen, Ernst 427
Klussmann, Paul Gerhard
  428
Kniebiehler, Yvonne 235
Knipovič, Jewgenija F. 522
Knüfermann, Volker 429,
  682, 869, 870
Koch, Franz 683
Koch, Hans-Gerhard 684
Koelwel, Eduard 309
Kofta, Maria 685
Kohn, Hans 262, 263
Kolbe, Jürgen 871
Koopmann, Helmut 5, 310–
  312, 430, 686–689, 872,
  873
Korell, Dieter 431
Kortstadt, Carl 313
Krämer, Helmut 690
Kraft, Werner 314, 432,
  433
Krahé, Peter 874
Kramer, Aaron 875
Kreutzer, Leo 691
Krogmann, Willy 434
Krüger, Eduard 692
Krueger, Joachim 99
Kruse, Joseph A. 100, 197,
  200, 201, 236, 574, 693,
  876, 877
Krzywon, Ernst Josef 101,
  102
Kubacki, W. 878
Künzel, Horst 435
Kurz, Paul Konrad 315
Kuttenkeuler, Wolfgang
  103, 316, 317, 694

Lahy-Hollebecque, Marie
  318
Lambert, José 878a
Landsberg, Abraham 879
Lauer, Reinhard 880

Laveau, Paul 3, 237
Lea, Charlene A. 605
Lebrave, Jean-Louis 202
Lefebvre, Jean-Pierre 104, 436, 695
Lehmann, Ursula 319
Lehnert, Herbert 881
Lehrmann, Cuno Ch. 105, 320
Lehrmann, Lucienne 882
Leja, Alfred E. 437
Leonhardt, Rudolf Walter 106, 264, 265
Leschnitzer, Adolf 266
Leschnitzer, Franz 696
Lévy, Madeleine 321
Lewik, Wilhelm 883
Lilge, Herbert 107
Lindner, Burkhardt 697
Liptzin, Sol 108
Lischke, Johannes 28
Loeb, Ernst 322-325
Loeben, Maria-Beate von 523
Löschburg, Winfried 884
Lüdi, Rolf 438
Lüth, Erich 109, 110
Lukács, Georg 698

Machado da Rosa, Alberto 885
Maché, Ulrich 111
Mackensen, Lutz 326
Magnani, Luigi 699
Maier, Willfried 700
Maliniemi, Irja 327, 886
Malsch, Sara Ann 701
Malter, Rudolf 702
Malycky, Alexander 29
Mandelkow, Karl Robert 328
Mann, Bernhard 277
Mann, Golo 267, 439
Mann, Michael 8, 203, 703-705
Marcuse, Ludwig 112, 113, 887
Mathes, Jürg 238
Maurer, Georg 524
Mayer, Hans 9, 114, 329, 330, 575
Mayr, Josef 706

Mayser, Erich 888
Meier-Lenz, D.P. 889
Meinhold, Peter 707, 708
Mende, Fritz 3, 30, 115, 116, 182, 204, 239, 240, 331-333, 709-716, 890, 891
Merkelbach, Valentin 892
Meyer, Raymond 440
Miller, Philip L. 490
Milska, Anna 717
Mitsuno, Masyuki 893
Mittenzwei, Johannes 718
Möhrmann, Renate 576
Möller, Dierk 334
Möller, Irmgard 3, 525
Moenkemeyer, Heinz 205
Mommsen, Katharina 441
Monz, Heinz 117
Motekat, Helmut 719
Mühlberg, Dietrich 20
Mühlhäuser, Siegfried 491
Müller, Beatrix 894
Müller, Joachim 442, 443, 577, 578
Murdoch, Brian 895
Musgrave, Miriam 720

Na'aman, Shlomo 118, 119
Nabrotzky, Ronald H.D. 896, 897
Nerjes, Günther 31
Netter, Lucienne 3, 120, 121, 206, 235, 721-724
Neubert, Werner 335
Nicolaus, Norbert 898, 899
Niehaus, Max 606
Noethlich, Werner 207

Obermann, Karl 725
Oehler, Dolf 726, 727
Oellers, Norbert 728
Oesterle, Günter 729, 730
Oesterle, Ingrid 730
Oosawa, K. 731
Owen, Claude R. 579, 900-904

Pabel, Klaus 580

Pageard, Robert 905
Paraf, Pierre 122
Paucker, Henri Roger 336
Pazi, Margarita 444
Pepperle, Ingrid 906
Perez, Hertha 907
Perfahl, Jost 4
Peschken, Bernd 908
Peters, Eckehard 732
Peters, George F. 445
Pfeiffer, Hans 733
Pfrimmer, Alfred 492
Pichois, Claude 3
Pörnbacher, Karl 1
Polak, Léon 32
Politi, Francesco 909, 910
Politzer, Heinz 446
Porcell, Claude 123
Porter, E.G. 493
Poschmann, Henri 911
Prang, Helmut 912
Prawer, S.S. 124, 125, 337,
    447-449, 526, 527, 734
Preisendanz, Wolfgang 10,
    338-341, 450, 735, 913
Prox, Lothar 914
Puppe, Heinz W. 451

Raddatz, Fritz J. 126, 528
Radford, F.L. 915
Radlik, Ute 127, 208, 209,
    219
Raphael, Jakob 128, 129,
    916, 917
Rappaport, S. 268
Rasch, Wolfdietrich 736
Reed, T.J. 918
Reese, Walter 919
Reeves, Nigel 33, 130, 342,
    452, 529
Reimann, Paul 920
Reiss, H.S. 34-37
Reissner, Hanns G. 241, 737
Rendleman, Neal 210
Reuter, Hans-Heinrich 530
Ribbans, G.W. 905
Richter, Karl 921, 922
Riemen, Alfred 531

Riesel, Elise 581
Rinsler, Norma 923
Rippmann, Inge 738
Robert, Frédéric 494
Rogge, Helmuth 924
Rømhild, Lars Peter 925
Roos, Carl 343
Ros, Guido 131
Rose, Ernst 38, 739
Rose, Margaret A. 453, 532-
    534, 582, 740, 926
Rose, William 39, 454, 455,
    741, 927
Rosenberg, Rainer 742, 928
Rosenthal, Ludwig 132-134,
    583, 743
Roth, Nathan 135
Rüdiger, Horst 535
Rümmler, Elise 136
Rukser, Udo 929

Salinger, Herman 344, 456,
    457, 930
Sammons, Jeffrey L. 40, 41,
    41a, 137, 138, 345, 536,
    537, 584-586, 744
Sandor, A.I. 346, 587
Santoli, Vittorio 347
Sauder, Gerhard 458
Saueracker-Ritter, Ruth
    745
Sauerland, Karol 588
Schäfer-Weiss, Dorothea
    42
Schanze, Helmut 10, 538
Schaub, Uta 931
Scheffener, D. 932
Scheibe, Siegfried 276
Scheiffele, Eberhard 348
Scher, Steven Paul 589
Schillemeit, Jost 590
Schiller, Dieter 933
Schlein, Rena 459
Schlüer, Klaus Dieter 460
Schmid, Carlo 269
Schmidt, Egon 934
Schmidt, Johann Michael
    746

Schmidt, Wolff A. von 139,
539
Schmitz, Gerhard 747
Schneider, Frank 495
Schneider, Manfred 140
Schneider, Ronald 591, 592
Schnell, Josef 461
Schöll, Norbert 748
Schönberg, Oswald 7
Schoenermark, Erna 935
Schönfeldt, Otto 936
Schoeps, Hans-Joachim 141
Schuller, Marianne 593
Schulte, Klaus H.S. 142
Schulz, Wilfried 614
Schumacher, Ernst 937
Schweickert, Alexander 938,
939
Schweikert, Uwe 4, 361
Seccia, Lia 940, 941
Seeba, Hinrich C. 749
Seifert, Siegfried 43, 942
Sengle, Friedrich 349, 540,
943
Senn, Alfred 944
Sieburg, Friedrich 462
Siegrist, Christoph 10, 463
Simon, Ernst 350, 750, 751
Snamenskaja, Galina 945
Snethlage, J.L. 351
Söhn, Gerhart 752, 946
Sourian, Eve 753
Spann, Meno 352
Spencer, Hanna 302, 353, 354,
464, 754-757
Sprinchorn, Evert 947
Stahl, Karl Heinz 1
Stanescu, Heinz 948
Starke, Fritz 758
Stauffacher, Werner 465, 949
Stein, Ernst 466, 467
Stein, Jack M. 496
Steinhauer, Harry 143, 950
Stekelenburg, Dick van 44,
951
Stern, Arthur 144
Stern, J.P. 355, 468
Stern, Martin 952

Sternberger, Dolf 356, 357,
759, 760
Stiefel, Robert E. 607
Stockhammer, Morris 358
Stöcker, Christa 3, 211,
242
Stöcker, Hans 145
Stöcker, Jakob 761
Storz, Gerhard 469
Streller, Siegfried 762
Strich, Fritz 763
Süskind, W.K. 270
Suzuki, Kazuko 953
Swales, Martin 470

Tarnói, László 359
Tesdorpf, Ilse-Maria 954
Thanner, Josef 594
Thomas, Barry G. 595
Thomas, Marcel 146
Thomke, Hellmut 45, 541
Tiedemann, Rüdiger von
955
Tieder, Irène 956
Tischer, Heinz 471
Töteberg, Michael 957
Tonelli, Giorgio 764
Tramer, Friedrich 765
Trilse, Christoph 11, 766,
767
Tronskaja, Maria 958
Truding, Lona 497
Turóczi-Trostler, József
608, 768

Ude, Karl 959
Überling, Wolf 360
Uhlmann, A.M. 147

Vajda, György M. 960
Veit, Philipp F. 148-153,
472, 473, 542, 596
Vermeil, Edmond 769, 770
Vogel, Carl Ludwig 46
Voisine, Jacques 3, 771
Vontin, Walther 154, 961
Vordtriede, Werner 4, 155,
212, 361

Wadepuhl, Walter 156-161,
  213, 362, 543, 597, 598,
  772-775, 962, 963
Wagner, Maria 474
Walter, Jürgen 277
Walwei-Wiegelmann, Hedwig
  838, 964
Waseem, Gertrud 475
Weber, Dietrich 476
Weber, Gerhard W. 214
Weber, Werner 477
Weidl, Erhard 215, 216,
  965
Weidmann, Helga 219
Weigand, Hermann J. 243
Weinberg, Kurt 363
Weiss, Gerhard 162, 217,
  609, 776, 777
Weiss, Walter 364, 365
Weiss, Wisso 218
Welzig, Werner 966
Werner, Alfred 271, 967-969
Werner, Eva 478
Werner, Hans-Georg 366, 778,
  970
Werner, Michael 47, 163-166,
  367, 368, 478, 599, 779,
  843
Westra, P. 479
Wetzel, Heinz 480
Wieland, Wolfgang 780
Wiese, Benno von 369-371,
  481, 482, 610
Wiesenberger, Fritz 971
Wikoff, Jerold 483
Wilczek, Stanislaw 781
Wilhelm, Friedrich 372
Wilhelm, Gottfried 48
Wilhelm, Kurt 782
Wille, François 167
Windfuhr, Manfred 5, 219-
  221, 373-375, 484, 600,
  783, 784, 972, 973
Winterberg, Inge 785
Woesler, Winfried 3, 244,
  245, 544-548
Wolf, Ruth 168, 485
Wolffheim, Hans 786

Wright, Charles P. 974
Wülfing, Wulf 376
Würffel, Stefan Bodo 549

Zagari, Luciano 486, 975,
  976
Zagona, Helen Grace 550
Zamudio, José 977
Zepf, Irmgard 377, 787
Ziegler, Edda 169
Zinke, Jochen 222-224
Zisserman, N. 788
Zlotkowski, Edward A. 601,
  602

INDEX OF WORKS AND SUBJECTS

"Abenddämmerung" 421
"Adam der Erste" 532
Adorno, Theodor W. 414
aesthetics 95, 278, 580, 590, 601, 614, 625, 626, 631, 632, 648, 653, 665, 668a, 672, 677, 682, 686, 692, 694, 700, 705, 714, 749
Allgemeine Zeitung, Augsburg 179, 203, 245, 618, 722, 724, 779
Almansor 605
America 660, 720, 776, 793, 827, 836, 912, 963, 967, 968, 969
Amphitrite, wreck of 226
"An die Jungen" 478
Andersen, Hans Christian 122
animals 306
anniversaries 17, 21, 24, 34, 46, 251, 255, 269, 338, 791, 802, 818, 855, 862, 876, 898, 899, 901, 927, 935, 937, 969
anthologies 30, 966
"Apollogott, Der" 473, 481, 482
Arabic poetry 403
Arminius motif 505
Arnim, Bettine von 242
Arnim, Siegmund von 242
Arnold, Matthew 811, 954, 974
art 8, 653, 665, 736, 752, 777, 787
Atkins, Stuart 44
Atta Troll. Ein Sommernachtstraum 281, 448, 481, 499, 504, 527, 529, 533, 536, 538, 540-547, 550, 764, 824
"Aus alten Märchen winkt es" 194
Aus den Memoiren des Herren von Schnabelewopski 574, 595, 600, 773, 922, 961
"Aus einem Briefe" 380, 381, 409
Australia 926

Babeuf, François-Noël 691
Bäder von Lucca, Die 128, 152, 552, 553, 575, 596, 651, 729, 757, 947

Ball, Hugo 870
ballads 388, 408, 417, 443, 474, 966
Banville, Théodore de 803, 805
Barthes, Roland 438
Baudelaire, Charles 727, 803, 805, 813, 818
Bécquer, Gustavo Adolfo 821, 823
Belgiojoso-Trivulzio, Cristina, Principessa di 235
Belinsky, Vissarion Grigoryevich 958
"Belsazar" 397
Béranger, Pierre-Jean de 895
Berendsohn, Walter A. 22
Berlin 98, 99, 155
Berlioz, Hector 86, 234, 236, 244
Bernays, Karl Ludwig 94
Betz, Albrecht 42
Bible 320, 444, 453, 534
Bibliothèque Nationale 193, 206, 214, 273
Bierbaum, Otto Julius 739
Biermann, Wolf 889, 964
"Bimini" 391, 420, 481
birthdate 96, 150, 151, 153, 157
Bloch, Ernst 614
Bocage, Pierre-Martin 227
Börne. See *Ludwig Börne. Eine Denkschrift*
Börne, Ludwig 335, 623, 632, 649, 662, 666, 668, 683, 696,
    709, 728, 730, 738, 748, 766, 843
Bonn 97, 98
Borries, Mechthild 42, 865
Boulogne 104, 226
Brecht, Bert 418, 804
Brentano, Clemens 649
Breza, Eugen von 101, 194
Briefe aus Berlin 661
Briefe über Deutschland 185
Briegleb, Klaus 192
Brunner, Carl 201
Buch der Lieder 83, 389, 390, 395, 398, 411, 425, 438, 441,
    447, 454, 455, 475, 888, 965. See also *Lyrisches Inter-
    mezzo*; *Nordsee, Die*; *Traumbilder*
Buch Le Grand. See *Ideen. Das Buch Le Grand*
Büchner, Georg 798, 799, 825, 869, 911
Bulgaria 863
Burschenschaft. See Fraternity
Busch, Wilhelm 938
Byron, George Gordon Noel Byron, Baron 905

Campe, Julius 47, 49, 55, 57, 159, 160, 169, 182, 211, 237,
    532, 808, 833

Carducci, Giosuè 909, 910
Carlsbad Decrees 441
Cartouche, Louis-Dominique 849
Casona, Alejandro 824
Castro, Rosalía de 885
Catholicism 91, 379
censorship 47, 55, 83, 84, 127, 180, 182, 211, 441, 508, 509, 532, 774, 779
Cervantes Saavedra, Miguel de 709
Chamisso, Adelbert von 895
Chernyshevsky, Anton Pavlovich 958
Chile 977
China 937
Chinese literature 739
cholera epidemic 706
Classical antiquity 295, 296, 835
Cobbett, William 744
Cogniot, Georges 882
Coleridge, Samuel Taylor 829
Cologne Cathedral 74
Communism 190, 249, 613, 638, 691, 711, 726, 727, 769, 897
Communist League 240
Constitutionnel, Le 239
conversations 163
Cotta, Johann Friedrich von 90, 179
Cousin, Victor 640
Cowper, William 895
Croce, Benedetto 941
Czechoslovakia 854, 920

Dallapiccola, Luigi 497
Damascus pogrom 723
dance 571, 604
Darío, Rubén 900
Daumier, Honoré 727
Davies, Robertson 915
De l'Allemagne. See *Romantische Schule, Die*; *Zur Geschichte der Religion und Philosophie in Deutschland*
Delacroix, Eugène 740
Desmoulins, Camille 911
"Deutschland" 512
Deutschland. Ein Wintermärchen 12, 212, 281, 439, 448, 498, 499, 505, 508, 509, 514, 518, 519, 521-523, 527, 528, 534, 536, 540, 546, 549, 613, 636, 678, 698, 761, 764, 827, 866, 889, 934, 964
dialect 173, 217
"Dichter Firdusi, Der" 416
Dilthey, Wilhelm 908

Dingelstedt, Franz 501
Dobrolyubov, Nikolai Alexandrovich 958
Döblin, Alfred 628
Doktor Faust, Der 28, 205, 603, 604, 606-610, 636, 915
"Doktrin" 249
Don Quixote, introduction to 83, 335, 709
"double" motif 337, 470
drama 11, 733, 767
Droste-Hülshoff, Annette von 840
"Du bist wie eine Blume" 437, 828
"Du hast Diamanten und Perlen" 212
"Du schönes Fischermädchen" 795
Düsseldorf 60, 71, 136, 156, 864, 946, 971, 973
Düsseldorf, University of 848, 936, 971
Düsseldorf conference (1972) 247, 330, 375, 565, 751, 855,
    862, 951

East Germany. See German Democratic Republic
Edel, Josepha. See Josepha
editions; editing policy 14, 40, 171, 178, 187-192, 198, 199,
    204, 215, 216, 219-221, 223, 230, 233, 243, 525, 791, 796,
    881, 963
Eichendorff, Joseph von 465, 470, 576, 872
Eisler, Hanns 487
Elizabeth, Empress of Austria 808
Embden, Charlotte. See Heine, Charlotte
"Enfant perdu" 530
Enfantin, Prosper 33
Engels, Friedrich 638, 681, 696, 747
England 162, 609, 667, 758, 793, 811, 912, 969
Englische Fragmente 744, 758
English language 30, 744
"Erinnerung" 460
"Es war ein alter König" 404
essay 282, 354
Europe 297, 369
Ewerbeck, Hermann 240
executioner motif 272, 621
exile 377, 826
existentialism 351, 856

Fairley, Barker 32
Faust. See *Doktor Faust, Der*
Federal Republic of Germany 17, 18, 187, 189, 219, 221, 246,
    257, 269, 373, 466, 762, 796, 831, 847, 852, 862, 868, 892,
    937, 942, 970
Feuerbach, Ludwig 674

Fichte, Johann Gottlieb 765
"Fichtenbaum steht einsam, Ein" 472
finances 164
Finland 886
Florentinische Nächte 556, 561, 571, 587, 589, 598, 718
Flying Dutchman motif 922, 961
folksong 395, 427
Fontane, Theodor 857
Fouqué, Friedrich de la Motte 596
"Fräulein stand am Meere, Das" 422
France 53, 64, 85, 179, 252, 320, 336, 385, 494, 608, 609,
    623, 624, 634, 635, 654, 665, 670, 713, 722, 777, 786,
    802, 817, 818, 853, 866, 891, 894, 912. See also Paris
Französische Maler 154, 653, 736, 740, 752, 777, 787
Französische Zustände 623, 624, 635, 706, 774, 891
Franzos, Karl Emil 29
Fraternity 75
Frederick William IV, King of Prussia 170a
Freemasonry 146
Freiligrath, Ferdinand 87, 526
French government pension 165
French language 30, 313
French literature 385, 550, 634, 803, 805, 813, 940
French versions 185, 544, 579, 642, 753, 819, 897
Freud, Sigmund 275, 363, 551, 553
Friedländer, David 152, 596
Friedländer, John 152
"Für die Mouche" 384, 385
Furtado, Cécile. See Heine, Cécile
Furtado family 231

Galley, Eberhard 16, 841
Gans, Eduard 241, 596
Gautier, Théophile 803, 805
Gebauer, August 194
Geibel, Emmanuel 426
Geldern, Simon van 92, 132-134
Georgia (Soviet Union) 795
German Democratic Republic 18, 187-189, 199, 204, 218, 233,
    247, 249, 258, 273, 276, 307, 308, 331, 335, 525, 565,
    652, 656, 676, 684, 712, 732, 766, 791, 831, 837, 844,
    847, 862, 889, 896, 897, 919, 927, 935, 942, 970
Germany 51, 64, 252, 274, 320, 336, 617, 633, 635, 644, 654,
    712, 778, 786, 797, 830, 832, 847, 850, 855, 858, 868, 873,
    888, 891, 908, 919, 938, 939, 972. See also Federal Re-
    public of Germany; German Democratic Republic; Prussia;
    Westphalia
Gerresheim, Bert 839
Geständnisse 123, 185, 195, 212, 324

Gide, André 790
Globe, Le 641
gods. See myth
Görres, Joseph 649
Goethe, Johann Wolfgang von 83, 111, 200, 328, 367, 403, 428,
    445, 565, 566, 603, 604, 608, 616, 617, 643, 655, 686, 701,
    710, 715, 757, 766, 773, 974
Götter im Exil, Die 940
Göttin Diana, Die 606, 607, 610
Göttingen 97, 98
Grandville (Jean-Ignace-Isidore Gérard) 541
Great Britain. See England
"Grenadiere, Die" 477, 961
grotesque 303
Grubačić, Slobodan 33
Gumpel family 128
Gutzkow, Karl 73, 730, 938

Haffner, Sebastian 864
Hamburg 100, 110, 128, 574, 879
"Hans ohne Land" 500
Harzreise, Die 551, 566, 568, 572, 576, 581, 585, 594, 602
Hauptmann, Gerhart 418
Hebbel, Friedrich 154
Hebräische Melodien 458
Hebrew 916
Hegel, Georg Wilhelm Friedrich 33, 98, 356, 436, 614, 615,
    640, 645, 648, 657, 674, 685, 692, 694, 704, 719, 754,
    780, 783. See also Right Hegelians; Young Hegelians
Heine, Amalie 148, 152, 455
Heine, Betty 140, 150, 304
Heine, Carl 143, 231
Heine, Cécile 143, 231
Heine, Charlotte 151, 228, 229
Heine, Fanny 175
Heine, Gustav 151
Heine, Mathilde 225, 497
Heine, Maximilian 151
Heine, Salomon 109, 231
Heine, Samson 142, 150
Heine, Therese 148, 455
Heinrich Heine-Archiv, Heinrich Heine-Institut 78, 174, 181,
    183-185, 196, 197, 200, 208, 209, 583, 841
Heinrich Heine-Gesellschaft 877
Hellenism. See sensualism and spiritualism
Henschke, Alfred. See Klabund
"Herbstwind rüttelt die Bäume, Der" 925
Herder, Johann Gottfried 612

hermeneutics 275
Herwegh, Georg 938
Hesse, Hermann 739
Hirth, Friedrich 131, 206, 230, 243
history 275, 281, 342, 355, 387, 456, 470, 481, 619, 622, 625,
   645, 648, 657, 687
Hölderlin, Friedrich 487, 912
Hörth, Otto 827
Hoffmann, Ernst Theodor Amadeus 175
Hoffmann von Fallersleben, August Heinrich 532
Holland 198, 637, 932
Houben, Heinrich Hubert 163
Howells, William Dean 836
Hugo, Gustav 69
Hultberg, Helge 14, 22
Humboldt, Alexander von 87
humor. See wit
Hungary 494

"Ich grolle nicht, und wenn das Herz auch bricht" 394
"Ich weiß nicht, was soll es bedeuten" 382, 396, 405, 423,
   434, 473, 480, 871
Ideen. Das Buch Le Grand 12, 172, 555, 559, 565, 569, 577,
   584, 590, 757, 789, 959
illness 135, 144
illustrations 809, 810, 833, 871
"Im wunderschönen Monat Mai" 353
Immermann, Karl 103, 364, 571
India 372
"Iris" gas company 58
irony 280, 285, 298, 319, 339, 365, 398, 424, 471, 480, 498,
   515, 763
Italian literature 785
Italy 599, 651, 941, 975, 976

"Ja, du bist elend, und ich grolle nicht" 394
"Jammertal" 527
Japan 861, 893, 953
Jean Paul 590, 869
"Jehuda ben Halevy" 485
Jewishness, Judaism 59, 70, 75, 96, 108, 110, 149, 152, 168,
   248, 256, 265, 266, 268, 271, 272, 274, 320, 321, 377,
   444, 458, 472, 473, 485, 605, 612, 627, 671, 679, 680,
   712, 723, 737, 741, 743, 751, 754, 782, 826, 850
Johann, Archduke of Austria 500
John, Karl Ernst 83
Josepha 60, 61, 79, 479
journalism 121, 131, 239, 611, 722, 724

Joyce, James 828
Jung, Carl Gustav 304, 457

Kästner, Erich 939
Kanowsky, Walter 33
Kant, Immanuel 630, 702
"Karl I." 387, 388, 418, 435, 464, 478
Kaufmann, Hans 22, 796
Keller, Gottfried 938, 952
Kerr, Alfred 939
Klabund 939
Klaproth, Heinrich Julius 141
Klein, Josef 491
"König Harald Harfagar" 443
Kolb, Gustav 245
Kraus, Karl 287, 807, 865, 931
Krzywon, Ernst Josef 42, 44
Kuttenkeuler, Wolfgang 22, 42, 44

Laforgue, Jules 803, 813
Lamennais, Félicité-Robert de 843
"Laß die heil'gen Parabolen" 433
Lassalle, Ferdinand 118, 119
Latin America. See Spanish America
law 650, 681
Lazarus, Emma 875
Left Hegelians. See Young Hegelians
Lenau, Nikolaus 364, 465
Lenin, Vladimir Ilyich 882
Liliencron, Detlev von 931
Liptzin, Sol 32
literary theory. See aesthetics
Lithuania 944
Loeb, Ernst 33
London, Ontario conference (1978) 302
Longfellow, Henry Wadsworth 829
"Loreley, Die." See "Ich weiß nicht, was soll es bedeuten"
"Lotosblume ängstigt, Die" 440
Low German 217
Lucca 554
Ludwig Börne. Eine Denkschrift 120, 180, 543, 632, 666, 668,
    676, 688, 708, 728, 737, 738, 756
Ludwig Markus 772
Lutezia 8, 170, 190, 203, 618, 634, 642, 673, 721-724, 735,
    771, 779, 897
Luther, Martin 324, 325, 633, 956
Lyrisches Intermezzo 353, 386, 394, 440

Maeztu, Ramiro de 904
Maier, Willfried 22
Mallarmé, Stéphane 803, 805
Mann, Heinrich 617, 945
Mann, Michael 14
Mann, Thomas 617, 682, 842, 845, 846, 881, 918
"Marie Antoinette" 435
Markus, Ludwig 772
Martínez Estrada, Ezequiel 901
Marx, Karl 113, 117, 130, 139, 511, 518, 613, 638, 657, 668,
    674, 681, 695, 696, 708, 725, 747, 751
Marxism 45, 287, 293, 295, 335, 359, 366, 393, 399, 410, 471,
    520, 521, 548, 622, 623, 631, 634, 638, 655, 656, 665, 666,
    676, 684, 692, 697, 698, 729, 732, 733, 758, 765, 767, 778,
    893, 919
Marxsen, Eduard 491
Mayakovsky, Vladimir Vladimirovich 524
medal 962
Meissner, Alfred 884
Memoiren 61, 62, 79, 158, 195
Mende, Fritz 14
Menzel, Wolfgang. See also *Über den Denunzianten* 54, 730
Merckel, Friedrich 160, 229, 232
Mérimée, Prosper 813
meter 402, 412, 547
Mexico 806
Meyer, August 238
Meyer Collection 174
Meyerbeer, Giacomo 50, 284
Michelet, Jules 956
Mörike, Eduard 465
monarchism 713, 764
monuments 250, 794, 808, 839, 844
Morgenblatt für gebildete Stände 179
Morgenstern, Christian 938
"Morphine" 459
Mu'allaqat 403
Müller, Wilhelm 452
Müller-Schösser, Hans 959
Munich 66
music 8, 179, 203, 589, 663, 699, 703-705, 718
Musset, Alfred de 818
myth 295, 346, 481, 482, 534, 673, 689, 760, 955

"Nächtliche Fahrt" 457
Napoleon I 96, 170, 320, 324, 325, 572, 577, 601
nationalism 355, 369, 762
nature 386, 465, 539, 615

Nazarenism. See sensualism and spiritualism
Nerval, Gérard de 803, 805, 813, 819, 851, 878a, 923, 955
Netherlands. See Holland.
Neue allgemeine politische Annalen 177
Neue Gedichte 383, 445, 483, 508. See also *Verschiedene*;
    Zeitgedichte
Nicholas I, Czar of Russia 788
Nietzsche, Friedrich 262, 617, 682, 731, 755, 798, 835, 845,
    881
Nordsee, Die 421, 442, 444, 482, 944
Norway 801

Oesterle, Günter 44
orthography 5, 223

Paganini, Nicolò 589, 718
painting. See art
pantheism 364, 365, 615, 622, 701, 955
paper types 218
Paris 67, 82, 131, 146, 252, 623, 624, 818
Parnasse 805
parody 453, 526, 757, 887
Pastor, Ludwig von 170a
pessimism 358, 456, 798
Petöfi, Sándor 960
Petrarchism 484
philosophy 316, 351, 358, 640, 644, 647, 656, 658, 674, 690,
    692, 702, 707, 745, 765, 780, 784
picaresque novel 600
Pissarev, Dmitri Ivanovich 958
Platen von Hallermünde, August 575, 729, 909
Poland 81, 101, 102, 628, 675, 685, 717, 781, 878. See also
    Über Polen
politics 9, 45, 107, 260, 262, 266, 278, 324, 328, 342, 355,
    356, 374, 380, 388, 427, 435, 441, 451, 506, 511, 515, 517,
    524, 530, 531, 539, 548, 570, 591, 592, 616, 618, 626, 650-
    652, 661, 688, 689, 701, 705, 706, 712, 713, 715, 716, 725,
    741, 742, 759, 764, 765, 769, 784
Politische Annalen. See *Neue allgemeine politische Annalen*
"Pomare" 486
Portugal 814
posthumous papers 207
Pottier, Eugène 849
Pound, Ezra 815
Prague 58
Pressburg, Sara Lea 129
Prussia 54, 83-85, 141, 508, 509, 598, 746, 774
Prutz, Robert 928

psychology 140, 304, 363, 551, 561
Pushkin, Alexander 788

Raabe, Wilhelm 792
Rabbi von Bacherach, Der 557, 573, 582, 583, 586, 680, 723
reading 71, 78, 97
"Red Sefchen." See Josepha
Reed, T.J. 881
Reise von München nach Genua 559, 651, 757
Reisebilder 83, 84, 281, 558, 560, 562, 564, 567, 570, 579,
    580, 588, 591-593, 597, 601, 602, 651, 799, 850. See also
    Bäder von Lucca, Die; *Englische Fragmente*; *Harzreise, Die*;
    Ideen. Das Buch Le Grand; *Reise von München nach Genua*;
    Stadt Lucca, Die
religion 65, 80, 88, 91, 108, 124, 241, 324, 351, 365, 437,
    458, 459, 529, 604, 650, 668, 674, 684, 707, 708, 713,
    732, 746, 754, 909, 955. See also Catholicism; Jewishness;
    pantheism
Rellstab, Ludwig 495
"Return." See Jewishness; religion
revolution 534, 580, 618-620, 626, 635, 655, 689, 697, 843,
    911
Revolution of 1789 630
Revolution of 1830 623, 624, 688, 713
Revolution of 1848 500, 677, 698, 725
rhetoric. See style
Rhineland 89, 145, 173, 194, 217, 712
Richter, Jean Paul Friedrich. See Jean Paul
Right Hegelians 658
Rimbaud, Arthur 813
"Ritter Olaf" 220
Robert, Friederike 596
Robespierre, Maximilien 630
Roger, Dolorès 229
romances. See ballads
Romanticism 262, 281, 299, 300, 349, 350, 359, 372, 385, 393,
    399, 419, 422, 423, 427, 428, 430, 442, 466, 476, 480, 504,
    538, 576, 593, 616, 625, 636, 648, 649, 655, 664, 693, 698,
    736, 750, 763, 778
Romantische Schule, Die 186, 614, 636, 646, 655, 668, 670,
    693, 731, 739, 799
Romanzero 28, 385, 388, 408, 430, 436, 448, 449. See also
    Hebräische Melodien
Rossini, Gioacchino 284
Roth, Joseph 867
Rothschild family 114, 161
Ruge, Arnold 890, 906
Rumania 907, 948

Runge, Phillip Otto   386
Ruskin, John   874
Russia   397, 410, 494, 522, 567, 581, 698, 712, 788, 816, 820,
    856, 859, 860, 883, 958, 970
Russian language   30

Sainte-Beuve, Charles-Augustin   813
Saint-Simonianism   33, 155, 356, 618, 641, 669
Salome figure   550
Salon, Der   211
Sammons, Jeffrey L.   14
Sand, George   52, 227
Sandor, A.I.   22
satire   281, 285, 345, 395, 526, 527, 533, 591, 701, 913
Scandinavia   343, 800. See also Norway
Scheffel, Joseph Victor von   938
Schelling, Friedrich   647, 674
"Schelm von Bergen"   449
Schiller, Friedrich   200, 370, 402, 860, 881, 918
"Schlachtfeld bei Hastings"   443, 474
Schlegel, Friedrich   682
"schlesischen Weber, Die"   467, 507, 520
Schloss, Michael   49
Schmidt, Julian   908
Schmitz, Gerhard   16
Schnabelewopski. See *Aus den Memoiren des Herren von Schnabele-*
    wopski
Schocken Collection   214
schooling   156
Schopenhauer, Arthur   798
Schubert, Franz   491-493, 495, 496
Schumann, Robert   321, 487, 488, 492, 497, 718
Schwabenspiegel, Der   639
Scotland   957
"1648--1793--????"   435
sensualism and spiritualism   295, 301, 324, 511, 580, 604, 610,
    622, 632, 662, 707, 967
Serbia   880
Shakespeare, William   533, 659, 667, 734, 775, 874
Shakespeares Mädchen und Frauen   198, 631, 659, 667, 775
Shelley, Percy Bysshe   602
Sichel, Julius   229
"Sie sassen und tranken am Teetisch"   527
"Signature" motif   371, 673
"Sklavenschiff, Das"   406, 895
slavery   660, 720, 895
Slessor, Kenneth   926
Snethlage, J.L.   305

socialism 629, 765, 919, 934
Solger, Karl Wilhelm Ferdinand 590
Soviet Union. See Russia
Spain 824, 885, 902, 903, 905, 929
Spanish America 821, 834, 902, 903, 929
Spann, Meno 22
spiritualism. See sensualism and spiritualism
Spitteler, Carl 949
Srūoga, Balȳs 944
Stadt Lucca, Die 554, 651, 757
Staël, Germaine de 212, 670, 753
Stahl, Joseph 973
Stahl, Lorenz 973
Stalin, Josef 882
Stehle, Hansjakob 628
Steinmann, Friedrich 213
Sternberger, Dolf 33, 314
"Still is die Nacht, es ruhen die Gassen" 470, 493
Storm, Theodor 938
Storz, Gerhard 42, 44
Strähl, Wolfgang 843
Strauss, Salomon 120, 543
Strauss Collection 221
Strindberg, August 947
style 170, 202, 279, 309, 313, 326, 327, 334, 336, 340, 347–
    349, 354, 376, 401, 428, 462, 523, 531, 547, 558, 562
Suarès, André 826

Tableaux de Voyage. See *Reisebilder*
Tacitus 505
"Tannhäuser" 451
Temps, Le 226
theater. See drama
Thiers, Adolphe 121, 165, 239
"Tod, das ist die kühle Nacht, Der" 432
Toller, Ernst 418
Tonelli, Giorgio 33
translations 30, 819, 822, 875, 883
Traumbilder 428, 463
trochees. See meter
Tucholsky, Kurt 939
"tugendhafte Hund, Der" 212

Über den Denunzianten 83, 730
Über Polen 675
United States. See America
"Unsere Marine" 526
"Unterwelt" 402, 482

"Valkyren" 456
Varnhagen von Ense, Karl August 155
Varnhagen von Ense, Rahel 596
Verein für die Cultur und Wissenschaft der Juden 485, 782
Verlaine, Paul 805
Vermischte Schriften 49. See also *Lutezia*
Vernet, Horace 154
Verschiedene 415
Vischer, Friedrich Theodor 938
"Vitzliputzli" 535, 915
voice 125

Wadepuhl, Walter 16, 44
Wagner, Cosima 921
Wagner, Heinrich Leopold 418
Wagner, Richard 93, 914, 921, 922, 961
"Wallfahrt nach Kevlaar, Die" 400
"Wanderratten, Die" 502, 510, 516
watermarks 218
Weerth, Georg 938
Weidl, Erhard 44
Weimar conference (1956) 791, 927
Weimar conference (1972) 276, 308, 933
"weiße Elefant, Der" 379
"Wenn ich in deine Augen seh" 440
Werner, Michael 772
West Germany. See Federal Republic of Germany
Westphalia 89
"Wie die Wellenschaumgeborene" 394
Wilhelm, Gottfried 16
will and testament 617
Wille, François 167
Windfuhr, Manfred 14, 22, 42
Winther, Christian 925
wit 318, 365, 376, 527, 551, 590, 591, 913, 930
women 106, 555
word index 222, 224
writing habits 216

Yiddish 173, 917
Young Hegelians 629, 740, 906

Zeitgedichte 483, 503, 513, 515, 517, 525, 530, 531, 537, 548
Zur Geschichte der neueren schönen Literatur in Deutschland.
    See *Romantische Schule, Die*
Zur Geschichte der Religion und Philosophie in Deutschland
    622, 630, 644, 656, 668, 799, 843